1st edn

$30

CAT G

TO COLORADO'S RESTLESS GHOSTS

TO COLORADO'S
RESTLESS GHOSTS

INEZ HUNT
and
WANETTA W. DRAPER

SAGE BOOKS

Sage Books are published by
Alan Swallow, 2679 So. York St., Denver 10, Colo.

INVITATION

Inez Hunt and Wanetta W. Draper

request the honor of

your presence to meet

COLORADO'S RESTLESS GHOSTS

PLACE CARDS

W.S. Stratton

Ouray

Martin Bowden

J.C. Osgood

Stephen Decatur

Annabelle, Stark ward

Nikola Tesla

Soapy Smith

Captain Jack

Grace Greenwood

Cy Warman

H.H.

Nora Gaines

Les Girls

Sky Pilots

Bathhouse John Coughlin

Milton Franklin Andrews

Frank Hamilton Rice

Otto Mears

Prairie Dog O'byrnne

To the memory of
Irving B. Bruce and Walter Colburn
who remembered when but left before . . .

Foreword

We invite you to sit down at our table to meet some of Colorado's divergent personalities.

For more years than we care to acknowledge, our hobbies have led us along the ghost trails of Colorado but our paths have never stayed in dull statistical ruts. With a penchant for getting off the track and a tendency to wander from the paved highway, we have encountered so many ghosts who were much too vital ever to lie buried in six prescribed feet. These were the restless vibrant souls for whom a lifetime was too short and who probably made their exits, "shrieking to the south and clutching at the north."

History, to us, has always been separated into its component parts—"his story,—and hers!" History is only people: dates and data are indexes and dividers.

We tend to be tolerant of human frailty and see no need to supply the insincere halo that is so often awarded even to the unvirtuous after death. Such sentimentality we repudiate.

We are not beyond listening to legend and folklore and hearsay with tongue in cheek. If a story has lasted a hundred years, it's a good one and should be heard though not necessarily believed. True or not, it should not be forgotten. It should be remembered that few historical facts are unmingled with legend and few legends are without historical origin. This is our premise for the inclusion of legend wherever it clarifies character. It might have been; perhaps it was.

Life is full of choices, each of which imposes certain limitations. So, too, in writing a book or giving a dinner party, one of the most difficult decisions is the matter of selection. One would like to include a multitude of interesting people but space will only allow a specified number. Should we invite only the famous? Do we dare include a few who are controversial, or must we consider the drab who are important only because of social pressure? May we include one whose table manners and graces will be unacceptable to the other guests but whose personality will cancel out his flaws? Dare we seat the saints with the sinners with millenium hopes of the lion and the lamb?

If we have omitted or minimized some of the great, it was not for personal reasons but because they had so many previous engagements and their names have appeared so often before in the historical social register.

So we have selected our guests on the basis of personal likes and mutual interests, and we offer no apologies for the inclusion of a few Philistines. Some readily qualify among the immortals—others were simply piquant personalities.

We invite you to sit down with these rakes and wraiths, heroes and horse thieves, and the whole motley crew. The guests may have dangerously little in common, but they all share a compulsive energy. In some it was explosive and unconfined—in others it was the channeled power of dynamo intensity.

Among them are the best and the worst, the crackpots and the clowns, the saved and the damned. This is the way we saw them.

INEZ HUNT and WANETTA W. DRAPER

Contents

Illustrations

Stephen Decatur,

Dry Land Commodore

From the beginning men have had a tendency toward a double life. For Stephen Decatur Bross the final score might have been totaled as doubled, redoubled, and vulnerable. He might have been known as "The Remarkable Mr. Pennypacker of the 1870's." He even put Mr. Pennypacker to shame; two families proved inadequate for Stephen.

It all began in 1825, in Sussex County, New Jersey, when Joseph Bross, the shoemaker, bestowed the distinguished name of Stephen Decatur Bross on his second son. Much of the boy's childhood was spent in Milford, Pennsylvania, where he learned the trade of shoemaking from his father. This was good enough for the moment but Stephen, even as a youth, was beginning to strain at the confinement of the cobbler's bench. He preferred to walk in the luring paths of other men's shoes. He was a naturally gifted boy who made the most of his chances for a liberal education, and he was ably abetted by his glib tongue and natural charm. He became a student at Williams College, Massachusetts, and a teacher and later a principal at Chester Academy, Orange County, New York. History does not record whether the dormant seeds of unrest which were a part of his personality were beginning to take root then. From later observation one might well believe that the constant procession of students growing tall and going on to exciting lives must have fretted such a nature. On late spring days the restlessness of his students may have kindled his own. The textbooks were unchanged and irksome to an adventurous mind.

It was about this time that Evalinda Hall came into his life and no doubt he was reluctant to relinquish any of his small measure of freedom, but Evalinda Hall must have been the type of

"Commodore" Stephen Decatur. *Photo courtesy Library, State Historical Society of Colorado.*

14

girl who could be attained in no other way; so vows were made and bonds were accepted, and who is to say he may not have been sincere at the moment?

To this union a daughter was born, and the story could have taken on the conventional lines of "love, honor, and obedience." Stephen Decatur Bross apparently accepted this responsibility of family and first child graciously enough, but when Evalinda started knitting booties again, the seeds of unrest took full flower and he must have felt that universal feeling of being hopelessly trapped, deluded, and sentenced to life at hard labor. He looked at the little town of Chester and must have visioned years of monogamy suddenly assuming synonymity with monotony. To this he must have added the picture of eternal diapers, grocery bills, mumps, measles, and mortgages. There are many ways of escape, but not many respectable ones. Divorce was unthinkable in Chester, and he had no reason that the average person would understand.

Did the local milk train whistle down the track early in the morning to fill him with the longing to follow any road or train, no matter where it was going? How did he arrive at his final decision? Did he invent a reason for going to New York on business, and was his mind made up before he left that he wouldn't be coming back? No one can answer this but it is known that he never went back to Chester.

Supper grew cold the night he was expected home from New York, but no one believed a man like Stephen Decatur Bross woud desert his family. Surely he must have been the victim of foul play. His relatives throught that he had been murdered and although they sought him they found no trace. Three months after his disappearance his son was born and Evalinda, in full faith, named the boy Stephen Decatur Bross. Mrs. Bross never married again.

If Stephen ever thought of Evalinda and the new baby, old chains were too far away to hold. He had relinquished them for a moment and he could not pick them up again.

The Mexican War caught his attention and he enlisted. War entailed discipline, yes, but a kind of freedom, too. His mind

15

must have turned toward the border where a soldier might find adventure—where a soldier might love a señorita beneath a magnolia tree or in a cantina with no obligation save that of the moment. No reason or excuse required. War was reason enough for anything.

In Doniphan's Regiment, Stephen Decatur Bross became one of those who made the famous march under Stephen Kearney to Santa Fe and Chihuahua. He was in the company of Colonel Clay Taylor, who remembered him well in after years as a brave and gallant fighter. He was a born soldier of fortune, but wars come to an end as does everything and the close of the Mexican War found him taking up residence on the banks of the Missouri.

From the journal of Rudolph Frederich Kurz of June 4, 1851, and from war records, we learn that the name of Bross had been dropped. It was never again to be used in connection with the renegade Stephen, in life or death. Whether it was bitterness or self-incrimination is a question never to be solved. At any rate, here he claimed to be simply Stephen Decatur, nephew of the famous commodore, who said, " . . . my country right or wrong . . ."

Kurz said of Decatur:

> He is employed here now as clerk. He is most courteous and obliging. Two months ago he served as sailor on a ship but owing to the illness of his comrades on their way to California, he got stuck fast in this region. He was earlier a teacher in the east. . . To provide me, (Kurz) with a position as clerk, in the event that the captain on the company's boat, that we are expecting, cannot take me with him, Decatur made me an offer at their trading post with the Pima, on the Fauquicourt.

Inevitably the path of one of his former pupils converged with his own. It was near Omaha in 1857 or 1858 that David Moffat was in the audience and heard Stephen Decatur speak. He was positive that it was his former professor and notified William Bross that his lost brother had been found. To substantiate the information John A. Bross, a prominent lawyer from Chicago, started at once for Nebraska. If the brother had any illusion that

16

he would take home a repentant prodigal, he was destined to disappointment for Stephen stoutly denied any relationship and professed great surprise and indignation at the claim. If he remembered New Jersey and Evalinda, it may have been with guilt or with regret, but the attempt to imprison him must have been traumatic, for, ever after, the name of Bross would set him afire. Later entanglements he could slough off with a shrug. Perhaps in the language of Dylan Thomas, "After the first death there is no other."

In Nebraska he became a prominent pioneer and a successful farmer. Here in 1856 he was trapped by a woman who insisted on marriage vows, and by this "marriage" they had three children. Records show ownership of a ferry and a shoeshop near Council Bluffs. Decatur was one of the first citizens in the community, a noted public speaker, and man of education.

But wagons kept going by and wheels turned and gouged their mark into the hardpan, and only the ruts and Stephen were left behind. Whispers of gold blew back on the wind. One day he came to the conclusion that he had exchanged one set of chains for another and it was time to move on again to greener fields and younger girls, and off he went. By nature a gambler, the adventurer turned his eyes where the fever was at a pitch. But if matrimony was too confining for him, celibacy was too dull. This time it was the black-eyed Indian girls who drew his attention. Here was adventure of a different kind and shade with women who made fewer demands and carried burdens as their lot, and expected nothing. It was what they got.

For a time, in utter abandon, he made his home with the Indians, but Mormon pushcarts were going through. A different kind of fervor caught his attention, and he pulled up stakes for Mormon country. But even the Mormons found him difficult competition and an upsetting influence in the home, and he was expelled and driven from a Mormon colony, barely escaping with his life.

Back in Nebraska, the second Mrs. Decatur had ceased to expect him. Later she took her family to California, where it is said she fell in love again but refused to marry, holding with puritanical tenacity to her marriage vows which she knew by now had never been legal in the first place.

Why did women marry Stephen Decatur? He was handsome, devil-may-care, and charming, with an air of mystery to whet a woman's curiosity. He had community prestige and most of all, an unquenchable virility. It may be noted that Stephen's wives never married again. He either killed or cured. He was Yul Brynner with whiskers.

Military history in Colorado included his enlistment in the Third Colorado Regiment. This gave him participation in the notorious Sand Creek Massacre. One might wonder, with his previous intimate experience of Indian life, how the brutality of this slaughter of Indian women and children affected him.

Georgetown, Colorado, became a focal point for his interest. Here his activities ranged over a large territory and it is said he loved the Snake River Valley best of all. On arrival in a new community, one can become a new personality and it was here that Decatur assumed the title of "Commodore."

Usually these Colorado hills form the profile of a man and his code and his personality become defined. This was true of Decatur and it was clearly discernible that his code became:

> To be an individual,
> To take life and popularity in big gulps,
> To paint in broad strokes,
> To love, when and where and whom the whimsy of the
>   moment provided,
> To gamble with life in his own coin,
> To wash his slate clean of any accumulative guilt,
> To steal the spotlight and the center of the stage,
> To bask in life's applause and publicity,
> To give account to no man, but especially to no woman.

Decatur was a prospector and the first to take ruby silver out of the Summit County area. This was from the Anglo Norman in the Peru district and the almost pure mass weighed seven pounds. Here he found the variety that he had craved all his life—no monotony, no monogamy—no matrimony. He was a born promoter and although he was never one of Luck's favored ones in

18

On the way to Argentine Pass in June. Argentine Pass was one of Stephen Decatur's promotions.

Stephen Decatur's stamping ground near Peru.

19

the matter of bank account, his life continued to be rich in experience. He built a road over Argentine Pass and another town was named for him. Already a town in Nebraska bore his name as did a county in Kansas. The Colorado mining camp founded by him in 1868 was located about thirty miles west of Georgetown and was later renamed Rathbone. It existed for only about three years after that, yet all who search for the story of Stephen Decatur pass over the name of Rathbone and to them the name of Decatur is as indelible as his personality. Who was Rathbone? No one cares.

Some say that Stephen Decatur named the town of Silver Plume; others have different stories. Perhaps it received its name because the ore was found in the shape of a silver plume, or perhaps there was a miner who promised his wife silver plumes for her hat. Or again, it may have been named for James G. Blaine, known as "the plumed knight." But those who live in Silver Plume lean to the Decatur story.

The *Colorado Miner,* December 5, 1867, records his activity in procuring salt for chlorodizing ore in the area.

> Last week, Commodore Decatur looked out the route for a new trail from Georgetown to Hepburn's Ranch on the Platte, where the proprietors of the South Platte salt works agree to deliver salt for $20 a ton. The Commodore estimates the distance from Georgetown to Hepburn's at twenty-five miles, by a good trail free from precipitous ascents. Salt should be delivered here, from Hepburn's at a price not to exceed two cents per pound, thus making a total of sixty dollars per ton. We learn that this route will be used for supplying Professor Martine with salt for chloridizing ores.

In his spare time Decatur achieved political prestige as a representative in the Colorado (territorial) legislature.

In the silver queen city of Georgetown, he became the favorite orator, always in demand and called for from miles around to preach a sermon or preside at a burial, and to hand out verbal bouquets on all occasions. There was no better speaker to give the two silver shields as prizes for declamation to the public school children and to present medals to the top spellers.

20

This gift for the spoken word carried over into the field of journalism and he became associate editor of the *Colorado Miner* from 1869 to about 1873. He took the *nom de plume* of "Old Sulphurets." A description of him at the time said he was

> . . . short, stocky, iron gray, bushy eyebrows and whiskers. Energetic, enthusiastic, sociable, a raconteur with an inexhaustible bag of stories, ready on a moment's notice to make a speech . . . .

Van Wagenen called him "the gray old man."

Samuel Bowles in *Colorado, Its Mountains and Parks* stated:

> Commodore Decatur, the prince of prospectors, the character of all characters, dropped in to bid us welcome to his principality (the junction of the Snake River and of the two trails from Georgetown) on his way from mine to cabin.
> . . . . but the "Commodore" who, to thirty years of schools and civilization, has added twenty of border life in Mexico, in Nebraska and in Colorado, living at times among the Indians, and for many a season in his solitary cabin in these elevated valleys, kept me entertained with his original experiences, his keen observations on men and manners, and his quaint yet rich philosophies. He is an old Greek philosopher, with an American variation; as wise as Socrates, as enthusiastic as a child, as mysterious in life and purpose as William H. Seward or an Egyptian sphynx, as religious as a methodist classleader; he ranks high among the individual institutions and idiosyncrasies of Colorado.*

Decatur was called a master of verbal castigation. In the *Colorado Miner* he wrote:

> For a mass of unintelligible, hotch potch nonsense in the shape of correspondence from this place, we commend our readers to the *Lawrence Kansas Tribune* of the 20th inst. The concoctor of that mass of garbage should have the hole in his head filled with lard, or some material that will give truth at least to his emanations. For a consummate falsifier he is one ahead of any and all of the rubbish, in the shape of correspondents, that ever visited this section.

---

*Mystery—Lieutenant Governor William Bross was one of those accompanying Bowles on this journey. Why is there no mention of relationship between Bross and Decatur?

But when dealing with the weaker sex, his flowery prose became gentle and soft, for on July 20, 1871, he said:

> Two smiling divinities, blue-eyed and fair-haired, intelligent young ladies, while pleasuring and sight-seeing among the glens and cañons of the Rockies made us a social call and by their cheering conversation sent dull care whirling to the misty land of forgetfulness.

In his promotion of the town of Sunshine we find the following quotation:

> The outlook to the east is one of great interest. See how the hills from this wonderland filled with rich ore channels of surprising richness, gracefully slope down and kiss the great plains with fond and loving embrace. . . There are our brothers, the grangers who struggle with the brown dust of the "Great American Desert."

Here he was attempting to arouse interest in this area for the Philadelphia Centennial Exposition in order to send a mining exhibit to the fair. Colorado recognized his ability as a promoter and knew that he was the logical choice to represent the state in the Centennial Exposition of 1876. He went at his own expense and, as usual, a busy young state forgot to repay until shortly before his death.

Decatur wasn't without recognition in his own town and at one time a monument to him was suggested. But men get busy and forget. Until just recently his sword and photograph hung in the office of the *Georgetown Courier*.

Although the Commodore did not marry again, he maintained all his charm with the opposite sex. Grace Greenwood, famous lecturer of the day, was one of his cherished friends, and the only one to whom he ever told his full story. If he relayed to her any regrets of his Bluebeard closet of bloody hearts, we do not know. Whether he ever opened the most secret door which was marked "Evalinda and Stephen Decatur Bross" no one has been able to find out. The name was erased but the erasure showed, and no one ever looked within that door unless it was Grace Greenwood and she, unlike most of her sex, never told.

Although Decatur had been a frequent orator on the temperance stage, he took no part of his own advice. He developed an insatiable appetite for liquor. Record says:

> He drank early and late; he drank constantly. Impoverished, and without any means for a livelihood, he drifted out of Clear Creek County, and almost out of the memory of many of his old friends.

He was an old man when he turned up at Rosita in Custer County. Rosita had always had a charm for every conscious or unconscious seeker of beauty. From his front porch the Commodore could see the little rose-bedecked town. Not too far up the draw, at one time, stood the brewery that bottled beer and labeled it "The Beer That Made Milwaukee Famous." The valley held its quota of pungent wild garlic adding its distinctive flavor to the cheese. However, at this early date, garlic cheese was not a gourmet's delight and the local cheese factory was forced to close down.

Molasses was a staple food in the early diet of the westerner. The molasses factory at Rosita caught fire one night, and much as it seemed a disaster to the grown-ups the children were delighted because the burned molasses hardened and formed into taffy to furnish good chewing for weeks. From the out-jutting timbers of a house in plain sight of Decatur's home had hung two outlaws who had quarreled at a square dance with one of the law-abiding residents and were later carted off and buried in a common lot in the cemetery.

Such little incidents made up the personality of the small community which still breathes its air of individuality.

Stephen Decatur, too, fell under its spell. His days of promotion were past and he sought nothing more glamorous than the political office of justice of the peace. Whether he ever performed a marriage ceremony is probably lost to record. If he did so, was it with tongue in cheek, fingers crossed, as he blessed the tie that had bound him, more or less, and with varying degrees of irritation?

Straitened circumstances made him willing to accept a war

pension which came mercifully at that time. Colorado could not have remembered her debt from the Centennial at a more opportune period. The thousand dollars from the state was a cushion in his declining years. Equally welcome were the little gifts of a community which saw his need and sent the children with bowls of warm soup and wedges of pie to the bearded old man. These may have been offerings of charity but they were wrapped in the warmth of hospitality. Rosita looked after her own and left a semblance of dignity even to the poverty stricken.

His cabin, with its foundation of flat native rocks, overlooked the main street. It wasn't far to the saloon. School boys who were recovering from epidemics of measles and mumps went by the old man as he sunned himself in front of his cabin.

"Hello, Commodore," the children would call, and many of them didn't even remember to say "Decatur."

One day on the hill, neighbors gathered to dig a grave for the old man who was a mystery to them but now one of their own. The next day, June 1, 1888, men who were bent under the burden of families and mortgages and shackles, covered the grave for one who had never been able to accept bonds.

Long before, Stephen Decatur *Bross* had died. From that first fateful journey to New York, Bross had ceased to exist. From that day on he had lived as Stephen Decatur. Death did not strip him of his stolen title but granted him the name of Commodore by which he had chosen to live.

POSTSCRIPT TO STEPHEN DECATUR,
DRY LAND COMMODORE

For two years we searched the little cemetery at Rosita for the grave of our Dry Land Commodore, but to no avail. Time and again we were teased by information of historians who claimed to have seen the marker but couldn't remember whether it was wood or stone, but who remembered that it said, "Commodore." We were plagued every trip to the cemetery and seemed haunted

24

Faintly discernible grave of "Commodore" Stephen Decatur.

Wheel rim frames the view of Sangre de Cristos from the Wet Mountain Valley near Commodore Stephen Decatur's final home.

by the ghost of the man we sought. How could we finish the story?

Every trip was marked with some kind of elemental disturbance. At one time the holes dug by badgers to the coffin lids made the trek a hazard since we were exploring at night with insufficient light.

Another time brought a cloudburst which washed out the road making our search a travesty on the term "dry land commodore." The day an old-timer located the outline of the foundation of the Decatur house, the rain came down again and blurred the picture.

It was through a series of newspaper articles which we had authored that we reached the solution. We stated our inability to find the grave. A rash of letters followed asking if we didn't know that this was not the Commodore Stephen Decatur who said, "My country right or wrong—" The result was that everyone appeared to be looking for the mysterious grave. They came from as far away as Tennessee. Rosita residents were plagued with questions.

A nearby ranchwife whose family is buried in the Rosita cemetery was visiting there one day when she saw one of the newspaper articles in the hands of a searcher. She wrote a letter to the paper telling them that she knew where the grave was. She concluded the letter with the question, "What do you want with him, anyway?"

We lost no time in driving into her yard. A conducted tour of the cemetery convinced us that she knew. Both her husband and her aunt vouched for the spot which gave no evidence of a grave. They insisted that they remembered the wooden marker which had stood in a direct path between the graves of their relatives. They recalled the inscription, "Commodore Stephen Decatur." We were still doubting Thomases. Death seemed to have outdone himself in the leveling process, and we were not convinced that it was even a grave. Knowing that we must put our fingers into the nail prints, we literally dug with our hands where she said the wooden marker had been. The rotted bits of the old slab lay just below the grass roots. What could have happened to the rest of the marker, we asked, and she explained. Some

time ago the residents, in a burst of civic pride, had cleaned up
the cemetery and burned all the old rotted and broken board
markers. (Historians weep at this point!)

So ended the two-year search for the final chapter of Commodore Stephen Decatur. We have replaced the old marker with a
new wooden one which reads:

Commodore Stephen Decatur,
died May 31, 1888
Colorado's Representative
to the
Philadelphia Centennial, 1876
Marker replaced in 1960

SOURCES

Silver Town, John Willard Horner, Caxton Printers, Caldwell,
Idaho, 1950

New Overland Tourist, Crofutt, 1878, page 86

Journal of Rudolph Frederich Kurz, June, 1851

Colorado, Its Mountains and Parks, Samuel Bowles, 1868,
pages 98-100

Stampede to Timberline, Muriel Sibell Wolle, University of
Colorado, Boulder, Colorado, 1949 (1952 printing)

Nebraska Summit County Leader, January 1, 1881, page 6,
col. 2

Georgetown Courier, June 7, 1888

Colorado Miner, July 27, 1871, July 20, 1871, December 5,
1867

Colorado Magazine Vol. 17, no. 5, September, 1940, page 190
Vol. 3-4, page 83
Vol. 21-22, pages 262, 215-217
Vol. 17, pages 190-191

Story of Transporation, p. 349

Daily Central City Register, vol. IX, April 19, 1871, page 4,
col. 2

And interviews with the Vickerman family, Mary Loens and
Molly Eichelman, and the Myron Chesleys at Westcliffe,
Colorado; Vern Thompson of Evergreen, Colorado; Mr. and
Mrs. John Hobby, Jr., of Rosita; and the Custer County
Coroner and the Custer County Clerk and deputy.

Cy Warman,

The Colorado Minstrel

Not all Colorado characters were badmen, outlaws, gamblers, or bunco artists, although we are inclined to forget the ones who led the normal unheadlined lives. There were a few with the lighter and more lovable graces, who made their lasting marks in history. Among these came Cy Warman to man the headlights of the locomotives and enlighten the rowdy camp of Creede with the brief flame of the *Creede Candle*. He was also to spread the light of journalism in the offices of the Salida paper *(The Frog)* and to man the desk of railroad editor of the *Rocky Mountain News*. Cy's pencil was inclined to rhyme. Beauty was in the eye with which he beheld this country, and music and rhythm were qualities born in him.

It all went back to southern Illinois where Cy Warman was born June 22, 1885, near the little town of Greenup in a community known as Timothy. He was born a farmer—but was not a born farmer. The fever of the times lured him westward. Coming to Colorado in 1880, for a time he was fireman and later a locomotive engineer for the Denver and Rio Grande Railway. Here the speed of the train and the rhythm of the rails made background for the mountain lyrics which were to gain for him the title of "Poet of the Rockies."

His railroad experience enabled him to get a position as editor of *Western Railway,* a semi-monthy magazine published in Denver. It was doomed to a short life and with it was buried some of Warman's none too ready cash. With his disappointment was born experience. He became railroad editor for the *Rocky Mountain News* in the 1890's, but the coverage for the railroad column was as wide as the horizon. As he complained in a poem (as poets are wont to do) about his editorship, he listed the

28

duties of the railroad editor as encompassing the police court, the prize fights, the concerts at the churches, a column on "What Old Timers Say," and the state house. The latter may not have been so far fetched. Many things have been railroaded through the state house.

Warman was described by his contemporaries as a lighthearted, sensitive, genial fellow, admired for his sterling qualities and his achievements in literature. It is said that "he attached friends to him with bands of steel."

His daily paper in Creede, established in 1892, died a sudden death. He assumed editorship of the *Creede Candle* which lent its light to that bawdy town at the time when Soapy Smith was in control of the uncontrollables there. It was to Cy Warman that Soapy Smith confided the news that he had found a petrified man. (Actually a cement figure shipped from Denver.) Cy believed Soapy. Cy was a believer.

It was Creede that became the subject for his most famous poem, "It's Day All Day in the Daytime and There Is No Night in Creede." Historians differ about the reason for Creede's perpetual illumination. Some say it may have been cheap power which allowed the lights to burn all night and all day. Others say it was the scintillating night life of the town, but a poet needs no reason.

There is an understandable confusion about Warman's married life. Both of his wives were named Marie. Some say his first wife was Myrtle Marie Jones of Salida. Also there was a Myrtle, later, in Denver. Some historians claim *she* was the Myrtle Marie Jones. There is a story that he courted one of these two Maries from the cab of an engine where he waved a columbine to a girl who always waved back.

It is an established fact that his first wife and their two children died in the 1880's.

Some believe it was the second Marie who inspired the poem "Sweet Marie" which was later set to music by Raymond More. About 1895, this song was number one on the "hit parade." If you passed an open window, you were likely to hear,

29

> Sweet Marie,
> Come to me . . .

and farther down the street you might hear the final words,

> Every daisy in the dell,
> Knows my secret,
> Knows it well,
> But to you I cannot tell,
> Sweet Marie.

This song made money for the author.

Warman became a popular poet and copies of his poems were sold on the trains. One book was called *Mountain Melodies*, and had this preface:

> The author makes no apologies to the public for publication of these rhymes. They were inspired by Nature and Nature's God. If you have a kick coming, kick higher.

According to the *Colorado Springs Gazette* of November 19, 1892, he became a resident of Colorado Springs and lived at 712 North Tejon. The paper stated:

> Mr. Cy Warman who has lately become a resident of this city left yesterday for New York City to superintend the publication of another book of poems.

Warman became a traveler and visited Canada, Europe, and the Orient.

His poetry was recognized as a contribution to Colorado minstrelsy. Warman's "Canyon of the Colorado" won first prize for the best poem about the scenic attractions of the state.

Warman's writing was accepted by the best of eastern publishers and he published with such noted firms as Century, D. Appleton & Co., McClures', C. Scribner's Sons, Boston Rand, and *Youth's Companion*. Among the books that he published were, *Frontier Stories, Last Spike, Mountain Melodies, Songs of Cy Warman, The Story of the Railroad, Weiga of the Temagani, Snow on the Headlight,* and *Rhymes of the Rail*.

Cy Warman died in Chicago in 1914.

Cy Warman. From *The Great Divide,* November, 1892. *Photo courtesy Denver Public Library, Western Collection.*

POSTSCRIPT, A PERSONAL NOTE ABOUT CY WARMAN

Cy Warman held a mystic fascination for us. Then we found his birth place listed as Greenup, Illinois, which was familiar stamping ground. We had business in the little town one spring, and decided to follow his story into the land of his origin. The waves of time cover footsteps quickly. The library seemed the natural place to find information about a home-town author who had made national history. The librarian was able to give only limited help. When asked whether they had any of his books, she answered, "We did have, but we do not have them now. Last year, one of his relatives living in the Southwest wrote and offered us twenty dollars for his books. We sent them and we're going to get a Sandburg collection. There will be more demand for it." True—but it seemed a pity to trade something which could not be replaced for something which could be purchased any day from a book store. Yet from a practical point of view, it was right. The library felt that it was better for the family to have and treasure his books, than for them to stand unused and forgotten on the shelf. It often takes time and perspective for prophets to be recognized by their own families.

The librarian directed us to the postoffice where we went to call on Rufus Carroll. He was a nephew of Cy Warman and knew about the old farm house where Cy was born and which was still standing out in the country near Timothy. Carroll said he remembered people telling of Cy's brother who used to play for all the dances. He was a left-handed fiddler and always strung his fiddle left-handed. Maybe so no one else could play it. Maybe just because he played it left-handed. All the family had that strain of inborn music which becomes a song of one kind or another.

Cy Warman had fit his gift for words and music to make rhythmic ballads that seemed to catch the patterned beat of jointed rails, the atmosphere of coal oil lamps, and warm pot-bellied stoves, the hue of columbines, and the face of a girl who waved to an engineer.

32

His flickering *Creede Candle* burned longer in the pages of history than the lights of the gaudy camp itself. We remembered how he came to Colorado with a headlight down the track. We remembered his favorite railroad story of an engineer, who in his dying hour and fading sight was sure that snow was obscuring the headlight. We took that little favorite book, *Snow on the Headlight*, from our bookshelf and sent it to the Greenup Library. He's back here now.

SOURCES

Poems of the Old West, L. J. Davidson, Sage Books, Denver,
    Colorado, 1951
Trail, April, 1914
        January, 1920
Colorado Springs Gazette September 24, 1892
                        November 19, 1892
Colorado Magazine, Vol. 1, 1923-1924
Interviews with
Rufus Carroll, nephew of Cy Warman
Myrtle Lydia Hiles, Librarian, Greenup, Illinois
William Crosby

Soapy Smith,

The Slippery Kind

Most bad men can furnish reasons, if not excuses, for their misdeeds. It is doubtful if Soapy Smith ever stopped to analyze how and where he missed the turn.

Jefferson Randolph Smith was born in Georgia about 1863, the son of a charming, cultured family. Because war had depleted the family fortunes and there were no longer slaves to till the farm, the sons of the family went to work in the fields. Young Jeff at ten was already doing a man's labor. Apparently discouraged by the lack of opportunity in the south, in 1878 the Smiths pulled up stakes and moved to Texas.

Here responsibility for the entire family fell on the shoulders of young Jeff. The father became an alcoholic and totally irresponsible. As runner for a hotel and clerk in a general store in Roundrock, Jeff was able to steer customers from the trains to both establishments so persuasively that he was soon earning the unprecedented salary of seventy-five dollars a month.

Not much glamor went with the position, however, and the advent of a street fakir with a flair for friendship and fine words held stronger appeal for the youngster. The street "artist" cheerfully taught the boy all he knew— how to play the guitar, to do sleight of hand tricks, and even to sing, although here Jeff did not prove to be so adept.

Determined to improve his lot, the lad ordered a hundred dollar traveling outfit from St. Louis and set up in business. His profits soon ran to 300 or 400 per cent which brought the wrath of local merchants. They protested so strongly and were so united in their forces that they soon established a law requiring itinerant merchants to purchase a license. Seventeen-year-old Jeff was supporting his mother, brothers, and sisters, but the move on the part of the merchants hampered his activities. With $1000 in his pockets, he set out for Leadville, Colorado, where he figured that the stakes would be higher with the free-spending crowd in the raw mining camps. The smoothness of his speech and the deftness of his hands combined toward his success in operating the old shell game, three card monte, and even a trick with fake gold bricks. It was with the sale of Sapolion soap that Smith achieved his greatest success—and it looked like a clean occupation. At twenty-five cents a bar there were few takers at first. Born an amateur psychologist, Soapy knew the lure of something for nothing and he had no pity for a loser. Offering his stock with a ballyhoo that would have done credit to Barnum, he urged men to "wash their sins away" and employed such clichés as "cleanliness is next to godliness." Smith coaxed his customers with his soft speech, but most of all, he lured them with bills of various denominations (up to $100) wrapped around an occasional bar of soap. (The lucky bars were always purchased by one of Soapy's henchmen, but the suckers were unaware of that.) The sale of soap in Leadville took an unprecedented jump and the soap box orator cleaned the suckers and moved on to Denver.

Here Soapy fell in with the worst element, but despite his companions he himself was well regarded and numbered friends among the more socially acceptable of the city. Handsome and debonair, Soapy was no student but could pass as a scholar. He even quoted Shakespeare when the occasion called for it.

In Denver he married a well-born St. Louis lady. They had a family of three or four children. Jeff was considerate to his family and generous with them, but he was a strict disciplinarian. He insisted that the children be brought up according to the strictest rules of morality .

Denver was a wide-open and fertile field for the smooth-tongued Soapy. The greenhorns coming from the east offered an unplowed field for his harvest. Political corruption gave Denver's underworld the upperhand, and political offices were frequently secured by the vote of opium addicts who were aroused from their pleasant dreams to vote repeatedly at various precincts.

One man, who very nearly became a victim of the soap salesman, described him as being dressed in a

> Prince Albert coat, a silk hat with cane and gloves. He had
> a close-cropped beard and displayed a heavy gold watch
> chain. He might have been mistaken for a preacher had it
> not been for his bold look, his shifting eyes and nervous move-
> ments.

Although Soapy was offered large opportunities to fleece
richer victims he seemed to feel that there were more five-dollar
suckers— and perhaps the game was more fun. He moved easily
between the underworld population of Larimer and Market
Streets but was just as much at home in the company of uptown
business men.

Soapy entered into such colorful civic strife as the war against
"Bloody Bridles Waite." In 1893, in a long overdue enthusiasm
for reform, Governor Waite pledged to "fight iniquity if I have to
ride through blood to my bridles." Denver's corrupt officialdom
would have none of this reform movement and called on Soapy
Smith and his henchmen to protect them from the avenging angel. Filling the city hall with armed thugs, Soapy held off the
militia in spite of the cannons trained on the building. The
forces of reform withdrew in ignominious defeat. Crime chalked
up a victory.

Like most gamblers and prosperous westerners of the time,
Soapy gave large donations to the poor and to the churches. He
was accustomed to sending twenty-dollar bills as Christmas gifts
to a long list of needy friends. He was credited with giving $1500
at one time to Parson Uzzell for the poor at the Tabernacle to
have a Christmas dinner and it was said that he donated over
$200 on one occasion to the same parson for the benefit of a
stricken family and even donated a fuzzy French poodle for the
kids. Ministers were forced to accord him credit for his generosity and quoted, "The Lord loveth a cheerful giver."

Parson Uzzell, who seemed to feel that a man of such generosity must have some innate goodness, requested Soapy to speak
before a Bible class at the Tabernacle. Surprised and bewildered,
Soapy accepted. The gist of his sermon was that he appeared

before them with some humility as a bad example, a man who had thrown away good opportunities in exchange for temptations of the devil. Soapy spoke with authority on his subject. He told of constant association with the failures of the world, and although he was not a teetotaler he offered the observation that "the smartest men in the country are men who do not indulge in liquor." The parson pro-tem spoke of the brief glory of the sinner and in cold business evaluation told how he often discharged men in his service when liquor interfered with their efficiency. He said, "Even in my profession the drinker cannot hold his own. He can't find his wits when the time comes to use them." He warned sinners that you couldn't beat the dice or the cards. He told young men that there was a chance for hope for them, but he held out no glowing promise for old-timers in sin; these, he said, were past redemption and down and out. Soapy insisted that he was poorer than the ones to whom he preached. He admonished them to keep their minds and bodies clean and to follow the parson's advice to walk the straight line. If men came to scoff, they left respecting the gambler's sincerity. It was the sort of sermon which might have been labeled, "Do As I Say, Not As I Do."

With the advent of the silver strike in Creede, a verdant field was spread out for Soapy's gleaning. And here again, in direct competition with Bob Ford, Soapy took over control of the entire community. He brought nearly a score of handpicked men with him. Bob Ford, the "dirty little coward" who was operating Ford's Exchange, was irked by the newcomer and developed an active hatred for him. Soapy ignored Ford's supremacy, and set up a protection system which paid him fifty per cent on the take of all underworld operations. Recognizing his superior and knowing that he was no match, Bob Ford came to a kind of cold agreement with his successor, and to an on-the-surface truce. Yet Cy Warman told, just before the shooting of Bob Ford, of a rather revealing incident. One of the girls, described as a "sorry looking young woman," came with a paper and pencil to get subscriptions for the funeral expenses of a sister-in-sin who had died the night before. Someone had to pay to have the hole dug and for the

Jefferson Randolph "Soapy" Smith. *Photo courtesy Denver Public Library, Western Collection.*

38

express wagon to carry the girl's body to the mesa. As the young woman pushed the paper toward Ford, he glanced down at the column and saw among the contributors, "Soapy Smith, $5.00" and because he hated Soapy, he immediately raised him five, gave the woman the money and wrote, just under his name and the figure ten, "Charity covers a multitude of sins." It was Ford's last contribution. Shortly after, a man with a gun let go both barrels with a shot which carried Ford's gold collar button "out through the back of his neck."

Various localities noted Soapy's activities after Creede and Denver. Texas and Mexico were included in his wanderings, and when he finally decided to turn north to Alaska it was not because things had grown too hot for him in the west, but because the field and the suckers in the new camps were greener. Actually, Soapy had a very definite plan which he outlined to his Washington cousin, Colonel Edwin B. Smith—that he hoped to make one more big haul and then he would settle down to a more respectable life. Accompanying Soapy to Skagway on his last venture in 1897 were old friends and accomplices. And it was the same story in Alaska.

Reform is inevitable when the pendulum of crime swings too far, and Soapy's over-zealous activities led to his final defeat in 1897 at the hands of the self-appointed One Hundred and One Club, a vigilante organization. Soapy's bravado in organizing The Three Hundred and Three Club was to no avail, and Smith finally met death at the hands of the engineer, Frank H. Reid, who fell at the same time, a victim of Soapy's gun. Soapy's last words were, "My God, don't shoot." But neither the Almighty nor Reid heeded the prayer.

Smith's funeral was held in a church which he had helped to found. The sermon was delivered by a minister who had often received financial aid from the gambler and the text was "the way of the transgressor is hard." The minister spoke of Smith's good works with appreciation but pointed out that they had not balanced with the wrongdoing which had been the keynote of the man's life. As a warning to all, a thirty-foot replica of a human skull was carved on a rock hill above the city and inscribed "Soapy Smith." On the simple wooden marker in the Skagway cemetery he was accorded the dignity of his christened name, Jefferson R. Smith, but curious tourists left him no such dignity, and chipped off splinters from the marker until the name was nearly obliterated. Not far from Soapy's grave was that of City Engineer Reid. It was just about a draw.

Although Soapy had taken over a million as he dug into the pockets of the suckers, he died practically penniless. His widow could find no trace of his belongings. Soapy's theory had been "money was to spend." He had made no provisions for old age or for a future life. For him there was only today and today was now yesterday.

Sources

Frontier Stories, Cy Warman, Charles Scribners Sons, New York, N. Y., 1898

The Reign of Soapy Smith, William Ross Collier and Edwin Victor Westrate, Doubleday Doran & Co., Garden City, N. Y., 1935

The Wildest of the West, Forbes Parkhill, Sage Books, Denver, Colorado, 1951-1957

The Trail, January, 1920, Barkalow Barnacle (in an article quoting Soapy Smith's cousin, Colonel Edwin B. Smith)

H. H.

Straws show which way the wind blows. It must have been a New England northeaster which was blowing when Helen Maria Fiske, second child of Deborah Waterman Vinal Fiske and Nathan Webly Fiske, made her appearance on October 15, 1830, in Amherst, Massachusetts. This was no child of calm. This was a being of hurricane potential.

Deborah and Nathan's first child had lived only a short time. The parents had attributed the baby's death to "God's needed chastisement." Helen's birth eased the parents' grief and the two other children who followed were tractable as summer breezes. Helen was different. It is said that even as a baby, she was something of a problem, with a mind of her own, inclined to "laugh in church, crow boisterously during the singing" and to snatch the spectacles from sharp New England noses. A feminine tendency to pull hair was an early characteristic.

As a small girl she was rebellious and consistently gave unconventional answers. When asked if she loved her parents, she exhibited none of the New England propriety which would have brought the accepted answer. Helen said, a mischievous, "No!" She always preferred her baby brother to a doll. Although she was to live in a world rich with imagination, her flights of fancy were always to be rooted solidly in reality.

A little sister who was born in 1835 was named Anne Scofield Fiske. She was often spoken of as "good little Anne." There was always a close relationship and deep affection between these two girls and it is doubtful if Helen resented it when family and friends said, "Helen is the witty one and Anne is the pretty one."

Helen was brought up in a traditional New England background of propriety, classical literature, and intellectual discussion. A female academy was foreordained as the accepted pattern for her education. Naturally she was a problem to Deborah

41

and Nathan, who never ceased to try to smooth off the rebellious corners and make her fit the mold. They never succeeded. They may never have had her complete confidence. Never was anyone sure which way she would turn. She had a half-dangerous delight in "sudden frolics," and a more dangerous tendency to question the unquestionable.

In order to guide her, the parents equipped her bookshelf with the following books: *The Pastor's Daughter*, *The Child's Book of Repentance*, *A Child's Scripture Question Book* (two volumes), *Scripture Animals*, *The Reformation*, *The Deaf and Dumb*, and *Temperance Tales* (five volumes). No wonder she wrote her own books!

Naturally, with her piquant personality, in her young girl years, she was one of the most sought after in her wide circle of friends. There was an aura of color and magnetism which set her apart from the drab flock who never ventured beyond the safety of the fence. She was described as "impusive, intensely emotional, vivacious and witty."

Her classic features and her attractive wardrobe had only a small part in her popularity. Some called her eyes green; some said, "they were beaming and candid." Moncure Daniel Conway declared, "I guess I'd say they were more alive than those of anyone else's I ever knew." Her taste was impeccable, and she could wheedle a sufficient allowance from an indulgent grandfather to satisfy it. Her clothes revealed a love of beauty, but did not exploit it.

On the outer circle of admirers stood Lieutenant Edward Bissell Hunt, "a man of strong physique and intense nature, a large forceful man with the creative spirit." Never one to be patient, Helen agonized while he took his time before declaring his intentions, but he finally put it in writing. On October 28, 1852, Helen and Lieutenant Hunt were married in Mount Vernon Church in Boston.

Early in the marriage Hunt exhibited a desire for certain restraints of opinion from his wife. He abhorred all abolitionists and forbade Helen to defend Harriet Beecher Stowe. In fact, he

Portrait of H. H. over the Ramona desk.

43

preferred that she remain out of all controversial issues which might have made his military career a precarious one.

At about this period, Helen became better acquainted with Emerson, whose influence did much toward sobering her volatile nature. At this juncture she was giving no evidence as an author, yet she must have been accumulating expression and experience.

Among the Hunts' acquaintances was a Mrs. Botta, whose home in New York had been called the "house with expanding doors," and whose guest lists included such names as Emerson, Poe, Anna Maria Child, and Grace Greenwood. It was said that Helen was delighted to be included. These new friends offered a kind of intellectual retreat from grief caused by the death of her first son, Murray. These gatherings were a godsend as she prepared for the birth of a new baby who was born in Newport on December 11, 1855. The child was called Rennie.

Helen always blamed herself for the tragic loss of her first son, who died from a brain tumor. She felt that having taken him to an unhealthy spot she had contributed to his early death. Her paradoxical New England conscience came to the fore with her personal feelings of guilt.

There have been conjectures that Edward Bissell Hunt and Emily Dickinson met in Washington in 1854 and fell in love— there have also been denials.

Josephine Pollitt states in her book, *Emily Dickinson, The Human Background of Her Poetry*, that

> . . . she (Emily Dickinson) met the husband of Helen Hunt, that they became interested in one another, that he was call- ing upon Emily Dickinson in Amherst afterwards, and that when she was forty, and living upon a long memory, his was still the name of consequence to her, are matters of record.

Colonel Higginson, literary friend of both Helen Hunt and Emily Dickinson, in a letter to his wife recalls a confidential talk with Miss Dickinson in 1870 at which time Emily stated, "Major Hunt interested her more than any man she ever saw."

It has been said that *Mercy Philbrick's Choice*, originally in the "No Name Series" could never have been written "by a Helen un-

44

aware of Emily's love story." The fact remains, Helen did not forget her childhood friend nor forego her interest in Emily "whose whole world was mirrored in a dew-drop."

With Emily's gift for oblique expression, many people put their own interpretation on such Dickensonian quotations as

> When I said I would come again sometime, say in a long time, that will be nearer. Something is nothing.

Soon after Major Hunt was transferred to the Navy Department, a series of disasters followed and he was accidentally killed on October 2, 1863. An even greater disaster followed for Helen Hunt, for, much as she had loved her husband, the love of Rennie, her second son, was even more intense. Rennie, too, was snatched from her by death. Old-timers said, "Never dote on a child—it will be taken from you."

On the unlucky day of April 13, 1865, Rennie died of "malignant diptheria," aged nine years, four months, and eleven days. It was said that he exacted a promise from his mother that she would not kill herself and avowed that he would manifest himself in spirit form after his death. Spiritualism was commonly accepted at that time and Helen's later life indicated that such doctrines had made a lasting impact.

Many an author has found expression necessary after a great grief. "Some souls need to be harrowed." Helen took up her pen. In that era that blossomed with anonymous writers, Helen Hunt's signature "Marah" marked the odds and ends of verse that appeared. She had said, "Writing is the only digging for which I have any capacity."

False Victorian modesty caused the anonymous writers to give the impression that they had no concern for their writings, but let an impostor claim their bastard child and they rose to its defense! Women writers were particuarly cautious because of the stigma attached to the profession. Even Henry James lifted his voice against the fluency of feminine authors.

Colonel Higginson was an admirer throughout Helen Hunt's literary career. He spoke of her as:

The ill-starred staircase.

Flirtation Corner

..... brilliant, impetuous, and a thoroughly individual woman
of her time and one whose very temperament seemed mingled
of sunshine and fire.

Although Higginson's wife declared her husband to be given to
superlatives, his extremes of expression ranged at both ends of the
scale for he labeled Emily Dickinson as his "cracked poetess."

Higginson was inclined to want to exploit Helen and he wished
to include her in an article on "The Female Poets in America."
Helen abhorred such publicity and said in a letter that she had
succeeded in keeping away from the "bevies of famous women."
Emerson, always one of her admirers, was said to have declared
when asked if he thought her the outstanding woman poet in
America, that it might be well to omit the term "woman." Emerson's choice of Helen's poems tended toward the obscure. This
choice he defended, with Coleridge, as being a compliment to the
reader.

The travel letters of Helen Hunt were published in the *Atlantic
Monthly*. Observations on a European tour furnished further
grist for her mill. In addition to her poetry and travel letters she
turned her energies to novels. These, too, were anonymously
credited to "Saxe Holm," or sometimes simply "No Name."

On Helen's first California trip, the old missions caught her
heart. However, Colorado was recommended for her health, but
she hesitated to make the change to that rugged state. After two
months of semi-invalidism she inquired of her friend Emily Dickinson about living quarters in Amherst. When Helen Hunt became increasingly ill, her homeopathic physician again insisted
on Colorado because he was concerned with the potential threat
of tuberculosis which had taken her mother. Helen was frankly
terrified of the barren place which looked to her like "Scandi-
navian hell." Denver she called "horrible." Colorado Springs
was recommended to her and so she registered at the Colorado
Springs Hotel. Soon her attitude began to change. Among the
boarders was an interesting man, William Sharpless Jackson, a
banker, and well known citizen of the growing community.
Helen took drives with him up the canyons and renewed her
acquaintance with Grace Greenwood who entertained her at her

"snuggery" in Manitou. Helen tasted the flavor of Central City, Georgetown, and Bergen Park. She discovered that Colorado was indeed the crossroads of the world, for whom should she meet in Denver but Professor and Mrs. Botta of the "house of expanding doors." With the acceleration of living among people of common interests and the scintillating atmosphere and the improvement of her physical condition, life took on a new meaning. She forgot she was an invalid and climbed Mount Lincoln and Mount Bross, and went down into the Dolly Varden mine, and found herself again capable of the heights and the depths. Her poems and *Colorado Sketches*, she began to sell to the *Christian Union*. She thought nothing of asking an editor for thirty-five dollars for a poem and getting it. The "Saxe Holm" stories which had been printed in *Scribners* brought in good money.

Colorado was becoming her second home, yet no one ever forgets New England, particularly in October, and she went back. Her restless nature kept her torn between the east and the west until, as the *Colorado Springs Gazette* stated, on September 12, 1874, she took the train east again and it just happened that also on the train was William S. Jackson. The paper speculated as to whether they would return together.

In the meantime, Helen was thinking and balancing her present freedom with the pros and cons of another marriage. Granted, W. S. Jackson was intelligent, successful, gentlemanly, and an important figure in the western world, highly regarded by all who knew him. Still, marriage makes demands. Writing was also a love and she had not dared to write in her first marriage. Again she hesitated because hers was a gay nature and she loved pretty and frivolous things. William S. Jackson was a Quaker with a tendency toward the plain life, thrifty and serious. She considered the combination. Then, too, there was that house which Jackson had just bought.

The house had been built by Stratton, the prospector-carpenter of Colorado Springs on the so-called "red-lot" on the corner of Kiowa and Weber Streets. It was understood that the lot was to be the site of a first-class residence and Stratton had complied with all the pride in construction of a master carpenter, but without the imagination of a woman. The front windows didn't even face Cheyenne Mountain! There were not enough closets for a woman's fripperies. It was Spartan simplicity with no trace of feminine frivolity in the structure. Something about that old house would have to be changed if Helen could even consider living in it. Could she do all this and still devote time to her writing which was by now her second nature?

Her decision was made evident when the news of a wedding ceremony held on October 22, 1875, reached Colorado Springs. The ceremony had taken place at the home of her sister, Mrs. Everett Banfield, in Wolfeboro, New Hampshire. It is very likely that she was married under a loved red maple tree at her favorite time of all the year.

The *Colorado Springs Gazette*, October 30, 1875, reported:

> Mr. and Mrs. William Jackson came to us from the East today.
> We welcome them and offer our congratulations.

As though fate were drawing together the characters for a later drama, the same column also mentioned that Miss Rosine Meeker, daughter of N. C. Meeker, had arrived and called upon the editor of the *Gazette*. These two were to become representatives of opposite sides of a burning question.

It was probably two years before Helen was satisfied to live in the Jackson house and not until it had been made to front on Kiowa instead of Weber with the windows opening toward Cheyenne Mountain. Inside the house she exhibited an almost feverish urge to put her mark on every part of it. A little entry way was converted into a whimsical corner with bookshelves lining the walls and with a south window determinedly facing Cheyenne Mountain. "Flirtation Corner" it was called and the floor space was barely large enough for two. It might well have borne the signature of H. H. Little corner cabinets began to appear and new shelves popped up for "Helen's traps," as Mr. Jackson called them. Bits of sculpture graced the walls and art treasures from all over the world found a friendly niche. Vases with fresh flowers adorned the tables. A wedding-gift fire screen of glass with pressed ferns, shielded the rug from the sparks. A

The Regal Tabby

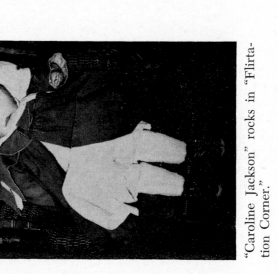

"Caroline Jackson" rocks in "Flirta-tion Corner."

50

portrait of Rennie was set in a prominent place. The Della Robia Singing Boys' Chorus was recessed above the fireplace. A Governor Winthrop desk became her writing place, where she corresponded with old friends. The pigeonholes possibly held letters from Emily Dickinson and other friends.

The staircase to the bedrooms was star-carved, in a reminiscent flight of fancy. It was copied from a house she had admired in Newport. The tall wooden beds with chests to match were all a part of the furnishings. In lieu of no upstairs bathroom, handsome matching sets of bowl and pitcher formed a part of the decor. A Lazy Susan bedside table held little books which were mostly of poetry and philosophy. No bedtime detective stories in that era!

The back stairway which ascended from the kitchen was equipped with a dumb waiter—the very latest in step-saving devices by which Maggie or Effie might increase her efficiency. Even with Effie or Maggie to help, Helen found that it took nine hours to groom that ogre of a house. The kitchen did not escape her ingenuity. It was modernized with a sink and drain boards. Semi-indoor plumbing consisted of a water closet inside the woodshed. A two-year campaign conducted by Helen finally won her the upstairs bathroom. The house was beginning to be hers —she had plans for a few more traps.

She entertained friends, but not all her acquaintances. There were some who thought her snobbish. The fact probably was that she could not afford to give herself to every cause or to every individual to deplete her energy and waste her time and talent. Somehow she felt the pressure of time and of her writing. Helen enjoyed the company of Grace Greenwood and a few intimate friends including several from the east who were attracted to Colorado Springs. Mr. Jackson loved to have the house filled with congenial guests and was a delightful host. Later, one winter, Helen's niece, Helen Banfield, the daughter of "good little Anne," came to be hostess for her Uncle Will while H. H. was away. Helen Banfield was fated to return.

Although churches were conveniently near, Helen Hunt Jackson did not attend, but avowed that she worshiped God in Nature's cathedral of Cheyenne Mountain.

On a trip to Boston, early in November, 1879, Helen heard the story of the Poncas from a lecture by Standing Bear and Bright Eyes. Perhaps it was an unconscious journalistic acumen and natural sympathy that stirred her interest in the cause of the Indians. The common sentiment was that the Indian was less than human. To the more sympathetic the Indian was replacing the Negro as a "cause." Helen had always shrunk from women with "causes" and could not ally herself with groups, but was a single crusader. She had no sympathy with the suffrage movement, although she did not deny the right of women to vote. She approved of temperance as such, but she had no interest in championing it as a "cause." It was a complete surprise to many when she picked up the banner for Indian justice. The result was her book *A Century of Dishonor*, which she hoped would inflame the public sentiment against the unfair treatment of the Indians.

The idea that the California missions would furnish her with material for another wedge in the solution of the Indian problem was still in her mind. She was drawn irresistibly to the California coast. Here her novel *Ramona* became the realization of a dream and a compulsion. It is said that she visited San Juan Batista; that she attended six o'clock mass at an orphan girls' school kept by the Sisters of the Sacred Heart. It is probable that she tried to rent the wing of a mission. She succeeded in antagonizing the priest of the mission. Many of the priests did not share her sympathies toward the Indians.

Ramona was written at lightning speed. Helen appeared to be driven by an invisible power. She became ill but her correspondence concerning the Indian problems did not abate. *The Critic* on April 12, 1884, announced that Mrs. Helen Jackson would soon release her first full length novel to appear over her own name, and on May 1, the *Christian Union* announced they would publish the serialization of *Ramona* in an early issue.

She was placed again on the list of American Augustans in the *Youth's Companion*. The novel was eventually to go into 300 printings and was to be called "The Uncle Tom's Cabin of the Indians."

Helen became ill during the following winter in Boston and Cambridge and her illness diagnosed as nerve exhaustion. The doctor warned her against overwork and advised her to stay out of Colorado for two years and to abstain from brainwork. Helen could comply with none of his orders.

Coming back to the house in Colorado Springs, her unexplained restlessness caused her to occupy herself in renovation. She decided the house needed new shades, rugs, furniture, covers, curtains, and a few more "traps." On June 28, 1884, Helen fell on the ill-starred stairs and broke her hip. She apparently recovered from the injury but she was never really well after that fall. She thought perhaps she would venture to California again to enjoy the air and sunshine there.

By now, Congress had passed a bill enabling Indians to take land under the homestead laws without fee and Helen was beginning to see the first fruits of her labors. She began to plan an Indian story for children.

California failed to provide the cure she hoped for. She began to suspect malaria, and all kinds of imaginary illness haunted her, but she apparently did not suspect the true cause of her progressive weakness—that cancer was gradually taking her strength. "Nerve exhaustion," as the doctor called it, had caused her to lose forty-five pounds in seven weeks. With stubborn refusal to yield to her condition, she planned a wagon trip to Mount Shasta. She was tired of the bed. She made elaborate plans for "eight horses and an ambulance, two camp wagons, a phaeton, her maid, her doctor, and four servants," but complete inability to sit up when the time came made it evident to her that she must bow to defeat.

It is said that she prepared everyone for her death except her husband whom she wished to spare. She was surrounded by the flowers and the friends she loved and she refused to be depressed and said she didn't mind considering herself a ghost. She only regretted, "the dying part of death" (words she had once written

Exterior of Helen Hunt Jackson's Colorado Springs Home, 1960

in *Mercy Philbrick's Choice*)—and the fact that she was so late in getting started on her serious writing.

When it became evident that death could no longer be held back, the doctor sent a telegram to her husband who arrived August 2, 1885, and shared her final ten days with her. It was recorded that:

> . . . her last conscious act before morphine was administered was a note to President Grover Cleveland in which she said, "I am dying happier in the belief that I have, that it is your hand that is destined to strike the first steady blow toward lifting this burden of infamy from our country and righting the wrongs of the Indian race."

She was buried above Seven Falls in South Cheyenne Canyon, near Colorado Springs. Her marker became a heap of stones placed by those who paid a pilgrimage to the spot where she had worshiped in Nature's cathedral and where she had translated beauty. It came to be the custom for those pilgrims to bring two rocks to place on the grave and to take one away. Even in death she was a giver, and one who profited by giving. Six years later her body was removed to Evergreen Cemetery in Colorado Springs. There were understandable reasons for the family to move the body from what had become a toll-gated tourist attraction. It seems ironic that, restless as she was in life, H. H. moved again.

The cairn remains on her favorite mountain to remind one of the always incompleted journey and of her poem which expressed that thought when she penned,

"Alas, for the song I never wrote."

H. H.

SEQUEL TO H. H.

Helen Fiske Banfield, a dearly loved visitor to the Kiowa Street house, became the second mistress of that home. She was the niece of H. H. and became the bride of W. S. Jackson three years after the death of Helen Hunt Jackson. Seven children were born to the union and additions were built onto the house for the grow-

55

ing family. Helen Banfield Jackson died quite young in 1899, leaving six surviving children, the oldest of them aged ten. Although the children had never seen H. H., they were acutely aware of her presence in every nook and cranny. At the "Ramona desk" they penned their childish correspondence.

After the death of William S. Jackson in 1919, the house was occupied by the oldest son and his family for nearly a quarter of a century. Three generations of Jacksons have lived in it.

Today it sprawls on the corner across from the City Auditorium, in the middle of a growing city. It is quaint, faded, mellow, and as outmoded as a Victorian novel. As it suns itself it seems to shudder at the parking meters lined up in front of the home where hospitality was always an unmetered gift. The trees grow tall—too tall for the heavy snowstorms—and the present owners grieve with each breaking branch. Green grow the lilacs and purple are their blooms each spring. There is a pervasive air of aristocracy. Even the house cat, a silver tabby, pounces with regal air and grows fur of quality. The old house draws its curtains against the commercial business crowding in on every side. The police department across the alley casts a longing, speculative eye on the location. The third Helen Jackson to live in the house is the daughter of William Sharpless Jackson and Helen Banfield Jackson.

Very little is changed from the days when Helen Hunt Jackson trailed the carpenters with determination. A furnace proves easier to cope with than the original fireplaces in each room. A portrait of H. H. hangs over the "Ramona desk," and her dominant spirit pervades the scene. The kitchen is equipped with a few conveniences. A utility room gives evidence of the same old laundry tubs and hand-wringer and a rusted laundry stove, complete with sad irons on racks by which they were once heated against the sides of the stove. Only one modern improvement stands out like a bandaged thumb—the white automatic gas water heater. Helen Jackson III calls it "the White Witch."

Time goes on and Colorado Springs knows in the back of its mind that it should find some way to preserve this building as a shrine, but the pressure of the times is causing the story to fade.

Some patriotic societies talk about taking it over as a project, but there are so many more urgent things to do. So it stands. In "Flirtation Corner," "Caroline Jackson," the handmade rag doll of Helen Jackson III, sits life-sized and complete even to cotton embroidered lingerie and rocks in a child's rocker and offers no solution to the problem.

H.H., who always wondered what to do with *that house*, smiles from her portrait over the "Ramona desk" and probably wishes she could do something— a few more "traps," or something! Someday the community will wake up, as communities do wake up to opportunities they missed—sometimes, too late.

SOURCES

Helen Hunt Jackson (H. H.), Ruth Odell, D. Appleton-Century Company, Inc. New York, N. Y., 1939

Emily Dickenson, The Human Background of Her Poetry, Josephine Pollitt, Harper & Brothers, New York, N. Y., 1930

The Life and Letters of Emily Dickinson, Martha Dickinson Bianchi, Houghton Mifflin Co., Boston and New York, 1924

World's Popular Encyclopedia, World Syndicate Publishing Co., New York, N. Y., 1937

Mercy Philbrick's Choice, Helen Jackson (H.H.), Little, Brown & Company, Boston, Massachusetts, 1904

Colorado Springs Gazette, 1874, 1875.

and interviews with Miss Helen Jackson, daughter of Helen Banfield Jackson and William Sharpless Jackson.

Nora Gaines, Tugboat Annie

of the Tourist Drivers

No one who saw Nora Gaines ever forgot her. She left her impact on "Li'l Lunnon" because she was an ink blot on the portrait of a city which called itself "cultured." But ask those who lived in Colorado Springs during her time and those who never knew its founder, who were utterly unaware of "Midas" Stratton, who never came nearer Penrose than the foyer of the Broadmoor, and they will catch their breath and smile and say, "Oh sure, I remember Old Lady Gaines." After a pause, they usually say, "Of course, I didn't know her well." With an apologetic manner they explain, "She was pretty rough, not our kind, you know." Most of them will add, "And what I do remember you couldn't put in print!"

So there are gaps and holes in the story because no one really knew her well and few tried. Nora Gaines made people aware of her presence forcibly and brashly. She rubbed "Li'l Lunnon" raw.

Nora Gaines was born in Michigan, probably about 1863, on August 7. Like many women she didn't tell her age. The death certificate guessed about seventy and the undertaker underestimated by a sizeable number of years. Nora was born to Charles Edwin Miller and Sophie Baer Miller. How she happened to come to Colorado is not known. She married Daniel Gaines, a large, burly policeman. It is rumored he eventually lost his job because he wasn't as tough as he looked. At first they lived in a downtown apartment but later moved to Cedar Street, between Platte and High. The cottage was on the west side of the street and was a square, red shingled house, immaculately clean. There was a barn in the back where children watched Nora hitch her team in the barnyard hollow. Their mothers said, "Don't go over and don't talk to her." The mothers didn't call.

Mrs. Gaines was in the most competitive business in Colorado Springs. Moreover, she was competing with men in a field that a woman had never entered in the area before. Tourists were the life-blood of Colorado Springs and she was out for blood. She took her place with twenty or thirty hack drivers who met the D&RG every day and almost snatched the flatlanders bodily off the train. Her sharp tactics were the dismay of her male competitors who resented a woman muscling in and would have preferred that she be more of a lady. What's more, she was a good driver, better than many of the men. Scrupulously honest with her patrons, infuriatingly competent with her horses, she gave her customers even more than their money's worth.

Yet, she was not above petty chicanery. It was the custom for managers of tourist attractions to furnish free passes to relatives of drivers. Ticket-takers became suspicious when Nora Gaines produced a surplus of cousins on her tours. She was passing her customers off as blood kin.

Effete Easterners looking for a thrill and not knowing what to expect in the west were bowled over by the novel experience of a trip with her. She delighted in sharing her mountains with them. They recommended her highly to other Easterners. This did not endear her to the other drivers.

As the tourists arrived, they were pounced upon by the bulky figure. She had a deep booming voice and wore khaki-like masculine appearing clothes and a man's hat. Hitched to the post was a team of well-groomed bay horses, harnessed to a surrey with a fringe on top, and with a buggy whip in the whip socket (seldom for the horses, occasionally for people). It is said she used the whip upon a fellow tourist driver who had baited her. It was common practice for most of her competitors to heckle her as much as possible. It was their defense against a woman who could hold her own. She could swear like a pirate and drive like the devil. Her dark, weatherbeaten face under a man's hat made a contrast to the eastern ladies who shielded their complexions under veils and parasols and who accentuated their feminine curves with lace and ruffles, and who smelled faintly of cologne.

Loading up the four-seater with her victims, Mrs. Gaines proceeded at a fast clip through downtown traffic, swearing at people to get out of her way—they did. It used to be in Colorado Springs that it rained a sudden summer shower every afternoon. Ma Gaines was amply prepared for this and as they trotted toward Manitou she covered her precious charges with old black rubber lap-robes and rain coats. The eating place to which she usually guided them was Edinger's in Manitou. One of her routine tours was over the High Drive where Captain Ellen Jack, another eccentric, had her kingdom of little cottages and some mining properties. The two unusual women were friends of a sort, but the kind of friends who could enjoy each other but without any of the amenities. They fought like tigers but neither cared for the opinion of others or for personal appearance. Each could hold her own. Each had a healthy respect for the other and there was no competitive feeling.

Those who remember at the turn of the century the flower parades recall seeing Nora Gaines, an incongruous figure, with her rig loaded with blossoms—and Nora in her usual outfit. The flower parade was the chief event of the summer time before the city woke up to its heritage and began to boast of its Indian background with Shan Kive, to be superseded eventually by the rodeo.

As Mrs. Gaines's clientele built up and she prospered, she purchased more rigs and horses and moved them to Peck's Corral at the rear of 112 East Cucharras Street. There she became a good friend of the owner of the feed lot. She hired more drivers and treated them honestly. They respected her square dealings and they overlooked her crudities. It was said that her personal habits even in public bordered on the continental. No one actually accused her of indecency. The few who knew her best asserted she was not morally loose, but merely standing her ground in a competitive world. She was meeting men's competition with a man's tactics—they could neither understand it nor accept it.

Naturally such behavior bred enemies. At one time it is said she had taken a group of tourists to Seven Falls. While there, some man in the crowd made audible remarks about Nora Gaines. She reacted with such a virulent vocabulary that the owners of the attraction feared for their reputation and forbade her to bring her tourists there any more. This was a severe punishment, for the Seven Falls has always been one of the most popular scenic trips. At one time she decided to ignore the ultimatum and drove brazenly with her load toward the Falls. She was met halfway up the Canyon by employees who unhitched the horses, turned the surrey around, and headed her back home. Nora Gaines had her revenge in her own way. About this time tourists met at the Busy Corner area in front of the Exchange National Bank to wait for the streetcar which ran to the end of Stratton Park (two fares). At that point, they might either walk, ride a burro, or take a hack to the Falls. Admission cost twenty-five cents but you could stay all day. Such a group was gathered in town one morning. It was a dry season and the bright sky gave no promise of rain. Trotting up the street came "Old Lady Gaines" in her rig. Pulling up before the crowd she yelled, "Where are you going?" and some unsuspecting tenderfoot replied, truthfully, "To Seven Falls." At this point Ma Gaines made an unquotable, pithy observation which had to do with the present drouth, the small stream of water trickling over the Falls, and an odious comparison of a natural phenomenon.

Come fall and the departure of the greenhorns, the town began to hibernate for the winter. The loveliest season of the year belonged to Nora Gaines. With her rig and horses she was often seen on the Old Stage Road and on the High Drive gathering evergreens and red-berried kinnikinnick. She kept them moist in her bathtub. As the days grew shorter toward December, she cut her supply of Christmas trees and she handled the ax as capably as a man could. Then just before Christmas she fashioned her greens into wreaths and took her stand in front of Robbins-on-the-Corner. No one had brighter berries or better trees, and many a beautifully clad woman bought her wares hurriedly and forgot to say "Merry Christmas."

The fringe wore off the surrey, the top came down, but such

transportation was becoming outmoded anyway. With the end of the horse and buggy days, Mrs. Gaines kept pace with the times by buying a few cars for her tourist trade and hired her nephew, Charlie, as one of her drivers. Sometimes she deceived her customers by meeting them at the train with a car and then driving a few blocks and transferring them to her waiting rig. She began to lose color as a character. Femininity was on the wane. She stood out less distinctly.

One of her first cars was a Lincoln. She also had a green Studebaker. The Lincoln was a good investment for the tourist trade but she had no desire to impress home folks. It was merely a business investment for her. Sometimes she would go to the coal yards and load a sack of coal which she would heave into the back seat and cover with a blanket.

People faintly remember Daniel Gaines but no one recalls whether he was aggressive or meek. There is a story told of the time Nora framed him. He was a spiritualist and she connived with a medium to tell him that he would soon feel a blow on the chest and that it would be a signal for the end. Then Nora proceeded to whomp him a healthy blow on his chest in the middle of the night. Gaines woke, sure that the end was near. The raconteur said, "There was always a little bit of hell in her."

In spite of her deviltry she must have been genuinely fond of Gaines. When he died, she buried him in Evergreen Cemetery and it is said she often visited the grave and sang hymns. Again she was an individual doing an unusual thing and people considered it abnormal behavior.

There are those who say she did and those who say she didn't marry Louis Whittaker. Louis is remembered as a mousy sort of little man, and a miserable driver. Folks said there were gears in his cars when he started, but he just preferred to ignore them. No wonder Ma Gaines used to call him at the Cave of the Winds on each trip to check and tell him what to do. Perhaps the relationship had an Oedipus flavor. Certainly Ma Gaines mothered and smothered him. Conjectures continued to be made as to whether she was married to Whittaker—later evidence in her death certificate bore out the name of Whittaker, but she was indelibly labeled Old Lady—or Ma—Gaines. When Louis died she buried him beside Daniel Gaines in the plot which she had bought, let the world say what it might.

Here is the portrait which the community saw and which it remembers: a woman who was not like a woman—one who was raucous, uncouth, tough as nails, honest, uncompromising, uninhibited, and socially unacceptable.

But this picture was not complete. There were a few who cared enough to see that there might be another angle to the portrait. Mrs. Gaines had no close friends, but from one who drew as near as Ma Gaines would allow came another picture. After Christmas it was the habit of Nora Gaines to go to Hermosa Beach and sometimes to the U.S. Grant Hotel in San Diego. At one time she invited her Colorado Springs friend to call on her at the beach. It was another personality who opened the door. Here was a well-groomed woman, dressed in a neat black dress, wearing earrings, diamonds, and heels. Her hair was marcelled and only the weather-beaten skin gave any evidence of "Old Lady Gaines." She was a different person and a different personality. She had cleaned up her person and her language. Apparently when she relaxed she put on her corsets!

Two other old friends verified this dual personality. One of her closest acquaintances, a former tourist driver, recalled how he used to give her a few customers some times, and on such days she declared him to be an angel. Then there were days when he had none to spare and on such times he assumed a cloven hoof and a forked tail. Once he recalled telling her of a movie that was running at the Burns Theatre. "The main character is called Apple Annie," he told her, "and she's just like you. You even look like her. Only the movie version is *Lady for a Day*. With you," he said, "you are a lady for six months."

Ma Gaines left her rig hitched in the street and went to the Burns Theatre to see herself in the movies. She was pleased with Apple Annie. What woman doesn't believe she could have been in movies?

Police department officials recall that she did much charity in the city and that undoubtedly the sacks of coal in the back seat

63

of her Lincoln were for some unfortunate family. She often called on the police for names of those in need.

Another friend who knew her well said that most people did not understand her and maintained, "People do not tell the truth about her because they did not know her. Actually," she said, "Nora Gaines was a shy person." There are others who laugh at this story and say, "Shy?—Hell!" and they shrug. There are some who venture to guess that she was aggressive to protect what might be hurt—that she might have been an embittered person with something traumatic in her past.

Only in the last two years of her life did Nora Gaines slow down, and then it was with reluctance. She asked her friends to place her "valuables," contained in a shoe box tied with twine, in their safe. They put them away carefully until she called for them shortly before her death. When the box was opened, it contained only useless papers and old receipts. Nothing of any value was left. She had given too much away. An acquaintance brought her an occasional delicacy in the final days and was urged to take home some memento but didn't, reluctant to let Nora Gaines know that her days were numbered. The friend said, "You'll be driving a hack again before you know it." So the little memento was left on the shelf and disappeared.

An old organ was promised to a special friend but it, too, vanished.

On October 14, 1933, Nora Gaines died. The funeral was held on October 17, an Episcopal service with six policemen as pallbearers. She was given the minimum number of lines in the vital statistics column of the local newspaper. Those who had laughed at her in life did not weep nor particularly notice her passing.

The tourists still come to Colorado Springs and the competition is still keen, but the approach is more subtle. No colorful, clamoring, cursing figure drags them off the train. But ask anyone in town who lived there during her time and he will say, "Old Lady Gaines? Sure I remember!"

POSTSCRIPT

One other woman entered the competition as a Colorado Springs tourist driver during the time of Nora Gaines, and old-timers tell us she was a lady and that she operated a rig and ran a cottage court over close to the old glass works and did a nice job—but invariably they have to stop and think—. She was a lady and that's all they can recall.

One interview concerning Nora Gaines was with the chief of police who has seen so many facets of life through the years. His parting admonition was, "Don't let them forget Mother Gaines!"

SOURCES

Colorado Springs Gazette and Telegraph, October 17, 1933
 Interviews with
Fred Murdoch
Mrs. Merton Robbins
William Crosby
Lieutenant Colonel Perry Parr
Mrs. William Tudor
Dora Foster
Mrs. Adele Denton
City and County Health Department
Mrs. Hazel Pickett
Albert Finney
Martin Drake
Law Mortuary
Walter Colburn
Mr. Roulette
Mr. and Mrs. Ted Beals
Nat Leonard
Clyde Snider
and particularly I. B. Bruce, Chief of Police, Colorado Springs
Springs
and correspondence with Mrs. C. D. Weimer, Taos, New Mexico

Captain Ellen E. Jack,
"The Fate of a Fairy"

At the turn of the century a mystery woman came to the High Drive above the city of Colorado Springs. Small of stature, of obvious education, but eccentric, she staked her mining claim, explored the mountains, and asserted that she had found a fabulous cave. Here she built a few cottages for a more certain income and became a kind of landmark to all who knew her as "Captain Jack." Here the elite of Broadmoor rode their thoroughbreds past her establishment, tour drivers stopped their rigs as they came up from Bear Creek Canyon, and children vacationing over at Laveley's summer camp came to gather the abundance of red raspberries in their straw hats. Here they found an aristocrat in the rough, clad in heavy skirts, with the scar from an Indian tomahawk still visible on her forehead.

Few people knew her story or asked. She wasn't the kind to answer too many questions, but she had a story.

It began in England on November 4, 1842, when Ellen E. Elliott was born to Quaker parents, William and Elizabeth Elliott, manufacturers of Nottingham lace curtains. The nine children of the Elliotts romped over the large family estate. From the beginning Ellen was a mystical child. Even the gypsies recognized her fey qualities.

It was at the Goose Fair at Nottingham when she was seven that the gypsy queen, tall and dark, took Ellen by the hand and led her home, to her mother. The gypsy turned Ellen's hair back from her forehead and said:

> The child was born to be a great traveler and if she had been a male would have been a great mining expert. She is a Rosicrucian, born to find hidden treasures. She will meet great sorrows and be a widow early in life. Fire will cause her great trouble and losses.

The words "born to find hidden treasure" rang in Ellen's ears and having overheard her father say that he put his money in the bank, she decided to dig in the bank of the nearby river Trent with an old knife. All she got for her pains was ridicule.

Great-grandmother was 107 when she foresaw her own death. For many years Granny had been a kind of neighborhood attraction for her advanced age and she resented small Ellen, who also drew attention for her looks and her intelligence. Granny was not above retaliating by snatching Ellen's hair out by the roots and mother became the buffer between the two. At Granny's death Ellen remarked, "Then I could go about without having my hair torn out."

Shortly thereafter the Elliotts left the ancestral home which had been in the family for 300 years. Misfortune followed the move. The brewery in which they invested in Manchester was a financial failure.

Even as a child Ellen was fearless and at one time while living with her married sister, all the bells in the house began to ring. Her sister refused to stay, but Ellen was determined to see the ghost and she discovered the rational explanation—rats running across the wires in the attic.

When she was quite a young girl romance came to Ellen in the form of a Russian lover, handsome and jealous and impetuous. On seeing her at the opera one evening with her male cousin, the enraged lover stabbed her three times with a dagger.

A sea voyage was prescribed for Ellen. Accompanied by her sister and brother-in-law, she went to New York, but there she became ill. It was on her return to England, weak and wan, that she met Captain Jack, who was the first officer on the ship. He said:

> When I saw her beautiful golden locks I was attracted to her and when I picked her up in my arms I knew she belonged to me, and I will have her, let the weather be fair or foul.

Charles E. Jack, the first officer, gave all his attention to blonde Ellen.

Captain Ellen Jack, from *Fate of a Fairy*

The weather on the trip home was both fair and foul and during the foul weather Ellen kept to her berth, but one moonlight night when the weather was fair the captain declared his intentions. Young Ellen did the proper amount of hesitating for the times. The captain cursed so foul a villain as her former lover who had caused her such pain. Captain Jack begged for an answer but Ellen was only interested in how long the ocean voyage would last and in whether this would prove to be just another shipboard romance. But on September 9, 1860, they were married in England and then returned to America where Ellen spent some time with her husband's family.

Captain Jack's step-mother, Ellen's new mother-in-law, was scarcely older than the bride herself, and unaccustomed to certain refinements. Most of the people Ellen met "wore diamonds and dressed in bad taste." One family ". . . had the finest cut glass decanters they could get. Madame put the champagne in the decanters." Such desecration was an offense to Ellen's breeding. "I pitied the poor foolish people who exposed their own ignorance in such a manner."

Civil War experiences followed close on the heels of the honeymoon, and like all young girls, Ellen waved at the troops as they went down the East River.

An unusual experience happened during the war. Her husband captured the Union steamer *Kate* which was trying to run the blockade. In the cargo on board was a personal object belonging to General Robert E. Lee. Since this had nothing to do with the war directly, and because he and Lee were brother Masons, Captain Jack returned the package to the defeated general. The general showed his gratitude by presenting Captain Jack with a diamond ring which bore the date of 1314 and which had been in many strange adventures. Accompanying the ring was a note, "Please accept from a gentleman and an officer who wears the Gray. Robert E. Lee." Ellen carefully guarded the ring and said she would give it to the South later on.

During the war period Ellen was introduced to the Lincolns and attended parties of the officers and their wives where she was struck by the contrast of their finery with the accounts of the suffering of the prisoners in Andersonville.

A share in the Elliott family fortune came to Ellen and she spent a part of it on an extensive European tour.

When her husband became ill, Ellen took over the financial responsibilities of their growing family. In Chicago, she dabbled in real estate to the tune of $25,000 profit in fourteen months. The captain attempted to support his family with a venture in the wholesale grocery business but found he was "all at sea" on land and not much of a business man.

On their return to Brooklyn, Captain Jack was put in charge of the Brooklyn Navy Yard. Here Ellen claims to have taken an active part in historic events. The Spanish ship *The Ariapolis* was to be blown up with all hands on board. Captain Jack could not bring himself to commit what he felt was the equivalent of murder, but Ellen came to the rescue—she slipped out of the house at night, went down to the Navy Yard, and cut the fuses so that when her husband and his men went forth to carry out their orders—it was to no avail.

The ensuing years of her life were to be marked by the death of her husband in 1873, the loss of her children, and disastrous fires which dissolved her savings. The gypsy's prophecy was working out. Ellen came to Pueblo, Colorado, from Brooklyn, and then to Denver. From this time on, Ellen herself was to be known as "Captain Jack."

Walking down Sixteenth Street in Denver she was hailed by a well-dressed woman who turned out to be her former nursemaid, Jennie. When confidences were exchanged, Captain Jack learned that Jennie had endured bestial treatment from a philandering husband and in revenge against the entire male sex had established herself in the house of Madame Clara Dumont and was bent on wrecking every man she could.

It was Jennie who advised Captain Jack to go to Gunnison— and she took the next available stage. Captain Jack was warned that her beauty and sex would be hazards on such a trip, but she declared that she carried an "equalizer" and could use it and that all women ought to be able to protect themselves against ruffians.

She kept her diamonds and government bonds sewed in her bustle and carried nothing of value in her satchel. She found the .44 a necessary piece of equipment and was called on to use it often, which she did with accuracy and dispatch!

There is a surplus of "Captain Jacks" in western history. There are those who say that Jack's Cabin north of Gunnison is named for Jack Howe. Ellen Jack herself said that she established the community of Jack's Cabin. There was another Captain Jack of Colorado history who was a capable writer and scout. Also, there was a Captain Jack, an Indian of the Ute-Meeker fiasco. Such similarity of names breeds confusion. And the "grave" on the High Drive labeled Captain L. Jacks? Five Jacks might be considered loading the deck!

Be that as it may, Ellen E. established herself on a mining claim in the Gunnison area. In 1882, she gained control of the Black Queen mine, a mile above Crystal, probably in the Lead King Basin area.

Ellen had thought for a long time that her life was controlled by spirits—that she had spirits all around her all the time, that good or evil, they influenced her. In business transactions she felt it an advantage to follow first impressions, but when she stopped to consider and to take advice, she was sure to lose.

When she decided to marry again, however, she failed to heed her voices. Walsh "was a tall, fine-looking old gentleman, and was a warden of the Catholic church, and a widower." He came right out and asked Ellen to marry him. Her first husband had been fifteen years her senior, and Ellen considered that since Walsh was twenty years older than she, he would be a father as well as a husband. She said, "Without thinking, I took my small satchel and not even a change of clothing, and took the train and went with him." In Denver, they went to the St. James Hotel and the license was purchased and he "made arrangements for Bishop Macerby to marry us the next morning." Ellen tended to slight inaccuracies in names of places and people—such as Scafield (for Schofield) and Crister Butte (for Crested Butte) so one is inclined to think that the bishop here referred to may have been the Catholic Bishop Machebeuf. Since Ellen was a member of

Scene along the Lead King Basin near the location of Ellen Jack's Black Queen Mine.

Crystal City, near Ellen Jack's mine.

the Episcopal church, special permission was required from the bishop for their marriage.

Ellen said, "I don't know, but I feel I am doing wrong in getting married, and I would rather go to the depot and go back as we came." Walsh called her a coward which infuriated her.

During the ceremony the voices of invisible children set up such a crying and a man's voice said, "No" so loudly that she jumped back and the ring fell to the floor and rolled to the priest. She couldn't understand why the others didn't hear the voices. At any rate, after the ceremony, Walsh left her waiting at the hotel for hours, until she picked up her satchel, went to the depot, bought a ticket, and left on the 6:20 train.

The ill-omened marriage went from bad to worse. Ellen found herself "in the toils of a robber and a murderer." It was to take many years and much money to clear her of the bonds of matrimony.

The Black Queen property she sold for $25,000; one year later it brought $3,000,000 and still later a valuation of $42,000,000 was placed on it.

A contemporary said of Captain Jack:

> A scar on her forehead, made by an Indian with a poisoned tomahawk, in the last days of the Gunnison uprisings, was a mark of her days spent among the din and confusion of frequent encounters.

The expensive litigations involved in her dealings with Walsh led Ellen to sell out her holdings in Gunnison. In 1900 she established her claim on the High Drive overlooking Colorado Springs. With her string of burros she combed the hills looking for the promised treasure and recording the memories of her early years in a book called *The Fate of a Fairy* which was published in 1908.

In her autobiography she revealed much of her own personal philosophy, that there:

> . . . is a power far stronger than that which forces us to our destiny, and we ought to be on our guard all the time for strangers that we know not, for some people carry a straight light around them that is destruction to one that carries the opposite light. For when a murder wave or a suicide wave

73

Another Captain Jack? Marker on the High Drive near Colorado Springs.

All that remains of the settlement of Jack's Cabin.

74

comes to a city you will know there will be many before it travels on . . . There is a triangle of three powers that govern both heaven and earth—electricity, vibration, and this force power, I know not what to call it,* but it comes in waves and in different colors and does its work according to its color . . . Nations rise and fall by it, and when the saints turn their attention to it we will have airships and farmers will use it instead of horses, and all trains and cars will be pushed by it. . .

After twenty-seven years of wandering through the Rocky Mountains in the far West I drop amongst the people as though I came from the clouds, and what do I find: That our public schools are teaching both boys and girls to be sports. The girls feel degraded to go out and do housework and they know nothing of housework, and want a piano the first thing. The boys will not work and are looking for a soft snap, to be a doctor or a lawyer or a politician—anything to get a graft out of the public—and the brainy men that are fitted for these positions are at their wits' end to know how to compete with this army of grafters; and as I wander on I find a lot of people banded together as temperance unions, or different names, who have been reformed drunkards and had to take a big oath and have a mob at their backs to keep them from getting drunk. These are degenerates, for if man or woman cannot drink beer, wine, or liquor without getting beastly intoxicated, he has no will power and is a degenerate. These are a curse to the country, for they say, "We do not drink now and you shall not drink." So they want to take the rights of the level-headed people away, who do not say we drink and you must let these people go back to olden times. When we had good mothers they taught their children to drink without being drunkards, as they taught them to eat without being gluttons. Mothers, stay at home and teach your children to eat, drink and work and be good men and women, instead of drunkards, degenerates and drones; even the bees know enough to destroy their drones.

I look farther and I find they have built railroads under the rivers in New York and built buildings twenty and thirty stories high. In every city where there are large sheets of water there is danger of a volcanic eruption which they call earthquake. When they come, I would rather be in the mountains than near those high buildings.

*The Los Angeles Group of the Rosicrucian Order maintains that the third force of the triangle is the power of creation and perfection which joins the other two making the perfect triangle which is the symbol of perfection.

75

So she stayed in the safety of the West, making her home in summers on the High Drive and in the winter in her little cottage in town just below the Nevada Avenue underpass. Driving by, people would see her brilliantly colored parrots in the trees in front of her house. Sometimes she would confide to her few associates in the tourist business that she regretted the necessity for "ladies like us to have to associate with the likes of Nora Gaines." But then again in the loneliness of the High Drive it was good to see even Mother Gaines's rig coming over the top of the hill with its obstreperous driver, and to be able to exchange greetings or vituperations according to whether the weather was fair or foul.

Leakage of the heart was the final price for the strenuous life, and death the last payment. Captain Jack tried desperately to get back once more to her cabin on the High Drive, but the disastrous flood of June 3, 1921, washed out all roads up the canyon. There was speculation whether the road would ever be rebuilt and some maintained that Captain Jack's grief over the damage to her domain hastened her death. She died June 17, 1921. The ladies of the G.A.R. conducted the funeral service on June 20, and she was buried in Evergreen Cemetery in the same block with General Palmer.

Two years later headlines in the *Colorado Springs Gazette* read, "New Captain Jack's Place Now Being Constructed on the High Drive." Nora Gaines had purchased the property and a dance hall forty-two feet long was to be the main feature. The new Captain Jack's place was to serve as a resting point for hikers and motorists. Mr. and Mrs. T. D. Miller of Michigan (relatives of Nora Gaines?) were to be in complete control of the quarters. The newspaper offered the assurance that "Mrs. Gaines will not have charge of the place."

A newspaper picture in May of the same year showed two scenes at Captain Jack's on the Buckhorn Trail with Spencer Penrose, C. L. Tutt, and a Mr. R. K. Dougherty on the new trail. Extreme left was Cliff Frager, cowboy guide. Hubert Strang was in charge of nature study and wild life trips. One hundred and twenty miles of trails had just been completed in the Pikes Peak Region. It was the tourist drivers who had given the "High

Drive" its name because the people in the horse drawn vehicles wanted to go to as high a point as possible, but when the automobile came it was a wise precaution to drop the name "High Drive" and to refer to it as "Buckhorn Pass." It was eventually to revert back to the old designation of "High Drive."

The rotting cabins are only a fading landmark now, but the area still bears the name and personality of its former owner. The bridle trail still brings the thoroughbreds from the Broadmoor Stables, and cars pause at the top before descending into Bear Creek Canyon, but no children walk so far to gather raspberries in their hats. People look at a rounded bit of earth that bears the marker inscribed with the words, "Captain L. Jacks." Whether it is the work of a prankster or the grave of a burro—or one more Captain Jack is a mystery. People pause and say, "I wonder who *he* was?" The wind blows through the pines in the early fall; perhaps Captain Jack's voice is one of the whispers in the wind now. Over the hill at dusk does Old Lady Gaines come riding in her rig to disturb the peace? She will be late getting home tonight.

SOURCES

The Fate of A Fairy or Twenty-seven Years in the Far West, Ellen E. Jack, M. A. Donahue & Co., Chicago, Illinois, 1910

Stampede to Timberline, Muriel Sibell Wolle, University of Colorado, Boulder, Colorado, 1949 (1952 printing)

Guide to the Colorado Ghost Towns and Mining Camps, Perry Eberhart, Sage Books, Denver, Colorado, 1959

Colorado Springs Gazette, May 20, 1923

Colorado Springs Gazette Telegraph, November 15, 1959, article by Charles Dudley

Interviews and correspondence with
Fred Murdoch
Mrs. C. D. Weimer of Taos, New Mexico
William Crosby
Mrs. William Tudor
Mrs. Hazel Pickett
Walter Colburn
and assistance from Joan Shinew of Coburn Library, Colorado College

Martin Bowden,

The Hermit of "Purgatory" Canyon

"Something there is that doesn't love a wall," said Robert Frost, but the opposite is also true. Something about a blank wall invites a pencil and Martin Bowden never got over the urge to make his mark on walls. This tendency does not always endear one to family, friends, or landlords, but in the case of Martin Bowden it was different and he carried the habit with him into solitude.

He was born in Lyons, France, in 1884 of an Italian mother who was a gifted singer and a father who later become a miner. The Baudinos, as they were called then, came to America while Martin was still a small child. The family drifted westward where the father became involved in mining and farming. An uncle, on enlisting in the U. S. Army during the Spanish American War, changed the family name to Bowden because of the unpopularity of Latin-sounding names at that time. Life in Colorado took on the usual pattern with the Bowden children attending the little red school on the mesa. Martin showed an early talent with his drawing pencil. Sometimes he came to the assistance of his less talented brother, John. On one occasion, the family states that the untalented brother was given the home assignment to draw the schoolhouse, which task he relegated to Martin, who in turn produced an amazing likeness of the structure, exact in detail, including the outhouse. The teacher was overwhelmed and announced that tomorrow they would repeat their drawings—on the blackboard. The pseudo-artist was A. W. O. L. the following day, and somehow lost his touch!

School wasn't always exciting for Martin. At the age of fourteen he came home one evening and announced to his mother that he had decided not to go back, but to work in the mines instead. Maturity and the glamor of employment appealed to him but after two days of aching muscles, he again approached his mother with the announcement that he had decided to relinquish his new found freedom and go back to school. His mother informed him that since he had chosen the mines he could just continue. So ended the formal education of Martin Bowden.

Sometimes a man who loves the sun and color and animals and the outdoors finds himself assigned to an ill-fitting niche. So Martin Bowden found employment in the coal mines around the little southern Colorado town of Trinidad. It was not a vocation of choice, but one must eat. Yet, during this employment he never overcame the feeling of claustrophobia and the desire to push back the narrow walls. He brought his colored chalk sticks in his pocket to give a little color to the coal cars and the black walls of the mine. Somehow these crude and incongruous murals gave the feeling that the walls had been pierced and when he looked at them, he stepped through their adamant prison. This was his contribution—the way he brought Persephone to Pluto's diminion. But the day came when he decided to leave the mines forever. A man can stand only so much of a grave before its time.

So Martin became a cowboy and a blacksmith and a metal worker. He is still remembered for his skill with his hands in metal work. He made his own cuff-links from bits of metal and was even his own dentist, sometimes taking the shells from his 30-30 to fashion caps for his molars.

He acquired a ranch, but now that he had found opportunity to live above ground he was not at all sure that this was what he wanted. He soon learned that man never owns the land. The land owns him. Possessions become possessors. He was forced to conform to nature and to bow to her deviltry and pay interest to the banker between crops. He was confident that this was not what he wanted of life. Perhaps that is how he came to turn the ranch over to his nephews.

The hermit of Purgatoire Canyon, Martin Bowden. *Photo courtesy Mrs. Hal Russell.*

However, Martin was not averse to holding on to the land from a distance for a few dollars which a man must have, but he cared nothing for more than he needed. A place in the sun was what he literally desired, and that place not too near to men. Men complicated life. Women were worse. A dog was better. In choosing a site he wandered far out on the plains east of Trinidad. The prairies were hot and dry and barren but there were no permanent shadows on them. Few ranchers had the temerity to put a plow to those dry acres. An occasional windmill, sometimes showing the worst of combat with the storms, was the only high spot. Sometimes a heap of stones indicated the abandoned altar of a Penitente shepherd. An occasional herd of antelope could be seen lying near a murky stream. Eventually the prairie dropped suddenly to a sheer canyon, walling in a flat valley at its base.

Bowden descended the precipitous red cliffs of Purgatoire Canyon and spent days and weeks exploring the desolate flat valley.

The Purgatoire River offered a small relief from the summer heat. Strange sounds rose from the floor of the canyon. Indians long ago labeled the place haunted and early settlers vowed they had heard wails of trapped souls and had given it the sinister title of *El Rio de Los Animas Perdidos en Purgatoire*. Scientists made some sort of explanation of underground caves and water moving in them. Martin Bowden was assured the place was spirit inhabited but he had no fear of the spirits. From the valley the walls rose straight and smooth and high. Far up the stream there were strange Indian pictures cut into the cliffs, marking the old Indian trail. Farther on were hieroglyphics that might have been messages carved by early travelers. Martin Bowden became aware that here was a natural and unlimited canvas spread before him!

On top of the canyon rim was the crude hut of a homesteader. The place looked ideal to Martin Bowden and he visited the old man who occupied it. The old settler was not hard to deal with. He had had enough of frying and freezing and purgatory to last a lifetime. He relinquished his equity, shrugged into his jacket and left. Martin Bowden finished out the old man's term.

During the next forty years he spent his summer days painting some forty murals on the canyon walls. A brother came to live with him and occupy a part of the house, and a dog was his close companion. When the brother died, Martin closed the door to his brother's part of the house and the little dog became more important than ever.

It was in the late forties that a few people began to hear strange rumors of the hermit who lived on the canyon rim and painted huge murals there. People began to seek local guides to chart them across the unmarked prairie. Laden with lunch basket and water bottle plus an occasional gift of Scotch for Martin, they followed a rattler trail, sensing the way rather than seeing it. The guide took his bearings usually from a battered windmill, or a dry stream bed, all the time scanning the horizon for an infinitesimal dot of a house. If the visitors had any preconceived notion of how a hermit should look, they were destined to be disillusioned. A dapper looking little man with bright, black Latin eyes met them with a smile. His gray beard belied the evidence that there was no barber in miles. It was trimmed with precision to a sharp Van Dyke as crisp-lined as his features. He might have been an artist on Royal Street. A little mongrel dog tagged at his heels. Martin always appreciated visitors, and the Scotch, and urged guests to make themselves at home and sign his guest book. They were always amazed to find that as many as twenty-five people a day made the forty-mile trek and that the hermit welcomed them all.

He urged visitors to see his pictures. Martin Bowden was still escaping through walls.

On hot summer days, the travelers stepped cautiously in fear of rattlers, although the only one encountered was usually the painted one just below the cabin. Martin always explained that he had a live model for that picture. The first painting

Home of Martin Bowden on edge of Purgatoire Canyon.

Tiger, Tiger, burning bright. ... One of Martin Bowden's murals on Purgatoire Canyon.

above the cabin was that of a little bulldog. This startling mural was quite realistic and looked as though it might bark at any moment. He usually led his guests down a path to the edge of a cliff to peer over and see paintings which had been done in the most precarious spots.

"How did you reach these?" was the inevitable question, and he would reply that often he had to build scaffolding before he could begin. His first scaffoldings had been built for him by his nephews but after a near fall, he did most of his paintings from a homemade ladder.

"What kind of paint did you use?" he was often asked.

"Just house paint," he would reply, "used to bring it out from town and then spend the whole summer painting with it." Then he would add, "I haven't painted for quite a while. Not anything new, that is. I just touch them up now and then to keep them from fading. First thing I always did," he would continue to reminisce, "was to draw the outline and then chisel it into the rock. Sometimes I sharpened my chisels many times a day. Someday I won't be able to touch them up and the sand and weather will wear them down, but the chiseling is going to stay."

Maybe he chiseled these paintings deep into the rock to be sure they would last after he was gone just as every man tries to speak a little longer than his tongue can speak, and breathe past the time for breathing, and live past the time for living. Some men fulfill the same urge for immortality by writing a book, or making a will, or siring their children.

Eventually the trail led to a chimney-like hole at the edge of the cliff through which descent could be made to see a very special group of paintings. A crude ladder was anchored to the cliff wall. Only by means of this ladder could one see the paintings, practically secreted from the rest of the valley. It was in this particular section that he had painted the face of the one woman in the whole collection.

The first ladder came to an end and transfer became necessary to another ladder which led out of the chimney and down the

84

sheer vertical face of the cliff. A wire was the only safety measure in making the transfer. One invariably came up with the paraphrase about changing ladders in mid-cliff. It was no place for the timid, the overweight, or the ulcer-prone. It was hard to visualize that old man going up and down these ladders with the agility of one of his prairie animals, and making the trek several times a day with paint bucket, chisels, and brushes.

At the bottom of the cliff, Buffalo Bill and one or two others waited with stony stares, but it was the woman most people came to see. The portrait was that of a pretty face, but it was storyless. It appeared to be deliberately impersonalized. A few were bold enough to ask the artist about her. It seems every one imagined a romance, but the hermit always evaded an answer.

Occasionally a visitor, half ill from heat or fear, would remark upon climbing back up that dizzy cliff that he had really prayed to get out of purgatory!

There was another trail that could be taken. It wound below the cabin past the painted antelope, cowboys on horses, mountain sheep, the rattlesnake, tigers, kangaroos, and every animal that had caught the artist's imagination. An interesting mark by the rattlesnake was an arrow. "That," said Martin Bowden, "points to the rock where I saw him."

If Martin Bowden had chiseled his pictures into the heart of his canyon, he no less certainly chiseled them into the hearts of those who knew him best. His friends often felt concern for him, alone so much of the time. The winter storms were hazardous to a man growing older. Yet, he loved this strange home and could not have been coaxed away.

Once he had been very ill and had lain unconscious on the floor of his cabin for several days before a friend had found him and had taken him to the Trinidad hospital. The calendar which he turned religiously each morning gave clue to the length of time he had been ill. When he regained consciousness in the hospital, it is said that he looked around at his strange surroundings and made the classic observation, "Hell, this ain't the canyon," got out

Eagle and kangaroo, incongruous companions on the walls of Purgatoire Canyon were painted by Martin Bowden.

Mural showing Rocky Mountain sheep in realistic setting along the trail to Purgatoire River, as painted by Martin Bowden.

of bed, and was discovered as he was going out the back door of the hospital clad only in his short nightgown!

Until the year 1958, a growing stream of visitors called on Martin Bowden, but after August of that year, he no longer waited for them at his gate. He had been ill for some time and suffered intensely at recurring intervals. He became apprehensive of his condition and the shortening shadows, but he refused hospitalization. He declined to leave his home. All summer he became more and more aware that time was running out. He had always had a love for animals. You had only to look at his paintings to understand that. He must have dreaded the fate his little dog would meet if left alone on that prairie. It could be some time before his nephew would come with supplies and mail.

One August day, when the pain must have become unbearable, he picked up his shotgun and tried to kill his little dog. Perhaps he stunned it. Its ear was shot off. Then turning the gun in his own mouth, he put an end to the Martin Bowden story.

Late in the fall, visitors still came to find the cabin deserted. The door was unlocked and the half of the house once occupied by Martin's brother was still closed as it had been. Martin's bedroom was dark, dusty, and deserted. His books were piled on a nearby table. The kitchen recalled the family story of his culinary skill and his big feather-light biscuits and his specialty of chicken prepared with his own secret sauces. On the wall, the calendar was turned to the day of his death. A pan of beans sat on the cold stove, and a deck of cards was topped by the Queen of Diamonds. He had lost another game of solitaire. Did the Queen of Diamonds look a bit like the face on the canyon wall? Probably not. An unfinished crossword puzzle lay nearby.

There was kerosene in the lamp but the light had been blown out. The ashes were cold in the pan. The wood box was filled. A shaving brush and bowl near at hand told the story of a neat Van Dyke beard. The adobe fireplace was sealed against the cold. A dark blood stain spread over the linoleum in a darkening pattern.

The winter supply of piñon wood was stacked high against the house. The gate to the path was topped with a horseshoe to hold luck, but turned wrong side up.

Old friends still came but no one used the cliff ladder any more. It might be in need of repair.

Some of those who made the pilgrimage to the rocky shrine remembered a man who asked for little and who knew how much was enough. Below the deserted cabin the wind and sand beat incessantly against the murals on the canyon walls.

SOURCES

Interviews with
Mr. and Mrs. John Grosso
Frank Grosso
Mr. and Mrs. Hal Russell
Claire Gilstrap

Three Views of Redstone

There is an aura of mystery which pervades the entire Crystal River Valley from Carbondale to Crystal City. There are some who say there is an actual spell which still lingers there.

Nowhere is this sense of *Brigadoon* mystery more acute than in the little village of Redstone which appears as if it had been transported by a giant hand controlled by an imaginative mind; and so it was.

Here flower gardens and neat fences enclose the fairy-tale Swiss cottages. The unexpected glamor of a towered inn with whimsical gables is startling. The eye is carried naturally to the clock which tells the present hour but gives no clue to the minutes which have ticked away and the quarter hours which have struck since November 2, 1902, when the giant brought his dream to life.

The climax waits at the end of the lamp-lighted road which leads to a Tudor castle.

The giant of the valley and the lord of the castle was John Cleveland Osgood, a man whose background was an enigma. Osgood was born in Brooklyn, New York, March 6, 1851, of English stock. His family history included founders of Andover, Massachusetts, and Cleveland, Ohio. From them he inherited the qualities of leadership and perseverance which dominated his life. Orphaned at nine, he was educated in public schools and the Friends Boarding School in Providence, Rhode Island. All of these experiences and his life with Quaker relatives, bore their mark. Here were rooted the seeds of sympathy, mercy, and an undeviating purpose, which were to be the controlling factors in his life and which have not been erased from his valley even yet.

As a fourteen-year-old errand boy in a manufacturer's office,

Redstone Inn.

Cleveholm Castle.

at $1.50 a month, Osgood began his Horatio Alger climb. At such a salary scale the ascent had to be fast. It was. From a clerkship with the firm of William H. Ladd of New York City, Osgood undertook to improve himself with a bookkeeping course and position with Union Coal Company of Ottumwa, Iowa. When he became cashier of the First National Bank, he noticed the large bank balances of the coal companies. Wheels began to turn in his shrewd mind.

In the early 1880's the young clerk left Iowa for Colorado to scout for coal for the Burlington Railroad. He was impressed by the large coking coal deposits. Here he fell under the enchantment of the Crystal River Valley. From this moment his life took on new meaning.

At the age of thirty-one, John Osgood established an office in Pueblo, Colorado, which was later described by the *New York Times* as a concern of "one room and a boy." Here he maneuvered the consolidation of the Colorado Coal and Iron Company with the Colorado Fuel Company to form the Colorado Fuel and Iron Corporation. When demand exceeded supply, Osgood formed a precarious partnership with Rockefeller. There were now two captains and only one ship. Osgood extended his own holdings from Pueblo to Garfield, Gunnison, and Pitkin counties.

By this time the young upstart had brought himself to the attention of Wall Street and he was a financial figure to reckon with. The *New York Times*, 1902, carried this notice:

> Within the past ten days the sharp eyes of Wall Street have been raised for a few moments to contemplate a new figure in the world of control—John Cleveland Osgood, of Redstone, Colorado who enjoys the proud distinction of having whipped Chicago plunger John W. Gates in a desperate battle for the control of the Colorado Fuel and Iron Co.

According to Gates' biographers he was said to have lost $3,000,000 in two months.

The common impression of Osgood was that of a rather handsome young man, immaculate in dress, exact in manner, emotional, and somewhat dictatorial. He appeared to be smooth skinned, with wide set eyes and broad forehead. His hair and his mustache were always parted precisely down the middle. His eyes were shrewd and calculating, with narrowed lids.

In a day when exploitation of the worker was the order of events, John Osgood was already dreaming of an ideal community where the usual injustices would not prevail. His Quaker background must have equipped him with an inbred concern for those about him and his early struggles only served to enforce his ideals.

Here in Redstone, Osgood built his coking ovens which are used to this day, although not on such an extensive scale. And here in the Crystal River Valley he began his sociological experiment—a model community of eighty-seven Swiss type homes which the workers painted in colors to suit their individual tastes, in sharp contrast to the usual company regimentation. Here was a club house with showers, a billiard and pool room, a library and reading rooms, a bar, and an upstairs auditorium, and stage. There were lawns, and gardens where the miners could plant whatever they wished. (Redstone potatoes became famous.) There was a cow kept in the community barn. There were schools and plays and lectures—and a traveling art exhibit, and a brass band under an Italian bandmaster. Active members paid an initiation fee of one dollar, and six months dues were paid in advance, at fifty cents a month, so that the member might feel that he was paying for what he got and would be inclined to take full advantage of club privileges.

Across the valley was the Big Horn Lodge, a Swiss chalet building designed as a meeting place for the board of directors of the company. The finest linens and furnishings equipped the lodge. The sterling flatware was specially designed with the Big Horn crest in filagree. It is said that the lodge was used only once for a meeting because the fumes from the coke ovens made it untenable.

The board of directors did not always see eye to eye with Osgood. They more than hinted that they would like him to put in more time maintaining control of the company and less on his model community. Osgood was not one to brook criticism, and when he set out to do a thing he was determined to finish it, as witness the construction of his highline railroad. Both the railroad to Coal Basin and the one to Marble were built more from sheer determination than from feasibility.

Another illustration of his stubbornness was the occasion when a friend remarked that a car could never get to the summit of McClure Pass above the valley and Osgood, determined to be right, offered to take his friends for a "little drive." They proceeded as far as they could up the pass in a car, then on to the summit on foot— and there in a grove of aspen sat a Model T Ford—it had been carted piecemeal up the mountain and there reassembled.

Work at Redstone continued. Rockefeller must have looked with disapproval at the experiment, for his policies and Osgood's at this time were as opposite as the poles. Tax-deductible philanthropy was not yet expedient.

Under construction was the apex of Osgood's dream for his fairy-tale valley—his own Cleveholm. Here was a Tudor castle complete with paved, enclosed courtyard, an iron dragon on the horse trough, and a huge clock in the enclosure. Hydroelectric power from the village lighted the forty-two rooms, twenty of which were bedrooms with twelve accompanying bathrooms, and fourteen adjacent fireplaces which heated the house —more or less. The one hundred doors were ornamented with gold-crested knobs. The living room overlooked the valley and was dominated by a fireplace which extended two stories. Gold andirons caught the firelight and the sunlight of the living room. The walls were decorated by an Italian artist. The rooms were furnished with art treasures which the Osgoods selected in Europe. The dining room was resplendent with red plush and a fashionable crystal chandelier. In many of the rooms the draperies were lined with eider down to keep out the cold. In the library the walls were of hand-tooled green elephant hide. The long library table extending nearly the length of the room was covered with a leather throw to match the walls. Mrs. Osgood's

Clubhouse which J. C. Osgood constructed
for the workers at Redstone. *Photo courtesy
of Howard E. Smith*

Three school teachers who were Redstone residents, 1906-1907. Miss
Mueller, Mrs. Wright (who married the paymaster), and the teacher
from Denver, Miss Whitten, with whom Mr. Smith still remembers
dancing. *Photo courtesy Howard E. Smith.*

ornate piano graced the music room where the ceiling was frescoed with French cupids and the floor was covered by a white rug.

Mrs. Osgood occupied a suite with curving windows which faced on the outer court. The walls of her room were cream-colored silk with pink roses and the lamps bore shades to match.

The master bedroom was upstairs and adjoined the balcony which looked out over the living room. There was a small window through which the master looked out to see whether the company had assembled before he made his entrance. The Rockefeller suite was said to have been on the top floor. Morgan and Gould were also guests at various times.

Downstairs were the game rooms, with a gaming table in front of a huge stone fireplace.

Two and one-half million dollars was the amount poured into the estate shortly after the turn of the century.

Diametrically opposing forces gathered against Osgood. The break finally came. When the opposition consolidated to overthrow Osgood, Rockefeller moved in, taking control of the Colorado Fuel and Iron Company. On June 24, 1903, Rockefeller urged Osgood to continue as chairman of the board. Osgood turned his back and walked away. There was no meeting ground and he simply abandoned the thing he had created.

Although Osgood lost stature when he lost control of the C.F.&I., he was far from finished. He organized the Victor American Fuel Company and continued the construction of his dream castle. Italian and Austrian workers were brought in to quarry the red stone for the building.

About 1913, J. C. Osgood closed the castle and expressed his growing restlessness in extensive travel. His wife, called "Lady Bountiful" by the people of Redstone, had died, and he no longer cared to stay in his valley. He returned in 1925, after having undergone surgery for cancer in a Denver hospital. In the interim he had remarried. His new wife accompanied him on the visit to Cleveholm. She was to have only three years with him until his death. The king of the castle died at Cleveholm on January 4, 1926.

Those who thought they knew him best were found to have known him least and the obscure people spoke out with the many incidents of his kindnesses to them. There were several instances of his generosity which had been heretofore unknown— he had furnished a college education for the sons of many of his workers.

A biographer summarized:

> Despite an orderly mind that grasped and totaled figures with the accuracy of an adding machine, much of his activity was strictly off the cuff without advice from or explanation to anyone. He lavished deep affection on both people and things.

According to Osgood's last request, his ashes were scattered over the valley.

OUR VIEW OF REDSTONE

The first time we saw Redstone, we, too, fell under a spell. From the first turn through the green valley, the brooding presence of Mount Sopris was evident. The quiet was disturbed only by the rushing of the clear waters of the Crystal River. We, too, were enchanted with Redstone and had the rare opportunity to spend a night in the castle. We tiptoed to the door, feeling the spell of the place and were ushered into the hall, past the carved oak mailbox and into the spacious living room. The room was cold as an English castle; the fire was out. Italian lamps with marble bases decorated the tables. The windows opened out to a magnificent view of the mountains and a courtyard where a white statue, carved by one of the Redstone residents, stood out in the gathering dusk. We were shown to our room. A choice was offered of the former quarters of J. P. Morgan or those of Gould or Rockefeller. We chose one with a better view overlooking the valley. The room was comfortable with twin beds, which obviously were not the original furniture. Each bedroom was equipped with a basin of running water and facilities for steam heat, but with the steam noticeably lacking. At dinner time we were called to the dining room where three other guests were already assembled. Trout from the Crystal River made up the entree. We wore our sweaters as insurance against the chill of the room and welcomed the hot tea and food. After dinner, an employee invited us to the game room downstairs where a rousing fire was most welcome. The employee had been a maid during the regime of the Osgoods. She remembered the Mrs. Osgood who had worked so congenially with her husband in his philanthropic experiments. The maid recalled Christmases when the Osgoods sought to give every worker's child a gift. She remembered the air of *noblesse oblige* with which favors were dispensed. She recalled parties at the old mansion and games before this very fireplace.

We were reluctant to leave the dying fire and go to our chilling rooms. The only one who didn't seem to mind was an Englishman, doubtlessly inured to the tomb-like atmosphere of Tudor castles. We shivered through the night and it wasn't too hard to get up in the morning. Hot breakfast was welcome. With the other guests we toured the castle; since the tourist season was past, we were able to poke into every nook and cranny and to take in every luxury and the stories which lay behind them. There had been frost in the night. The entire valley had a Midas touch.

The last time we saw Redstone, the Inn had been expanded and modernized but with no sacrifice of atmosphere or artistic lines and no blot of vulgar commercialism. A swimming pool with tropical plants and a ski course were being installed and plans had been made for sleigh rides for those not equal to the more strenuous exercise. It gave promise of a year-round paradise.

We made our evaluation of the Osgood story before we left the valley. We thought of the kindliness of this feudal lord whose strength was pitted against the industrial giants in a turbulent revolution. That he was behind his time and ahead of his time was the paradox and an insurmountable one.

There would probably never be another such experiment in

97

our times. The pendulum had long since swung away from the iron hand of capitalistic management grinding the worker into the dust, but there had also been a resultant rise of labor to wrest the power into its own hands. Never again would culture be superimposed through the bounty of giving. Now giving has become tax expedient.

However one's sympathies might run and however hardened one might become to history and the natural evolution of man's fight for a place in the sun, one cannot fail to compare Osgood with a certain chapter in Rockefeller history which is recorded graphically on the monument at Ludlow, Colorado, the scene of one of the state's darkest labor incidents. It is not so much the eighteen names engraved on the stone which strike the heart, but it is rather the shocking age of the victims listed here, such as Elvira Valdez, age three months, Lucy Petrucci, age four-and-a-half years, Lucy Costa, age four. No such monument was ever necessary in the Crystal River Valley. Evolution is slow.

A REDSTONE REMINISCENCE

The many facets of Redstone would not be complete without the personal story of Howard E. Smith of Colorado Springs who can recall vividly a happy year there in the employ of J. C. Osgood. During the year of 1906 to 1907 Mr. Smith lived at the Inn and took care of business transactions. It was one of his jobs to go to Coal Basin once a week to collect the receipts for the clubhouse and to send them to Mr. Sage of the board of directors in Denver.

The coke ovens were going full blast. Howard Smith, like everyone else, fell under the spell of the beauty of this valley. One of the things he likes to remember is one trip down from Coal Basin during the thunderstorm when there was a rainbow over the valley below him.

He recalls that Mr. Osgood was a frequent visitor, leaving an impression of kindness but not intimacy. Smith remembered

Employee of Crystal River Ranch bringing milk into Redstone. Name of "milkmaid" unknown. *Photo courtesy of Howard E. Smith.*

Rock-climbing expedition near Redstone, 1906. Mrs. Paul being pulled up on the rock. *Photo courtesy of Howard E. Smith.*

99

"Lady Bountiful" and recalled certain hot springs on the east side of the road which had been made into a private bathhouse for Mrs. Osgood for the relief of her arthritis. He recalls many of the employees of the regime, among them Tom Gibbs, the superintendent of the whole railroad project and Mr. York of C.F.&I. importance and Mr. Peale of the Crystal River Railway, a Mr. Pearson who was an electrician, the porter, John Murray, and the pies baked by Irish Katie, the cook. He was happy to help her with her tax accounting and glad to accept remuneration in the form of apple pies. Dean Peck came from Denver to preach the only sermon during that year, at a service held in the schoolhouse. A priest from Glenwood Springs was an occasional visitor, and Mr. Smith smiled as he remembered the Friday when the priest ate pork chops before he thought of the day—but Katie's pork chops were apt to make one forget.

Dr. Paul was the black-bearded doctor at Redstone. The population was of varied nationalities. The bandmaster was Italian.

It was cattle country, too, and Placita, just to the north, was the shipping point for stock.

Denver society people were frequent visitors and were usually guests at the lodge across the valley. This was a luxurious edifice with the most fashionable furniture and the best of everything. Mr. Smith took personal inventory of its furnishings when it was closed.

Unmarried women were at a premium. The three school teachers were the belles of the valley. They had an enviable status. Nothing went on in which they weren't included. Two left the ranks of the unmarried before the year was over. Life must have been exciting for those girls, with the pick of the bachelors of the whole valley. There were dances, skating parties, ball games, picnics; and everybody went walking on Sundays. Mountain climbing was not up to present standards. Considering the attire the women wore, they were surprisingly adept at reaching the top, with the aid, of course, of their male companions. Picnics were the order of the day and at one time a huge valley picnic was planned at Marble. Everyone went by train. Three cabooses were attached to the little row of cars to give protection to the delicate skins of the women and children. The stronger sex was relegated to the open box-cars. The Redstone band, with its Italian leader, went along for gaiety, probably to play in the little wooden bandstand that now lies tilted crazily in the creek bed. The time-old custom for women to outdo themselves on a picnic lunch was the prescribed formula and one man went about the crowd declaring, "The more you eat the better you feel," which Mr. Smith vows is a cliché of doubtful truth.

Howard Smith recalls a bear hunt with Senator Robert La Follette from Wisconsin. He remembers a charge of two dollars and a half a day to guests at the inn for royal quarters and Katie's food. He remembers, too, the sixty-five oriental laborers who were housed on the third floor for a time.

Howard Smith was asked if he felt that the valley was jinxed or if he was conscious of a depressing atmosphere which is sometimes attributed to that area, but he recalled only the happy times and the beauty of the place, and the three school teachers—and Katie's pies.

His picture album was a sun dial which recorded only the happy hours.

SOURCES

Bet a Million, The Story of John W. Gates, Lloyd Wendt and Herman Kogan, The Bobbs-Merrill Co., Indianapolis, New York, 1948
Westerners Brand Book, Volume IV, 1948, "Redstone on the Crystal," Vaughn Mechau
Colorado Springs Weekly Gazette, October 2, 1902
Interviews with
Howard E. Smith
and assistance from
The Colorado State College at Greeley
Colorado Springs Public Library
Coburn Library, Colorado College

Prairie Dog O'Byrne

Prairie Dog O'Byrne was the nickname given to the diminutive Irishman who was railroad man, poet, author, historian, and owner of the most unusual team ever driven through the streets of Colorado towns. Whether he gained his name because of his size (he was waist high to a prairie dog) or whether it was because of his habit of driving his tourist hack accompanied by two tame prairie dogs on the front seat, remains a matter for argument.

John O'Byrne's parents were Irish Catholic. Patrick O'Byrne and Bridget Mulherin both left Ireland in 1847, on different boats, but were destined to meet in Sandusky City, Ohio, where they were married. Fate was weaving a strange western threaded pattern in the O'Byrne chronicles, for the ceremony was performed by Father Machebeuf, later to become bishop of the Denver diocese. "The Irishman was king of the shovel" in those days and as such Patrick O'Byrne helped to throw up the grade of the Lake Shore and Michigan Southern Railroad in Ohio. John was born in 1862, just before the O'Byrnes moved to Kansas. His memory of his family was one of Irish Catholic unity and the pride of a father who told his twelve children that he came from a part of Ireland that never produced a coward or a traitor. John O'Byrne was inclined to believe his father told the truth.

At twenty-one John found himself well established in a railroad career, but not with a shovel. He was a brakeman. After a few years in Kansas, Texas, and California, he came to Trinidad, Colorado. The rhythm of the rails has inspired more than one poet to think in patterned lines and he, too, began to form his rhymes and visual impressions which would some day become a book.

O'Byrne's love for the Pikes Peak Region was of such propor-

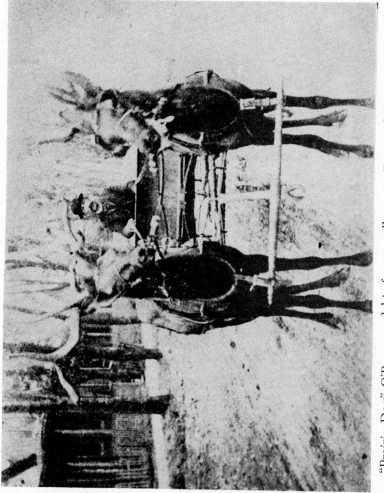

"Prairie Dog" O'Byrne and his famous elk team. From *Pikes Peak or Bust*.

103

tion that he became a missionary, in the guise of a hack driver. He was happiest when sharing Colorado's beauty with the rare tourist who could really appreciate it. Being a man adept with words, he found expression where many men were inarticulate. He wrote songs and told stories (which he came to believe himself) for the amusement of his passengers and they came back to ask for him time and again.

As he drove his hack to Manitou through Old Town (Colorado City), he often recalled the raucous days of the first capitol of Colorado and the times when he met Bob Ford, Eat 'Em Up Jake of Dodge (probably an escapee of Matt Dillon), and Soapy Smith and dashed off a rhyme that smacked of experience.

> And there stood "Soapy" Smith with three cards in his hand,
> And each word he uttered he spoke with command;
> "Now gents," he would say, "there is the ace
> And it is plain to be seen—
> And that's where I lost all my money—
> On the Ace and the Queen."

Then Prairie Dog would reminisce "Gone to Boot Hill and if the Divil hasn't come after them, they are lying there still."

He went on to tell about Old Town when it was

> in right full bloom and that's where we went to see the sights —it made no difference what time of day or night you came the excitement and amusement were continuous . . . If we did not see two or three gun plays or one or two shot, we considered business pretty quiet.

Thirty years of experience as a tourist driver gave Prairie Dog a rare insight into human behavior. He said of hack drivers, "Many are called but few are chosen. Very few of them would pass the test for a competent guide."

His tour equipment kept pace with the times and included everything from a team to a Pierce Arrow. He said of his passengers that they were all kinds, but men were the most nervous and biggest cowards. He remarked,

> if the car is working well and you are making good time, 25 to 30 miles an hour, then they think you are a reckless driver.

104

Some ask if you have ever had a wreck and when you tell them, "no," they will not believe you. For this class, it is best to side in with them. Tell them you have an interest in the undertaker's establishment at the foot of the hill.

Scenery wasn't the only thing that came in for discussion on his tours—the weather was always a vital topic to those about to depart for Pikes Peak. He maintained:

Do not ask the chauffer about the climate conditions on the trip to the Peak because he does not know; he might make a good guess, but he is more liable to make a poor one; the good Lord runs the climate on the Peak. The United States Government had a signal service station on Pikes Peak a number of years and they failed to be able to determine when storms were coming, so they gave the job back to the Lord and He can give you any kind of climate your heart may desire on the trip and sometimes on very short notice.

Prairie Dog expounded his advanced theories of archaeology, among which were his explanations of the original Cliff Dwellings. He was convinced that there had once been a strip of land between Siberia and Alaska, that the Indians had many similar characteristics with Orientals, and that they came originally from China but had been driven out six or seven thousand years ago.

Philosophy did not escape him and his analogy of life was that of man as a tourist traveling toward eternity:

We came from dust made after God's own image and likeness and as we start down the lane of life we enter the poet's sweet dream of love. Then we try to climb that Mountain of Hope and we pass on down through that valley of sighs and tears and on to that Cañon of Death and after we have crossed this Great Sea of Life we come up to the city of the Home of the Dead and there we are planted, and then we return back to dust.

His observations on social conditions he passed on for what they were worth, commenting on the number of men in jails that should be put to some useful work, and he deplored the account of a Colorado chief of police who made the report of

425 drunks and some $3,000 dollars collected in fines and commented that there would have been a better report if the drunks had had more money. (And in later years on a trip to California, O'Byrne observed, "The moving picture show is schooling the rising generation by the thousands; they see the gunman on the screen and the burglars, also, this disgraceful love-making and they try to imitate the movie men.")

Easterners were told how the Garden of the Gods was once called "The Red Corral" because the early pioneers used to camp there enroute to the Far West via Ute Pass.

He related the chain reaction of accidents which gave Cripple Creek its name. He was told by Mrs. Anna Faulkner of Colorado Springs about her home on the bank of the creek in 1872. Brother George fell off the roof of the house, hurting his back, brother Alonzo nearly cut his foot off with an ax while chopping wood, Ben Roberts, the hired man, was returning with bear meat when his Indian pony reared and fell on him, breaking his leg. Father went after cattle, saw a buffalo among the herd, dismounted, rested his left hand on the pommel of the saddle, struck his elbow, the gun exploded and the ball entered his left hand. To top it off, a prize yearling broke its leg when it stepped in a prairie dog hole. No wonder they called it "Cripple Creek."

Cripple Creek also came in for a quotation which O'Byrne attributed to Mr. Dooley, that the scenery on the trip to the gold area "bankrupted the English language," a statement since attributed to Theodore Roosevelt.

As he drove his hack load through South Cheyenne Canyon, Old John spoke of the original grave of Helen Hunt Jackson which had been on the mountain side but from which the body had been removed and taken to Evergreen Cemetery. O'Byrne said, "The poet never dies—she migrates."

Prairie Dog maintained his home at 427 East Bijou in Colorado Springs and worked as a passenger brakeman between the Springs and Denver on the Atchison, Topeka and Santa Fe, but continued his tourist business in the summer.

But the incident which makes Prairie Dog O'Byrne stand out in the memories of present day citizens was an Irish whim which seized him in 1889. Whatever possessed him to buy a pair of baby elk from Judge A. W. Rucker of Aspen, no one can surmise. The elk had been captured in North Park in the spring of the previous year. The judge, for some reason or other, had bought them at an auction in Denver. To O'Byrne the possibility of training the six-month-old elk became a tantalizing idea. He proceeded to break them to drive single and double and they became a familiar sight on the streets of Colorado Springs. Pedestrians gave the whole outfit a wide berth.

O'Byrne wrote:

> My Elk team got very familiar with the road between Colorado Springs and Colorado City. When returning from Old Town to the Springs we would not be more than 6 or 7 minutes making the 3 miles; there were no street cars here then and no speed ordinances to take the joy out of life.

When O'Byrne moved to Denver in 1889, he took the elk with him, but Denver took a dim view of the team. O'Byrne said he could drive them anywhere a horse team could be driven but that he had to drive them every day in order to hold them down. He said:

> My Elk team was always unwelcome in Denver, the society people of Capitol Hill had many fine turn-outs with blooded horses and expensive broughams and cheap drivers and they took many fast rides away from me and my elk team when their horses would get a smell of my elk. I have seen as many as three runaways at one time, women screaming at the top of their voices and the driver hanging on for dear life. As soon as those people reached their homes they would call Police Headquarters; some days three and even four would call up in the same hour and tell the Chief what a narrow escape they had in a runaway, their horses getting scared at a team of elk. They asked the Chief to take that elk team out of the city as it was dangerous for them to drive their horses down the streets. So I was ordered into City Hall. The Police Clerk read the city ordinance to me in a very strong voice. He said, "Young man, goats and other animals that are dan-

gerous to life and property must be kept off the streets of Denver, and now, young fellow, we will give you just one more chance. You keep those animals out of the city or we will lock you up." However, I was called to the City Hall so often that I became quite familiar with their traffic ordinances, as they were read to me many times, but I was never fined.

As the Christmas holidays drew near W. L. Van Horne, who ran a sporting goods store at 1525 Lawrence Street, conceived the brilliant idea of having Prairie Dog play Santa Claus and drive the elk through the streets during Christmas week. The only hitch was in the ultimatum which the City Hall had issued.

> I had been warned by the Chief that if he ever caught me down in the city with that elk team, he would lock me up and shoot the elk and feed their meat to the bears at Elitch's Zoological Gardens.

Mr. Van Horne brought his influence to bear on a friend who had worked in the City Hall for forty years and a statement was issued that there was no law in the United States to prevent anyone from driving anything that turned a wheel, so long as he made his living at it. This statement gave the fiery Irishman the courage to deck himself out in Santa's fur coat and woolly cap; and with his long whiskers he dashed forth behind the elk team.

> The very first day I drove we caused a runaway. An old gray horse hitched to a top buggy standing in front of a blacksmith shop on Holaday Street (now Market Street) got a smell of the elk. He broke loose, upset the buggy and dragged it to pieces. The owner of the horse went to Van Horne's store and demanded damage. He talked loud and fast and threatened us with the law but finally admitted the elk hadn't run into the buggy, but that the horse was scared.

In the five days that O'Byrne stayed with Van Horne, business boomed at the sporting goods store so much that it was necessary to expand into an additional shop.

City Hall stopped its haggling but the opposition went under cover and two mysterious fires were set in the barn that housed the elk. Realizing that he could not fight the invisible, O'Byrne decided to ship the team east and sell out.

In the meantime, he entered an advertising venture in Chicago. He appeared as a belated Santa Claus after the holidays in 1891, first for a clothier and subsequently for a fur company, but he did not like the advertising business, and listed the elk for sale in St. Louis and New York newspapers. Hundreds of replies and offers were made, the best coming from Pawnee Bill's Wild West Show at Philadelphia. O'Byrne sold the team for $500 and expenses from Chicago to Philadelphia.

On his way to the World's Fair in 1893, Old John stopped off in Streator, Illinois. Perusing a billboard which advertised *The Hettie Bernard Chase Opera Company* in "Alaska" with Arctic scenes, he recognized his elk team. He learned that they used the elk to draw a sled across the stage, a supposed Eskimo driving them. Prairie Dog thought of the days when the elk were small, and of their devotion, and of the years he had spent with them. He was sure his elk would remember, too. With high hopes he visited them.

He said:

> Yes, I went to see my elk and on the way to the car I said, "I will bet they will know me," but I was sadly disappointed in that, as they did not seem to notice their old master who raised them from little pets six months old and who used to think so much of them. This is the last I ever saw or heard of my famous Elk team.

Sic transit amor.

Old John died December 26, 1936, in Los Angeles, "one of the most colorful figures in the history of this section of the state." *Sic transeunt omnia.*

SOURCES

Pikes Peak or Bust and Historical Sketches of the Wild West, John O'Byrne, 1922

Colorado Springs Gazette, December 28, 1936
Colorado Springs Gazette Telegraph, April 4, 1920; December 6, 1925
And interviews and correspondence with
Fred Murdoch
I. B. Bruce, Chief of Police, Colorado Springs, Colo.
Bill Crosby, Territorial Mayor of Manitou
Mrs. C. D. Weimer, Taos, New Mexico
Walter Colburn
Dorothy Bartlett

Milton Franklin Andrews

In *Three's a Crowd*

The west is melodrama-crazy. Crowds throng the bars and theatres to relive the days when the villain was always pure black, the hero pure white, and the heroine just pure. The audience hisses the villain and cries in the beer over the woes of the innocent victims and cheers the inevitable triumph of justice— and wonders how a past generation could have been so naive. Actually the melodrama wasn't always overdrawn.

Look at the old files of the famous murder of Bessie Bouton and be convinced it sometimes happened that way. This old drama might have been entitled *Three's a Crowd*. The cast might have read as follows:

The Victim	Blond Bessie Bouton
The Villain (swindler, gambler, murderer, charmer, dastard)	
	Milton Franklin Andrews
A jockey	Friday Ellis
Chief of Police	W. S. Reynolds of Colorado Springs
The other woman (one of them)	Nulda Olivia, a New Orleans Creole

And incidental characters such as the surveyor, the doctor, and the coroner, who played bit parts, and also the San Francisco Police Officers.

Scene I: the slopes of Mount Cutler, near Colorado Springs.
The Time: 2:30 p.m., December 17, 1904

The curtain rises with the County Surveyor J. P. Woodside and Dr. F. C. Chamberlain strolling along the rocky trail surveying some property belonging to the physician. The two are brought up short by the sight of a nude body stretched over two logs. Every trace of identity such as clothing and jewelry

111

had been removed and an obvious attempt had been made to burn the face beyond recognition. "And she was very, very dead." Dr. Chamberlain declared the burns to be from acid. What was left of her hair was a soft, taffy color.

The following day, a strange procession wound up the mountain trail. Clad in long overcoats against the chill and wearing their customary four-inch stiff white collars, they pulled a reluctant burro behind them to bear the body down to the hearse at the foot of the canyon. The site was swept for evidence. A carbolic acid bottle and a gasoline container were found nearby.

The autopsy was performed by Dr. Peter Hanford, who found that the girl had been shot with a .38 caliber revolver. She was described as 5 ft. 6 in. tall, weight about 140 pounds, and she had been dead between two and six weeks.

Police Chief Reynolds commissioned a local dentist to send charts of her dental work to police chiefs and dentists all over the country. Ten thousand pamphlets were circulated from coast to coast. It was through these pamphlets and the recognition of the dental work that identity was established. Investigation brought to light the story of Bessie Bouton, who had been christened Duske Kempter. She must have been basically a timid child and poorly adjusted. Because the children called her "Darkie," she changed her name to plain old Bessie.

In her teens she married George Bouton, a Syracuse mechanic. Bessie's craving for fine clothes, travel, and excitement could not be met by her commonplace young husband. Apparently Bessie was not mechanically inclined! She looked over the fence at greener pastures and decided to leap.

It was in a "house" called the Globe that she met Milton Franklin Andrews, typical melodrama villain of 1904. His waxed mustache, his forty fancy vests, and especially his $5,000 worth of diamonds appealed to Bessie. He has been described as tall, dark, and handsome. People have called his eyes steely, black, grey, blue, and blue-gray. Probably he avoided a direct look into anyone's eyes and the color was of necessity conjecture. He assumed various aliases, among them,

DESCRIPTION OF NUDE BODY OF MURDERED WOMAN

Found on Cutler Mountain, December 17th, 1904.

The body was that of a woman well developed and apparently well kept, but discolored from fire and exposure to the elements. The face, nose, lips, chin, left side of neck, both ears, shoulders and breasts burned so as not to be recognizable.

She was probably between 25 and 35 years of age, weight about 120 to 130 pounds, height 5 feet 2 or 3 inches, light auburn or ash blonde hair, part of which was burned off; skin evidently fair, with no birth marks or scars showing; small bones, limbs well rounded, hips and thighs large, very small hands, nails clean, long and well manicured; feet small, toes even and straight, nails manicured; probably wore a number 2, 2½ or 3 shoe.

TEETH—The teeth were large, white and chalky. In the upper jaw on the right side the wisdom tooth had never developed; the second molar was present with no fillings. A bridge extended from the first molar to the cuspid. This bridge was of solid gold and worn with no fillings. A bridge extended from the crown. The first and second bicuspid being absent, their places were supplied with solid dummies. Two gold fillings of medium size in the Mesial of the upper centrals or incisors. The upper teeth protrude slightly. In the left upper jaw a gold bridge extended from the first bicuspid to the second molar; a peculiarity of this bridge is in the fact that the second molar is made of a bicuspid dummy. The third molar or wisdom tooth on this side is present. In the lower jaw on the right side the third molar or wisdom tooth is present, the second molar has a gold filling in the Mesio-occlusal surface. The first molar is absent, evidently for some years, as the space is almost closed. Slight overlapping of cuspid on lateral. Pyorrhea of lower teeth—centrals and laterals—with considerable tartar, showing that they had not been cleaned recently. Left side:—considerable overlapping of cuspid on lateral; all teeth present on left side lower jaw. First molar large gold filling on occlusal surface; second molar large gold filling on occlusal extending on to the distal surface; third molar or wisdom tooth undeveloped, that is, partially covered with tissue.

All clothing, finger and ear rings, and all other means of identification had been removed from the body and no trace of same have been found, and up to the present time we have been unable to identify her.

The above description and diagram is the only evidence we have for identification.

Kindly call the attention of dentists in your city to the above description and diagram. If possible, have your newspapers print it.

Address all information and inquiries to

W. S. REYNOLDS,
Chief of Police.

COLORADO SPRINGS, COLORADO,
December 28th, 1904.

Dental description of Bessie Bouton which led to her identification. *Photo courtesy of I. B. Bruce, Chief of Police, Colorado Springs Police Department.*

113

"George Burnett," "George Brush," and even that of "George Bouton," Bessie's husband! Andrews was suave, polished, and second to none in his gambling ability.

The lure of jewels and the promise of a life of ease inveigled our heroine Bessie to abandon "a fate worse than death" for one that proved not too much better. It didn't take Bessie long to make up her mind to conform to Andrews' ideals and standards of living.

Andrews later stated, "She was a good conversationalist. . . I met her at the Globe. I told her I was a gambler and she wanted to travel with me and when she promised to give up smoking and getting drunk and meeting men, I took her on the road with me. She agreed that if she ever met men or got drunk again I would take them (the diamonds) all back and we would separate."

Records later tell that Bessie welched on her promise—Andrews caught her playing sneak on him and they split up several times on the strength of it and each time, he said, "I took back the bag of diamonds." Back-sliding Bessie was relieved of her diamonds each time!

In Colorado Springs, Andrews decided Bessie's reform was impossible so he said, "Good-bye forever," to Bessie and took her "best friends" from her for the last time. It appears that he had in mind transferring them to a younger friend not so set in her ways.

In Colorado Springs, Bessie and Milton had been living at the old Gough Hotel on South Nevada. The people who remembered the pair spoke of their violent and repeated quarrels.

Tracing back, the police found that Bessie and Milton had spent May 15 to July 13 at the Albany Hotel in Denver, then traveled together to Salt Lake, Ogden, San Francisco, and for a visit with Bessie's sister at Santa Barbara. There they had a particularly violent disagreement and Bessie had returned alone to Colorado Springs while her lover is said to have gone to New Orleans. Bessie wired her parents from Colorado Springs for money. Andrews denied that he ever returned to Colorado

114

Springs, but the telegraph company maintained that he was with Bessie on September 17, when the money was collected.

Apparently with the couple separated, and Andrews in New Orleans, a dark-haired Creole by the name of Nulda Olivia supplanted poor Bessie and with only one set of diamonds to satisfy two women, it was obvious to Andrews that he had to remove the jewels from Bessie—one way or another. Three's a crowd.

Between October 3 and 7 a couple answering the description of Bessie and Andrews was seen going up the Mount Cutler trail, the girl wearing a pretty, thin dress and carrying a lunch box. Andrews is known to have suffered from stomach disorders. What was in the lunch box is only a matter of conjecture. It may be that upon climbing to the summit and working up a healthy appetite, poor Milton discovered that Bessie had packed only a couple of dried peanut butter sandwiches, and his ulcer medicine was back at the hotel. Perhaps he said, "Bessie, not peanut butter again—" and then shot her.

Regardless of the motive, the diamonds disappeared.

Months passed, and later evidence revealed that the Creole from New Orleans was wearing Andrews' set of traveling diamonds, as she accompanied him to Australia. There he sought to ply his trade at the track. Seeking his own kind, he fell in with a jockey and bookie at Kensington, a second rate proprietary race track in Sydney. Known in Australia as "Friday" Ellis, the new acquaintance's name should have signaled "bad luck." His career in Australia came to a climax when, rumor says, he welched and he, Andrews, and Nulda soon made a cozy threesome as they headed for America. Again three became a crowd and the two men quarreled over Nulda. Andrews threatened to kill Ellis "for what he had done to her." Once back in the States, the string of broomtails which Andrews had declared he owned proved to be mythical. Ellis took up residence with the couple for one night but when he heard them whispering became suspicious and moved immediately. Yet Nulda always drew him back, and one day he couldn't resist an invitation to lunch. Maybe it was her Creole cooking. It was while he was eating the

DEPARTMENT OF POLICE,
COLORADO SPRINGS, COLORADO.

WANTED FOR MURDER
$2,000 reward

The above reward will be paid by the County of El Paso for the arrest and conviction of Milton Franklin Andrews, alias George Bouton, alias George Barnett, alias Milton Franklin, for the murder of Mrs. Bessie Bouton, on Mt. Cutler, on or about the 5th day of October, 1904.

DESCRIPTION.

Age, 31; weight, 130 pounds; height, 6 feet 1½ inches, stocking feet; complexion, light; eyes, blue grey; hair, medium light brown and slightly wavy, generally worn medium length and either parted in middle or on right side; moustache, rather small and light brown—however, was smooth shaven when last seen. From tip to tip of fingers is 6 feet 2⅝ inches; measures 13½ inches around neck; upper chest, 33½ inches; lower chest, 31 inches; waist, 28¾ inches; hips, 35½ inches; breadth of shoulders, 16⅛ inches.

Has a very thin and pale face, high cheek bones, prominent nose and a very noticeable scar on either right or left cheek. Has deformed chest (measuring only 6⅛ in. through) which he claims was caused in childbirth. When walking, toes are thrown in. The above measurements were made stripped, and he will appear taller and heavier when dressed.

Andrews is a very neat dresser, usually wearing expensive clothing, and has numerous fancy vests. His laundry is principally marked M. F., M. F. A. and G. B.

This man has stomach trouble; buys quantities of malted milk and the very first thing he does on his arrival in a city is to look up a Battle Creek Cafe or store where such supplies are sold, and lives principally upon foods manufactured by the Battle Creek Sanitarium. Watch all branches of the Battle Creek Sanitarium, as he will, more than likely, be found around such places taking treatment.

Andrews is a noted gambler and pool shark, being known amongst the profession as "Longshot" or "Hi" Andrews.

If located, arrest, hold and notify me and I will send an officer immediately with necessary papers for him.

COLORADO SPRINGS, COLO.,
February 6th, 1905.

W. S. REYNOLDS,
Chief of Police.

Mystery: Whose hand rests on Milton Franklin Andrews' shoulder? *Photo courtesy of I. B. Bruce, Chief of Police, Colorado Springs Police Department.*

marmalade that his friend Andrews suddenly swung a blacksmith's hammer on Ellis's head. The villain underestimated the thickness of a jockey's skull. Later Andrews maintained that he didn't know Ellis had the skull of a gorilla, "or he would have used a pile driver." In the brawl that followed, Andrews managed to remove $500 from the pocket of the jockey although he declared later that robbery was not his motive. Ellis also received a deflected blow to the wrist and although Nulda had him covered with a pistol, he managed to escape. With the instinct of a jockey using good horse sense he headed for the nearest stable and fell in a dramatic faint. Andrews and Nulda disappeared.

To W. E. Atchison is accredited the denouement through the aid of an anonymous tip, probably from Ellis. It appears that Andrews and Nulda sought refuge, realizing the impossibility of escape from a tightened ring. They took up residence in a rooming house. Apparently the owners of 748 McAllister Street, San Francisco, were unaware that the woman was not alone. The pretty eighteen-year-old, with dark eyes, black hair, weighing around 115 pounds, went under the name of Mrs. Little. She modestly went about her grocery shopping but it seemed strange that she bought enough for two and that she threw out the center of all the loaves of bread. Apparently this final love nest was stocked with a crust of bread and milk for the ulcer and Nulda was the "thou." The doors were always locked, and a towel was thrown over the transom into the hallway; yet Andrews made a fatal error—he forgot to pull down the blinds, and thin lace curtains revealed their silhouettes to watching detectives. The pretext under which the police finally entered the house was disguised as a call from the plumbers. Nulda protested their entry but finally allowed them to come into the apartment. The detectives (in plumbers' clothing) noticed the bed pushed against the closet door and suspected that Andrews was probably the "skeleton" hidden there. Nulda was dressed shabbily, and a bottle of peroxide gave evidence that there were some changes being made and they deduced that Andrews' sleek black mustache was also headed for a change in color, by the hair dye on

117

Headlines and pictures of Milton Andrews, Nulda, and Bessie. *Photo courtesy of I. B. Bruce, Chief of Police, Colorado Springs Police Department.*

the sink. A bowl of half-consumed broth was on the table and an abundance of almonds, and ulcer food, added clues to tighten the net. A book of German was open on the table and it is possible that Andrews was contemplating flight abroad. The masquerading officers left to evaluate their findings.

When they returned demanding admission to the apartment, they were refused. It was said that Andrews, the experienced gambler, knew when the chips were down and the cards on the table. Two shots rang out and when the officers broke down the door they found Nulda dying, with her hands clasped on her breast—maybe in prayer to the Almighty, but likely in supplication to our villain. Andrews was already dead, a gun in one hand and a mirror in the other. He was cheating in the last act of his life, dying as he had lived, by violence.

A letter, concealed in one of Nulda's stockings, revealed that Andrews had wished to bargain with the officers, offering to give himself up to stand for trial for the murder of Eugene Bosworth in New Britain, Connecticut, and the death of a man in Chicago, and the killing of a woman in New York. (Bessie was said to have been in with him on the New York crime.) Perhaps he hoped to be cleared for lack of evidence on those old scores. His price was the dismissal of all the minor charges against him. In a last note he protested his innocence of the murder of Bessie. He insisted he had been a thousand miles away. Could there have been any mistake that Andrews was the man? Is there any explanation for the working of the criminal mind? Why with his disdain for law or code of convention did he at one time try to divorce a wife in the east (who still held legal rights) so that he might make Nulda an honest woman? Why—why—why?

So rang down the curtain on a tragedy of 1904. So justice triumphed and the dastardly villain and his dark-haired accomplice came to the customary denouement demanded by the theatre of that period. Maybe the old melodrama wasn't so exaggerated after all!

SOURCES

Interviews with
I. B. Bruce, Chief of Police, Colorado Springs, Colorado
Lieutenant Colonel Perry Parr
San Francisco Chronicle, November 7, 1905
Colorado Springs Gazette and Telegraph, December 18, 1904, and
  following issue
Inside Detective
Colorado Springs Free Press, Sunday Review, February 26, 1956,
  Article by Lillian de la Torre.

Grace Greenwood,

Dispenser of Culture

At the prim age of twenty-seven, in 1850, Sara Jane Clarke should have remained fixed in her New England orbit. Instead of that she took off, like Halley's Comet, for an unchaperoned, unprecedented, and unheard-of tour of Europe. From then on it was but one blazing tour after another.

Writing had been the lady-like pastime of a girl who had published poems and sketches in her early years, submitting her endeavors to what she sometimes referred to as the "Harper House of Doom." At twenty she sold her first prose to the *New York Mirror,* succumbing to the popular feminine practice of using a pseudonym. As Grace Greenwood, she achieved national popularity, and even her friends began calling her Grace. She claimed that her poetry was the result of the growth of her mother's mental influence—"the very ingrafting of her nature upon mine."

Sara Jane was one of a large family who could claim with pride their descent from Jonathan Edwards. Born November 23, 1823, in Pompey, Onondaga County, New York, Sara Jane was educated in Rochester, New York, and later moved to Brighton, Pennsylvania, with her family. However, she must have received some of her early education in Ohio, since many years later there was a letter written by a Colorado lady

> who must be on the shady side of fifty but who lives on the sunny side of the Divide, in the neighborhood of Edgarton, loves to dwell upon her experience as a teacher when, some thirty-five years ago, in the Buckeye state, she swung the potent birch above the head of Sarah Jane Clark, known to half the world today as "Grace Greenwood."

121

The need for the birch switch may have indicated an early mind of her own. Apparently Sara Jane remembered the potent discipline of her early years because in telling of her reunion with a brother, she said:

> It bears us back to those rare old times when we were inseparable companions; when, by night, the same roof-tree was over us, and a household of home affections encircled us; when, by day, the same "school-marm" swayed us with her ferule of despotic power.

Rochester was for some years her well-beloved home; she said of it:

> . . . here it was that I spent my few school days; received my first trifle of book-knowledge. It was here that woman's life first opened upon me . . . as a sphere of labor, and care, and endurance; an existence of many efforts and few successes, of eager and great aspirations, and slow and partial realizations.

Exuberant and self-sufficient in an era when frailty was the fashion, Grace grew too tall, was too vital and too clever. She simply didn't fit her time nor her place; she outgrew them all.

Leaning heavily on adjectives, her prose style was verbose, overly descriptive, but often characterized by flashes of wit and humor which were to become synonymous with her later fame. In an early publication, *Greenwood Leaves*, she employed floral whimsies to describe "A Touching Incident."

> A few months since, on going to our office, we every morning met a little girl, some nine or ten years of age. She was a slight, fair-haired child, with a colorless cheek and a large blue eye, beaming and humid. On her arm she carried a light basket filled with simple flowers, which she timidly offered to the passers-by. As morning after morning we met the young stranger, we grew more and more interested in her—the little bunch of flowers, which we always purchased, as it caught our eye during the labors of the day, brought that pale, sad face, and that fragile form vividly before us. We were confident that she must have a history to relate, touching and strange, it might be, and we resolved to question her concern-

Grace Greenwood (Sara Lippincott). From a *carte-de-vista* photograph by Matthew Brady, collection of Frederick Meserve, New York, N. Y. *Photo courtesy Denver Public Library, Western Collection.*

ing it. One morning, after purchasing the usual bouquet, we kindly inquired if she had always pursued her present employment.

"Oh, no, sir," she replied, "we were once respectable and happy, when father followed the carpenter's trade, and supported his family comfortably. We had a nice cottage home, and brothers and I went to school, and I had books, and flowers, and such darling little birds! Oh, sir, we were very happy then!"

"Did your father die?" we asked.

"No, sir, but he suddenly took to—"

Here the poor child burst into tears and sobbed bitterly. In a saddened tone we finished her sentence—

"To drinking?"

"No."

"To gaming?"

"No, sir, to writing books!"

"Alas, poor unfortunate!" we mentally exclaimed, "thy destiny is indeed a hard one."

Grace's impressions of Europe formed material for some of her early successful writing. Marriage came late to a girl who was just too, too—in every direction. Leander K. Lippincott, however, was confident that these qualities were not an impediment to marriage. He admired her raven hair and her "swanlike" neck, but even more he respected her rapid mind and advanced ideas. Married in 1853, the Lippincotts had one child, a daughter, Anne. The year following their marriage they established a magazine for children, *Little Pilgrim*. Leander became business manager for the publication. He was a man of culture and refinement, but of a retiring nature. The two were differently paced and he fell into the quiet, unobtrusive business life and let Sara Jane have her fling.

A born actress, she had been frustrated by parental disfavor of the stage. But expression would out and her exuberance could not be contained. Grace Greenwood wrote columns in the *Washington Post* for forty-seven years and saw fourteen books in publication. She became a potent voice in literary America. Historical writing had its pitfalls for her, as it has for many an experienced author. She confessed:

124

Soon after mailing my last letter, chancing to open a *Pennsylvania Historical Collection,* I saw, to my dismay, that I had made a misstatement respecting Fort Mackintosh. It appears it was not erected until 1778. I had never consulted authorities. I wrote from information carelessly given by some of the natives, and they ought to have known better, Heaven help them! It is, however, apparent that the historical is not my *forte,* nor my fort historical.

With the growth of a young daughter and the family's increasing financial demands, Grace Greenwood extended her talents to the lecture platform which was as near a stage career as she dared approach at this late date. With her dramatic flair, her brilliant mind, her quick wit and sense of justice, she took up every cudgel which came to hand to annihilate abuses and to support needy causes and to further her own popularity. She espoused such causes as reform of women's dress, an Asylum for Idiots, the Society for Alleviating the Miseries of Public Prisons, and the emancipation of slaves. Later writers have described her as being a combination of "Cornelia Otis Skinner, Dorothy Kilgallen and Eleanor Roosevelt, the most versatile woman of the last half of the 19th century." She was known and loved from coast to coast. She spoke to packed houses and the laughter rang.

The perils of the intellectual woman she described in an early letter "To an Unrecognized Poetess"—although she appears to have had an utter disregard at times for her own admonitions. She cautioned:

> The intellectual woman should be richest in "social and domestic ties;" she should have along her paths a guard of friendship, and about her life a breastwork of love. True feminine genius is ever timid, doubtful, and clingingly dependent; a perpetual childhood. A true woman shrinks instinctively from greatness, and it is "against her very will and wish transgressing," and in sad obedience to an inborn and mighty influence, that she turns out the "silver lining" of of her soul to the world's gaze; permits all the delicate workings of her inner nature to be laid open; her heart passed round, and peered into as a piece of curious mechanism . . .

125

> The radiant realms of her most celestial visions have always a
> ladder leading earthward . . . Never unsex yourself for great-
> ness. The worship of one true heart is better than the wonder
> of the world. Don't trample on the flowers, while longing
> for the stars. Live up to the full measure of life; give way to
> your impulses, loves, and enthusiasms; sing, smile, labor, and
> be happy . . . There is a joy which must, I think, be far more
> deep and full, than any which the million can bestow . . . .
> This is the joy of inspiration. . . . But this is for the masters
> of the lyre; it can never be felt by woman with great intensity.

Nearing the half-century mark, Grace began to feel fatigue
and to look forward and backward with some trepidation. She
took the current excuse of health to travel westward. She fell
in love with the country and became Colorado's first and most
avid chamber of commerce. Her Denver notes of travel were
published in the *New York Times*. She lectured in Golden,
Boulder, and Denver, where she was a guest of W. N. Byers
of the *Rocky Mountain News* and where she appeared at the
Denver Theatre on August 22, 1871. At Caribou she discussed
"The Heroic in the Common Life" and was rewarded by having
a lode 600 feet above town christened The Greenwood. When
the *Boulder News* mentioned that she would speak at the Con-
gregational Church, it said, "With Fanny Fern and Mrs. Stowe
her name has been for years a household word."

And the *Colorado Transcript,* announcing her imminent
arrival in Golden said, "Almost everyone has laughed and wept
with Grace Greenwood, as they have followed her through her
hundred beautiful tales."

She was entertained by the cream of society and on August
24, 1871, the *Rocky Mountain News* ran an account of a most
important civic celebration at which Grace Greenwood was an
honor guest. The *News* stated:

> A party of about one hundred excursionists including the
> mayor of the city, all the councilmen, several well known
> lawyers, twenty or thirty ladies and representatives of the
> press boarded the train of narrow-gauge cars at three o'clock
> yesterday afternoon and were soon whirling away in the
> direction of Littleton. Col. W. H. Greenwood (no relation),

director of construction, and Mr. W. S. Jackson, secretary and treasurer of the Denver and Rio Grande Railway Co. had planned an excursion as a complimentary benefit to Mayor Harper and his colleagues of the council chamber. Col. Bridges, Mr. W. Blackmore, and Mr. Neave, English gentleman who owned landed interests in Colorado, were of the party; also, Grace Greenwood.

The article went on to describe a sudden storm which came up as they left Denver but which must have subsided before they arrived at Littleton. A little engine trouble was also cause for delay. The *Rocky Mountain News* continued:

When the train reached the end of the track, three miles beyond Littleton, or say fourteen miles out of Denver, the excursionists tarried long enough to witness the manner of the placing of rails. Someone put a sledge hammer into Grace Greeenwood's hands, at the same time pointing to a spike in the ties. When, with a display of muscle quite alarming in a woman, she drove the spike home.

Grace's own comment was

Laying the rails of the D and RG the party was "Merry as a marriage bell."

She described the engine as an iron horse or a fiery mustang and said:

The remorseless officers of the road insisted that I drive a spike. It was a cruel task of my "muscular christianity." The newspaper report says that I drove the spike home triumphantly.

There were other difficulties on a train trip which she depicted graphically in her volume, *New Life in New Lands*.

Fortunately, our party started with the idea of roughing it and so were able to take things as they came, being all tolerably good-humored people. But we had our trials . . . As to the table, though it was always bountifully supplied, it was not, I must say, as elegantly and thoroughly appointed as one could wish. There was no epergne, no printed bill of fare. There were no finger glasses, and the supply of nutcrackers was limited. There was not even a full assortment

127

of wineglasses; and when, on the Summit, Mr. Joaquin
Miller treated to champagne, we were obliged to worry
it down out of lemonade goblets. We had, of course, nap-
kins, but the rings were evidently of plated ware. A pretty
idea would have been a set of solid silver lined with gold,
each one engraved with the name of a guest of the superintendent of the Union Pacific, and designed to be taken away
as a significant souvenir of California and Colorado. When
a man sets out to do a handsome thing, I like to see him do
it . . . We became satiated with oranges, bananas, apricots,
strawberries, peaches and cherries; but I missed black-
berries and pears, my favorite fruit; and the almonds were
all hard-shelled and I decidedly prefer the soft.

In July, 1872, she answered the call for encore and came
back for a brief visit.

She honored the excursion from Denver to Pueblo with
her presence, making a most humorous speech at the dinner,
(celebrating the dedication of the railroad to Pueblo) in
the course of which she remarked people had told her once
she had seen California she would not think so much of Colorado, but she declared she had lost none of her admiration
for her first love.

To prove it, she returned three months later with her daughter, Anne.

Grace became interested in the Greeley colony and paid it a
visit. She must have been half-fearful of that prairie town and
picked her way carefully, always afraid of rattlesnakes.

I always inquire about the rattlesnakes, for the subject,
like the reptile, has for me a fearful fascination.

She also said:

The usual reply to inquiry was, none here, but a little
farther on, look out.

Joaquin Miller, a good friend, presented her with a pair of
earrings made of rattlesnake rattles, mounted with gold.

It was the first time the lecturer had seen the colony system
in operation and she was particularly interested in it, although
she admitted that she did not care especially for the town itself.

128

In the first place, she disliked the temperance situation and told at one time of a man who went to buy snake bite remedy and was told to try the drug store where he could get spirits of ammonia. The man was said to have remarked that he would have taken that ammonia for whiskey—as good whiskey as he ever drank. Grace declared, "Bad Tammany politicians go to Greeley when they die."

She seemed positive that the feminine population of the colony was not actually happy.

> The women of Greeley seem to me to have great spirit and cheerfulness. Yet I felt that with their new, strange, wild surroundings,—the illimitable vastness of earth and sky,— with new labors and hardships and deprivations and discomforts—with the care of all the ditchers that cometh upon them daily,—they must be discontented, unhappy, rebellious; and I tried to win from them the sorrowful secret. I gave them to understand that I was a friend to the sex, ready at any time on the shortest notice to lift my voice against the wrongs and disabilities of women, that I deeply felt for wives and daughters whom tyrant man had dragged away from comfortable Eastern homes, neighborly cronies, and choice Gospel and shopping privileges. But the perverse creatures actually declared that they were never so happy and so healthy as they are here, right on the edge of the great American Desert, that they live in the sure hope of soon having more than the old comforts and luxuries around them; that, in short, the smell of the "flesh-pots of Egypt" has gone clean out of their nostrils.

Included in the Greenwood itinerary of mountain towns was Georgetown where her visit was not considered an unmixed blessing. The Georgetown *Weekly Miner* for October 31, 1872, fumed:

> And now the *Register* says Grace Greenwood telegraphs that she will be pleased to meet the people of the mountains and "entertain them with a variety of humorous readings from the poets and other folks." Now, what have the people of the mountains of Colorado done that they have to be read to and entertained so much? We wish that these graceful, entertaining and accomplished literary ladies of

The remodeled cottage of Grace Greenwood is said to stand at 801 South Tejon. The lines of this house are similar to her original Manitou house.

Grace Greenwood's Clematis Cottage (called a "snuggery" by the Denver papers). This house won a *Ladies Home Journal* prize for a most attractive mountain cottage. *Photo by Gumsey of Colorado Springs. Courtesy Denver Public Library, Western Collection.*

the east would visit us once, at least, especially when it is outside of the lecture season, without entertaining us at all. The mountain public are getting tired of this sort of thing, and the Press is weary of puffing these entertaining people, and urging sturdy miners and all sorts of people, to come down with their fractional currency to pay hall rent and kerosene, that these most excellent ladies may have room and light for entertaining purposes.

Now, ladies, try us for once as entertainers. Come up to the mountains without your old portfolios and well thumbed selections from the poets, and accept of the grand entertainment we can offer you in the shape of unrivalled mountain scenery, glowing beneath the wondrous wealth of glorious autumnal sunshine, or radiant under the wildering beauties and brilliancies of Indian Summer's moon-beams. And we will not ask you to be satisfied with sunshine, moonshine and scenery only, we will show you things more substantial and attractive, if not as beautiful as these—our wondrous wealth of precious ores—great fissure veins, deeper than the eternal depths of oceans, filled to the brim with metallic richness, and the huge furnaces, with stomachs of livid flames, that reduce this crude richness to precious, glittering bullion.

We, of the mountains, regard Grace Greenwood very highly, we love her genuine womanly qualities, and appreciate her superior literary attainments, and the use she has made of these in writing pleasant descriptions of our country, its scenery and resources, and we want her to come to Georgetown without any idea of entertaining the people, but as the honored guest of honest admirers. Visit us as Mrs. Lippincott, the lady of fortune, culture and rare abilities, whom we all esteem so highly, and it will not be in a dimly lighted, and not over and above cleanly hall, that we will give you welcome, but in the elegant and comfortable parlors of our best Hotels, or around the glowing hearthstones of cozy mountain homes.

Perhaps Grace did accept the invitation of the editorial writer to make her visit a personal as well as a professional one. This may have been the time she became acquainted with "Commodore" Stephen Decatur and declared him to be one of the most interesting men she had even known. This may also have been the time when, in an unguarded moment, he told her the real story of Stephen Decatur Bross, which was never repeated to another person and which Grace Greenwood either forgot, or was too busy, or too honorable, to tell.

Making her experiences in the west do triple duty, she compiled her western columns in a book called *New Life in New Lands*. It was one of her fourteen published books and she modestly vouched for its excellence, saying, "I know it's a good book because I wrote it myself."

Despite all her touring of mountain towns, Grace declared that she had spent a month of determined and unmitigated idleness! She then descended on Washington with renewed vigor and took up her pen to sketch the appearance of some of the more noted congressmen and the accoutrements of the galleries.

Following one of her regular Washington trips, a correspondent there said of her:

> What a natural actor the woman is! She comes from Colorado this winter younger and stronger than when she went; full of Yankeeisms and Yankee anecdotes and twang and idiom— a regular "Hosea Bigelow". . . . Eastern twang and Western slang are both easy to her. I have seen her by aid of a red bandana, slouch hat, pipe and stick metamorphise herself from an old man to an old woman alternately, while reciting, or rather, improvising a dialogue between two such characters with a facility that was marvelous. Mrs. Lippincott is a handsome woman—at least, she is to those who prize the meaning above the mere shape of feature. She is dark and rather pale. Her eyes are hazel, deep set, bright and like all hazel eyes, they vary with every emotion. Her face is strong and its character is decided by the beautiful eyes and forehead for her mouth belies the strength of her mind. She is tall, but stoops, a little, as is the wont of authors. She has in her rooms a portrait and bust of herself. The first is full length, vivid with gleams of rich color of ribbons and drapes that well became her Spanish face—the latter white and silent, but not cold for under Hiram Power's hand even the marble could glow into life. And as she, the living woman, stands between, we recognize the secret of expression that defies the most cunning hand and learn that

132

age may fade but cannot mar the face whose light shines from the soul within.

With the common fate of a man who is overpowered by a dominant female, Mr. Lippincott rated one brief paragraph in the article. It probably took some research to find that much material.

> Mr. Lippincott is a Philadelphian, connected with the well known Lippincott family of that city. He is one of the most delightful men, witty, cultured and accomplished, but with so little taste for society that he rarely appears out of his own immediate circle.

Grace was so enamored of Colorado, and particularly of Manitou Springs, that she bought an acre and a half of ground for a cottage and in mid-July, 1873, sent instructions to a Mr. Whipple, contractor, to build her a cottage upon the lot with all possible dispatch. She and her daughter spent some time as guests of their relatives, the Mellens, at Glen Eyrie, during the period of construction. What persuasive powers Grace must have wielded are revealed by the fact that as early as August her home was already approaching completion. The "honey of a cottage," "the charming snuggery," was soon ready for occupancy. The story of this small house in the cottonwoods is the story of Pikes Peak region days, with the carriage crowd as frequent callers; among them were the William S. Jacksons, General and Mrs. Palmer (Mrs. Palmer was a relative of Grace Greenwood), the Kingsleys, Dr. and Mrs. Bell, and, of course, the noted Eliza Greatorex. The atmosphere was right. The company was congenial.

The cottage stood on the banks of the Fountain qui Bouille until a flood in 1893. An old-timer describes the deluge which he says carried away the cottage, saying:

> For days it rained. Not sudden cloud bursts, but steady, hard, downpour. The water rose until a stream flowed through the old Cliff House Hotel.

He says that he stood on the banks of the swollen creek and saw Grace Greenwood's cottage collapse and float downstream,

There are other stories about its fate—one historian emphatically denies that the house was demolished, but says it was merely washed off its foundations and was later removed to a location on the 700 block of South Tejon Street in Colorado Springs. Others specify 801 South Tejon as its present location, and certainly the structure which occupies that corner now bears a marked resemblance in outline to the original "snuggery." There is a further controversy; the house on Manitou Avenue which is now labeled "Helen Hunt's Cottage" is said to have been the Greenwood summer home. This erroneous idea is further complicated by a picture of *this* Manitou Avenue house which appeared in a *Colorado Springs Gazette* issue of 1905 with the caption stating that it was the Greenwood abode which had been the winner of the *Ladies Home Journal* prize years before. The *Gazette* house pictured is the one now called "Helen Hunt's Cottage"—the one in the *Ladies Home Journal* resembles more the building at 801 South Tejon Street. All this is confusing. Attempts to capitalize on the names of Helen Hunt and Grace Greenwood only cloud the issue. The present location, if such it is, on South Tejon bears an "Apartment for Rent" sign, which recalls that in December, 1877, Grace Greenwood advertised her cottage for rent by the month until June 1, 1878, partly furnished, for thirty dollars a month. The rent has doubtless been raised!

Although Grace loved her small home, she didn't confine herself to it that first year. Instead, she took an extended tour with General Palmer, Eliza Greatorex, and General Hunt through South Park to Twin Lakes, Fairplay, and Mount Lincoln. Her friend, Greatorex, was busy making drawings for her book *Summer Sketches in Colorado,* for which Grace wrote the foreword. On one occasion when the two women were traveling by coach together, the vehicle overturned in a gulch. Badly shaken, they were taken to a small hotel "where Grace fainted from exhaustion." The landlady, who brought restoratives, stopped long enough to exclaim with pleasure, "Oh, what an honor to have Grace Greenwood faint on my floor!"

On another trip, when the lecturer rode to the top of Pikes

Peak to dedicate the new signal station, she came to the fore when it was discovered that most of the supplies had been left behind and demonstrated her more or less competence in the kitchen. She held up the laurels of her sex by cooking flapjacks for fifty, over an open fire. It is reported that they were not of the best quality, that some of the participants evidenced distinct distress, but Grace alibied by giving the usual regional excuse of the altitude. She said, "the flour had already risen to an altitude of 14,000 feet and couldn't be expected to rise too much higher."

The most popular Greenwood lecture of the day was "The Heroic in the Common Life" which was called both "grave and gay." She gave readings and recitations in costume at the Presbyterian Church, she stage-managed a production of *Babes in the Wood* with Anne Lippincott and a Mr. Cavender as the babes.

There were conflicting schedules on the social calendar of Colorado Springs one evening. The Fire Company thought it wise to postpone their regular meeting because it happened to fall on a night when Grace Greenwood was lecturing—and besides, the Utes were on the rampage. What chance did the fire department have with two such competing conflagrations raging?

Grace had no sympathy with the Indian as an individual.

> I am a sad infidel as to the regeneration of the average red man. I believe in original sin. I never grieve much for the lost tribes of Israel. So, perhaps, consequently, I have no strong affection for my kinsman, the unhappy Arapahoe. I don't believe he is my "long-lost brother." But I don't want him "deluded and abused" and toted back and forth in delegations any longer. I think the President should step between him and traders and treaty makers, powder and whiskey peddlers . . . and say, "Hands off, gentlemen." Leave me my savage in *purus naturabilus*, morally, at least. Don't imperil his wild virtues in Washington . . . Exterminate him, if you must, but don't put a stove-pipe hat on him.

At the same time she took up the banner for Colorado state-

135

hood, and pointed out the cultural refinement of the women of the territory. Women's rights were important to her, but Grace offered to settle for statehood alone, on the "half-a-loaf" theory.

The defeat of the Colorado Bill in 1873 aroused her righteous indignation:

> They have been and gone and done it! They have slammed the door of the Union in the face of Colorado by a vote of 117 to 61. There were also 64 dodgers. Well, we must all be patient and cultivate a christian spirit of generous forgiveness. I hope all those inhospitable M.C.'s will go out to Colorado next summer for a long pleasure tour. . . . May magnanimous farmers of the Platte Valley make a feast for them and kill the fatted prairie dog and pleasantly delude them into believing it wild antelope. . . . May they go hunting and fishing in Middle Park, and have the excitement of being chased by coyotes, cinnamons and Utes and of taking refuge in the hot springs up to their necks . . . May they all be left by the train over-night at Greeley, each man with an empty pocket-flask and not a euchre deck among them. (Letter to *New York Times*, 1873.)

In retaliation, the *Chicago Post* declared that Grace Greenwood had invested heavily in Denver town lots; the investment was, they maintained, her real reason for being upset over the defeat of the bill. She demanded investigation, saying that she owned nothing in Denver, that the gift of a lot promised her by Greeley had never materialized, but that she owned only her bit of land near Pikes Peak. "If my Chicago brother should speak well of Heaven, I would not suspect him of 'having treasures laid up there,' " she retorted.

Grace and her daughter Anne arrived in July, 1874, to spend another summer at the cottage. Newspapers took account of the presence of Bishop Machebeuf in town at the same time; he was making arrangements for regular services to be held in Colorado Springs. By early August the popular lecturer already had her schedule filled. Her new topic, "Indoors," which she delivered at the City Hall, was proclaimed by critics in New York, Washington, Boston, and San Francisco the best she had yet offered to the public. The program dealt with "Home Life and All Its Relations."

With her "charming pen" Grace described the night life at the Manitou bowling and billiard hall:

> . . . a mixed and motley gathering, picturesque and peculiar. Ranchmen, booted and spurred, miners and prospectors, tourists and explorers trying to look like mountaineers but betraying the counting house or college at every turn, weak looking but stylish young men wrestling with the big balls in the alley, endangering the shins of the pin boys, laughing young ladies lightly skirmishing with billiards while playing deeper games, Englishmen of high birth and rising inflectons, civil engineers, artists, editors and reporters—all made up the varied gathering.

Grace vowed that she was charged exorbitant prices in Colorado because she was mistakenly thought to be the wife of J. B. Lippincott, the eminent and opulent Philadelphia publisher, and she complained that she was burdened with manuscripts from ambitious young writers, accompanied by their requests that she intercede for them with her "husband." Apparently Manitou Springs' small underworld must have been confused about her financial status, too, because burglars once attempted to invade her small cottage. Grace took her Italian stiletto and went in hot pursuit, but the would-be thieves were frightened away. She gave due notice in a local newspaper:

> We now give warning to all gentlemen of burglarious proclivities that a good gallant friend having provided us with a six shooter, we intend to practice diligently with it, firing promiscuously from our balconies o'nights. I am not Mrs. J. B. Lippincott, and haven't any diamonds, our silver is plated, our money in the bank if we haven't over-drawn . . . I intend setting the shrubbery full of steel traps . . . no use for them to call again at Clematis Cottage and may be slightly dangerous. P.S. another friend has lent us a brindle-bull terrier—very powerful.

Bad weather cut into the attendance at her farewell lecture of that year and not many were present to hear the address on "Yankee Character and Humor" with its numerous illustrated recitations.

By this time Grace felt that Colorado cities and towns and neighborhoods had acquired their own peculiar characteristics and standards of respectability. She stated:

> In Denver, they would ask, "How much are you worth?" Colorado Springs looks severely at you and says, "Who was your grandfather?" Golden don't care much, but would like to know what church you belong to. Greeley says, "Do you drink?" while Boulder shakes hands coolly, "I will not grow sociable till you answer the question, 'how much do you know?' "

At the age of seventy, Grace Greenwood wrote her *Reminiscence of Washington before and after the War*. At the age of eighty-one she died at her home in New Rochelle, New York, on April 20, 1904. Notice of her death appeared in the Colorado Springs paper and the *Denver Republican*.

Her brilliant flash across Colorado skies had been meteoric and spectacular, but her flame burned out quickly and left no trace. This may be attributed to her penchant for spreading herself too thin over too wide an area. Had she concentrated on one cause, such as did her contemporary, Helen Hunt Jackson, she might have retained some of the same immortality. As it was, her trail was obliterated and became only a pleasant memory of a waning star.

SOURCES

Greenwood Leaves, A Collection of Sketches and Letters, Grace Greenwood, Ticknor, Reed and Fields, Boston, Massachusetts, 1849
New Life in New Lands, Grace Greenwood, J. B. Ford & Co., 1873
The Book of Colorado Springs, Manly Dayton Ormes and Eleanor R. Ormes, The Dentan Printing Co., Colorado Springs, Colorado, 1933
Westerners Brand Book, 1955, article on Grace Greenwood by Marian Talmadge and Iris Gilmore, Denver, Colorado
Historical Album of Colorado, Off Duty Enterprises, Colorado Springs, Colorado

Outwest, 1872-1873
Colorado Springs Gazette, 1873-1874, April 21, 1904, January 1, 1905
Racky Mountain News, August 24, 1871, September 2, 1873
Boulder News, August 26, 1871
Colorado Transcript, August 30, 1871
Weekly Miner (Georgetown, Colorado), October 31, 1872
Inter-Ocean, February 7, 1874
Interviews with
Bill Crosby
Mrs. Kenneth Englert
and assistance from
Joan Shinew, Coburn Library, Colorado College
Denver Public Library, Western History Department

Bathhouse John,

Poet Lariat of the First Ward

Stepping into the lobby of the Antlers Hotel one summer day in 1900 was a sartorial vision which popped the eyes of the natives and stunned the local visitors. A massive figure of over two hundred pounds, his burly head crowned with a bushy pompadour, his hard blue eyes surveyed Colorado Springs' outstanding hostelry; his voice boomed out a greeting in an Irish tenor that seemed to embrace the whole community. His immense torso was decked out in the type of garb with which he had just overwhelmed the guests at the Brown Palace in Denver— red, white, and blue vest, green pants, and a modest brown Prince Albert. The people in the lobby who glimpsed the newcomer were aware that this was some kind of *rara avis,* but were totally ignorant of the breed.

There was a story behind the man that was as gaudy as a sideshow and was to be the transitional stage between the tin horn gambler and the small-time crook, and the future with highly professional, organized gangsters. The hotel register identified the resplendent figure as John J. Coughlin of Chicago. It did not mention "Bathhouse," or "Ward One," or "Silver Dollar Saloon," or "Turkish Bath," or "Clark Street," or "Michigan Boulevard," or "the Levee."

The story which few Colorado Springs residents ever knew began August 15, 1860, in Connelly's Patch, the Irish district east of the Chicago River. John was born an Irishman, a Catholic, and a Democrat with both a large and a small "d." His formal education was cut short by the Chicago fire which wiped out the family store and home and which forced him into the school of hard knocks, a circumstance which he never resented. On the

Bathhouse John at his Colorado zoo. *Photo courtesy Pioneer Museum, Colorado Springs.*

contrary, according to his biographers, Lloyd Wendt and Herman Kogan, he was to say later, "Why, money didn't mean anything to me. I'm glad that fire came along and burned the store. Say, if not for that bonfire, I might have been a rich man's son and gone to Yale—and never amounted to nothing!"

During his brief period at Jones School young John's job as janitor earned him the nickname of "Dusty John," a title in which he took pride. From the first, his chief asset was a real talent for personal relations, and his trademark was a cheery wave of the hand. His sheer size made him an outstanding figure; his bull neck indicated tenacity, and his imposing jaw verified it. John's physical stamina and driving ambition permitted him to hold three jobs at one time.

It was the day of the popularity of bathhouses where prize fighters, jockeys, stew bums, merchants, and politicians came to scrub in the tin tubs, steam away in a cabinet the accumulated poisons, and get a rub down of salt or sand. John put his muscles to good advantage and became a rubber, and, in a short time, through the influence of a ward politician, found himself owner of his own bathhouse on Clark Street. His natural friendliness and his association with politicians who patronized the establishment helped him to form his philosophy for life—"The prominent citizen shucked down to the skin is much like everyone else. You could learn from everyone. Ain't much difference between a big man and a little man. One's lucky, that's all."

The day after buying his own place, John went to church at St. John's and prayed.

With the success of his first bathhouse, John was encouraged to open a second which he staffed with efficient help. He took on poundage, added a mustache, and gained the name of Bathhouse John.

His love of loud, friendly talk and his enthusiasm for politics made him a natural for the presidency of the Democratic Marching Club. His voice boomed out for Cleveland for President and Carter Harrison for Governor. Harrison was sometimes referred to "as the politician who kept his hands in his own pockets."

John was seen in expensive restaurants, but he rarely drank and never gambled—except on horses. His love of good clothes was an early characteristic. He felt that you couldn't wear good clothes unless you were clean on the inside.

Politics and horses were his two passions. In 1885, he bought a two-year-old and named her My Queen in honor of his first and only sweetheart, Mary Kiley of Connelly's Patch. Mary was studying to become a school teacher. She found John's grammar a never-ending challenge. They were married October 20, 1886, in St. John's Church and moved into a small Michigan Avenue apartment.

John's enthusiasm led him to accept a position as wheel horse of the First Ward. Of the thirty-five wards in Chicago, Ward One was a world in itself, consisting of churches, mansions, cheap gin mills, dime hotels, prosperous business buildings, cribs, and, on the southwest, the Levee habitat of the dregs of civilization. A section of the old Levee was dubbed "Little Cheyenne" for Cheyenne, Wyoming, then the wickedest town in the nation. Cheyenne later retaliated by naming its red-light district "Little Chicago."

John was gradually being groomed for the job of alderman, and Mary assisted by attempting to smooth off some of his rough edges. She brushed his clothes, made him change his vest, and bought him a big porcelain spittoon. She took this *objet d'art* to a nearby art school to have it decorated with pretty flowers. "Some red and blue ones," she suggested. "Mr. Coughlin is very fond of flowers."

With the growth of the city came the growth of crime, and this became the undergirding of the political kingdom which John Coughlin inherited. Politics makes strange bedfellows. Allied with this handsome, genial, blustery giant was the pint-sized, close-mouthed, dour Michael Kenna, known to everyone as Hinky Dink. They made an incongruous but perfect combination, with Bathhouse John the noisy front and Kenna the quiet operator and the brain behind the scenes.

For his coming out party, Alderman Coughlin chose to wear a vest made of his lucky racing colors of green and white checks. With this he wore trousers and coat of a delicate gray. His newly acquired mustache was waxed and twirled to pin-point perfection and his closely cropped hair stood up like a cockatoo's comb. In the background, Hinky Dink quietly chewed his black, unlighted cigar and laid plans for the two of them.

As a member of the reception committee for the Chicago World's Columbian Exposition of 1893, Coughlin made a pretty picture, resplendent in all his convention badges.

Coughlin and Hinky Dink became virtual rulers over Ward One and found themselves in a position to dispense "protection," for a fee, to the smallest city employee, to the street cleaner and to the owner of the richest "house" on the Levee. Coughlin always remembered early advice, "Don't take the big stuff, go after the little. It's safer." There was enough little stuff to add up to a big amount. He was a firm believer in "Live and let live" if it was profitable, and it was. The Levee, the organized vice area of Chicago, was a political plum for any politician clever enough to keep his eyes open or closed at the proper time.

At the time of the Columbian Exposition, the Levee took on a new spurt of prosperity which eventually ended in the pockets of its protectors. The brothel doors swung wide and Chicago reporters described the seething section.

> . . . new bordellos and crib shacks sprang up, and hundreds of sharpers, pimps, and strong-arm men lurked in every Levee street and alley to separate the visitors from their money. The entire Levee seethed with the most abandoned orgy of vice and crime the city had yet seen . . . Thousands of dollars poured over the gaming tables every hour, day and night. . . In the brothels beer flowed, champagne corks popped, the "professors" and Negro bands played gay tunes and the girls worked in double shifts . . . In Carrie Watson's brownstone establishment, the show place of the Levee, sixty girls, clad in shining silk, worked night and day, while Carrie's amazing parrot croaked in its cage by the door, "Carrie Watson. Come in, gentlemen." (Kogan and Wendt, *Lords of the Levee.*)

144

It is said that this same parrot later became a Colorado Springs resident!

As the pendulum of vice swung too far in one direction, the reform forces propelled it in the other. William Stead, a visiting English editor, shouted the facts which Chicagoans had only dared to whisper. His book, *If Christ Came to Chicago*, had world-wide effect and the city could not refuse to take note of the stranger within its gates. Stead's publication spared nothing in graphic detail—complete to maps of the areas under fire. The Presbyterians felt that was going a bit too far and that the maps might have something of the effect of a *Poor Man's Guide to Chicago*. As long as the sore spots of the city were not mentioned, they could be ignored by the respectable citizenry, but once they had been brought under Stead's microscope, surgery was required.

The fever of reform brought pressures within the party itself, and resulted in mob fights with clubs and beer bottles, and even straight-edged razors. When the aroused citizenry demanded an investigation, John Coughlin rose to the quick defense of his taxpayers and protested the expenditure of the $3,000 which a vice investigation would cost, saying that they could not afford it, since the party had already spent $100,000 in recent campaign funds to assure their successful election. It was a time for economy measures.

Alderman Coughlin proceeded to press enough ineffectual reform bills to furnish a sop for the reformers, and he also came forth with such distracting ordinances as the suggestion to place twelve-foot walls around all Chicago cemeteries. John felt that cemeteries had a deadening effect on neighborhoods, and as an economy measure the walls could pay for themselves by means of the advertising which could be placed on the outside. Coughlin said he was in dead earnest about it, but the bill never passed. However, the idea was accepted in part, and in some sections the walls were put up—however, without advertising.

In Mayor Carter Harrison II, the Bath found his ideal of the person he would like to be, but never could. The mayor was cultured, well groomed, and polished. Bathhouse looked up to him.

Tax manipulation was an accepted practice. An exposé by the *Chicago Journal* and the *Daily News* brought to light some shocking facts, according to Lloyd Wendt and Herman Kogan in their *Lords of the Levee*:

> . . . a suit manufacturer in the First Ward . . . paid two representatives of the First Ward machine $500 to effect a lowering of his assessment. . . (Thus effecting a saving of $1,500.)
> . . . A real-estate dealer testified he had paid $2,500 to have his property value reduced from $2,300,000 to $1,700,000. The Chicago City Railway Company was found to have been taxed on an assessment of $800,000, whereas the true worth of its property for tax purposes was $4,000,000.

Kenna and Coughlin began to be known as the "Rocks of Gibralter" and Coughlin's ambitions grew, even to aspirations toward the office of mayor, but he never quite made it. He was not beyond bribery, and the employment of thug tactics was the accepted political practice.

Following the reform turmoil, Bathhouse decided that he needed a rest. Probably Chicago did, too. For relaxation John decided to visit the watering places in the east, but this required a complete new wardrobe in order to give the eastern die-hards an eyeful. Bathhouse insisted he didn't want to look like an undertaker. He was too busy living to think about death. Passing up the current fashion for gloomy, dark clothes, he declared, according to his biographers Wendt and Kogan, that he wanted

> . . . a cross between a Bowery drop curtain and a Quaker gray . . . (With it he ordered) a silk hat of two gallon capacity . . . a straw hat with a blue band studded with polka dots, a Prince Albert coat with a plaid vest and plaid trousers . . . russet shoes with bulldog toes

and a stunning bathing suit of baby blue with heart's-blood polka dots.

He held a preview fashion show for the First Ward, who

seemed properly impressed, and Tom McNally remarked when John appared in his green dress suit, "It's a peach. You look like an Evanston lawn kissed by an early dew." One newspaper man declared that John would become a "lily of the valet."

Rounding out his eastern tour, John decided to make Kansas City one of his targets. He struck Missouri color blind with his evening vest of red and white polka dots, his summer suit with its pink silk lining, the gold necktie, and his gray "flush of morning" hat.

Bathhouse extended his sartorial tour to include the less humid area of the west. It was about 1900 that he first popped the eyes of the lobby-sitters in the Brown Palace Hotel in Denver with his red, white, and blue vest, green pants, and modest Prince Albert. Colorado Springs, of conservative taste, was given a brief glimpse of his gaudy coat-tails as he paused like a butterfly on a flower before flitting back to the political flame that was Chicago.

John's opponent in the Second Ward was stealing a march with the offer of free baths which heretofore had been Coughlin's sole right. The newcomer declared that there was nothing like a free bath for getting votes. After all, it wasn't a new idea. Nero, Agrippa, and Diocletian had done the same thing. It was good clean politics with a classic example.

John countered with something new. In the west he had become a changed man and had added another facet to his talents. He had set himself up on a "spavined Pegasus" and had become a poet. He declared that the west had the effect of making men and poets. His creation, "Dear Midnight of Love," was set to music and he promptly claimed the music, too.

Not one to hide his light under a bushel, John decided to present his maiden efforts in the largest opera house available and with the best singer obtainable to do the song full justice. He first thought of Madame Calvé, but she is said to have snorted at the suggestion. So John decided on a younger and more amenable *prima donna*. Miss May de Sousa, thirteen-

147

year-old daughter of a loyal First Warder, was chosen to perform the sacred task. Miss de Sousa was visited by the alderman.
She sang her school song for him, and the Bath knew he had
found the ideal one for the debut of his new masterpiece.
Hinky Dink, who either knew nothing about poetry and music,
or maybe knew too much, was sceptical but stoic. The show
ran for a week with the best seats priced at thirty cents and the
gallery at ten cents. With songs from Victor Herbert and a variety show, the crowd was assured of its money's worth, but the
piece de resistance was young May in a white dress with ruffles,
against the background of a palace, and with the accompaniment
of fifty voices from the First Ward, singing "Dear Midnight of
Love."

John modestly took several bows with May, and declared he
wasn't swelled up about it. According to biographers he declared:

> "There's nothin' to it! . . . . I'm certainly th' best there is,
> th' best anybody ever looked at. I'm doing a stunt right here
> now that no alderman can touch, no alderman in the world.
> Th' orchestra's all right, the singer's all right, the song's all
> right, the house will be all right . . . And I—well, I'm just Jawn
> and I ain't swelled a bit because I got it all comin' to me."

The *Chicago Journal* said, "From now on, it's Bathos John."

Mayor Harrison was puzzled and asked Hinky Dink if he
thought John was crazy or full of dope. Hinky Dink assured the
mayor that John wasn't "dotty or full of dope, but to tell the
God's truth . . . they ain't found a name for it, yet."

When the reporters told Bathhouse, mockingly, that he was
poet laureate of Chicago, he grinned and shook his head. "No,
boys, not Chicago yet. Just the First Ward, boys. Poet Lariat of
the First Ward, that's Jawn Coughlin."

"Dear Midnight of Love" achieved astounding popularity. The
cover of the printed music was adorned with a picture of John,
a church in the background, with a spray of flowers and two
doves wreathing him. The song was found on every "professor's"
piano on the Levee.

After John's glittering musical debut, things grew dull and he remembered the Antlers Hotel and Pikes Peak, and felt the need to get away from it all. What more complete change for the versatile John than to become a Colorado farmer? He set his agents to work, in 1902, to find the ideal farm, and with his flair for showmanship arrived on the scene in the midst of "Li'l Lunnon's" annual Flower Festival and accepted graciously the invitation to be a part of the parade celebration. Hiring a rickety carriage, he had it covered with blossoms, First Ward fashion, and he and Mary drove slowly up the street, waving to the crowd. Biographers said that Theodore Roosevelt, a visitor, watching from the stand, boomed out, "Hi, John," and Bathhouse boomed back, with tears streaming down his face, "Teddy, Teddy, me boy, Teddy," while the crowd cheered. If "Li'l Lunnon" knew the background of the Bath, they ignored it, and welcomed him with open arms.

John not only extended his interests to farming, but he also became involved in a mining project. There wasn't anything he couldn't do. He bought an interest in a mine from a broken miner for $300. For once John did not cut much of a figure with his haberdashery; out for gold, he dressed the part. Among the mining equipment he purchased was a string of burros, one of which he sent to Mayor Carter Harrison with a note saying that it was the finest emblem possible of the great machine party to which both he and the Honorable Carter Harrison belonged. Mayor Harrison was overwhelmed with the four-legged gift and at a loss what to do with the beast, particularly when it became surly with children. He thought he had found a neat solution when he put the burro to graze in a poison ivy patch, but the Chicago mayor wasn't very well acquainted with Colorado burros. The animal thrived on the ivy patch, and forthwith became poison ivy exterminator for the First Ward.

On John's next trip to Colorado, he reverted to type; it took five trunks to contain his togs, which set the community to thinking and buzzing. The local paper said:

149

John has an outlay that will startle the natives in these
diggings. He has just had made in Chicago a salmonhued
broadcloth vestcoat the likes of which has never been seen
here. It is one of those new creations and those who have
seen it say it is a stunner from way back—the hottest thing that
ever came down the Pike! John will don it some of these
evenings with his green clawhammer, then what a furor!

By July 24, 1901, John and Mary were cozily at home in a
pretty little cottage on the banks of Cheyenne Creek. Chatting
with his cronies one convivial evening at the Antlers Hotel, John
and his friends discussed the recent scaling of the Matterhorn
by an Englishman. With his customary reticence, John said,
"Let 'em try to climb Cheyenne Mountain. Now there's a hill,
ain't a man can climb Cheyenne except, maybe, myself." A young
Englishman, Winston Dunraven, rose to the defense of his coun-
trymen, and Coughlin squared off to wave the Stars and Stripes,
and the two agreed to a contest.

The local newspapers took cognizance of the contest and dispatches were filed daily in a dozen states. The *Colorado Springs
Evening Mail* of August 10, 1901, headlined its account, "Bathhouse John will Plant Stars and Stripes." It went on to say:

John J. Coughlin, Chicago alderman, politician, diletante,
poet, song writer, miner and farmer, which last roles he has
assayed since his advent in Colorado Springs, has broken out
in a new place. Bathhouse is a bundle of eccentricities. He
is just naturally built that way and can't help giving vent to
them.

Withal he is patriotic and yields to no man in defending
the laurels of his country. On this account he has agreed to
race an Englishman who is sojourning here, to the top of
Cheyenne Mountain and plant there an American flag. The
Englishman, Winston Dunraven, will attempt to beat John to
the crest of the mountain and plant there the English flag
first. In event that he beats the Chicago Alderman, the latter
will give a champagne dinner and vice versa.

The start is to be made from the Antler's stable on Cascade
Avenue some day next week yet to be determined. Both men
are to ride horses to the point north on the mountain over the
stage road. Then they are to dismount and climb to the sum-

mit. John will ride his celebrated full blooded Arabian steed
whose equal has never been seen in these parts. The animal
was bought by Bathhouse John several years ago, when he
crossed the desert and is swift as the wind. Of course, when
Dunraven entered into the agreement he did not reckon with
this fleet footed thoroughbred, and if he beats John, there
is a champagne supper in it for him.

"Say, I'll beat that guy in a walk," said John today. "I'll
hand him a bunch so hot it'll burn him, see. His steed will
stack agin my flyer like a burro. He don't know. Durhaven,
or Dunraven, or whatever his name is, might as well dig for
his long green and come up with goods now for the supper.
It'll be just like getting money from home to take it. But no
man can con me. If he throws any bull con at me, I'll call him
and if he can't deliver the goods then he'll have to do business
with me, see? I am always here wid the goods myself and no
mistake. And what's more I don't ever come up wid a four-
flush. I'll tell you those."

The way in which John calls it, Mr. Dunraven might as well
declare all bets off, for he's already beaten. . . . Mr. Dunraven
had heard of Bathhouse John and found him a veritable curiosity. Both are patriotic and this is what led to the race and
the feat they have agreed to perform.

Patriotism was quick to flame in the breasts of the local citizenry, and while John and Dunraven were debating what to wear
on the perilous ascent, unbeknownst to them, a dark horse entered
the competition. H. R. Van Meter, an old prospector, made an
early morning ascent of the mountain. The *Evening Mail* of
August 17, 1901, stated that Van Meter

    . . . rode his horse to a point half a mile beyond Kerr's ranch,
    then scaled the mountain side carrying a thirty foot pole at
    the highest point on the mountain.

The paper reported Van Meter as saying that he felt his record
could not be lowered by anyone else and quoted him as saying,
"I heard that a party of English people were going to make a
record for the climb and thought the record had better be made
by an American."

Another son of John Bull, J. L. Conway, was Dunraven's backer.
The paper reported that Conway was "somewhat disgruntled

Saturday afternoon. With the wager practically won, his joy was suddenly cut short on finding that on the summit of the mountain floated the Stars and Stripes from a thirty-foot flag pole . . . . Mr. Conway and Bathhouse decided to have the champagne supper and divide the expense."

It was about 1902 that a young sandy-haired lad, Walter Colburn, came to the attention of John Coughlin. The boy had been working at Mayhurst Lodge around the horses, adjusting stirrups and accepting tips from wealthy easterners to the tune of twenty and twenty-five dollars a day. It was a good job for such a small boy and the young fellow looked out for his employer's interest along with his own. On one occasion when an easterner attempted to catch a train without having settled his sizeable account, young Walt jumped on a pony, galloped across the fields to the railroad station, seized the man by the coat lapels, and demanded payment. The infuriated tourist vowed he would have satisfaction for the insult, but Walt persisted until the man settled the account just in time to leap on his departing train. When this came to the attention of Bathhouse John, he said, "I can use an enterprising young man like you in my business. Go home and tell your Mama you're going to live with me now in Chicago." So Walt Colburn became a member of the Coughlin household and a student in the Chicago trade schools. He came under the wing of Samuel Insull, to whom he reported each Saturday. Walt equipped himself with a thorough knowledge of dynamos and motors—and public relations.

John was grooming the boy to manage his Colorado Springs interests. Coughlin had deplored the inadequacy of the tourist transportation business in the resort city, so he wired Chicago for rigs and horses so people could have better service. Colburn was put in charge of the horses and rigs.

Bath thought again of farming.

Before plunging into barnyard technology, he sampled agrarian life by experimenting on the Dipp farm on Cheyenne Creek. The *New York Sun* took account of the alderman's accomplishments in an article headed:

152

. . . most versatile, accomplished and original of the Democratic statesmen of Chicago. He may have rivals or equals in that or this line of talent. The Hon. John Powers may be a greater financier, the Hon. Carver may be more technically beautiful, the Hon. Bobby Burke may be a subtler diplomatist. The Hon. Hinky Dink may be more sententious and idiomatic. But Mr. John takes the most points for the most events. He is pretty rich, pretty pretty, pretty diplomatic, pretty sententious and idiomatic. He is also the beau of Cook County Democracy, its leader in the matter of splendid and surprising clothes. He is a poet of much inspiration and suspiration, and his "Dear Midnight of Love" is familiar to all those who are familiar with it. He is a tiller of the soil, a doer of chores, a speeder of the plough, a Cincinnatus of the west. The buck and exquisite of the First Ward is also a bucolic hired man.

Richard Harding Loper of the *Evening Mail* in Colorado Springs also had something to say about John as a farmer:

He has been working on a Colorado farm on Cheyenne creek, a five acre farm, small, intense but intensive. . . . Mr. John wears a brown Norfolk jacket, a pair of neat cowhide shoes, a brown Fedora hat from Carter Harrison's own block. He milks the chickens, counts them before they are hatched, shears the cows, sets the sheep on the nest, leads the horse to water and makes him drink, makes the goat browse where it is tethered, gives anti-fat to the stalled ox, says boo to the geese, buys pigs in a poke, makes hay while the sun shines, and catches weasels asleep. He lives in clover, kills two birds with one stone and when he can't put salt on their tails, makes two bites of a cherry, puts the cart before the horse, goes all the way around Robin Hood's barn, acknowledges the corn, feels his oats and knows his beans.

He takes the bull by the horns, gives the calf more rope, and waits until the cows come home. He lets the grass grow under his feet, curries a short horse soon, lets the cat out of the bag and puts all his eggs in one basket. In short, there never was a more practical and ingenious farmer than this emigrant from Chicago's First Ward.

So they poked fun at the genial gentleman farmer, but John's two hundred leghorns were the finest in the land and he always

had fries on hand for his guests. A flag raising at the farm sig-
nalled his annual arrival in the Springs. He usually made a short
address, but avoided giving a political speech. The open air
apparently agreed with Bathhouse, for in December, 1902, he
completed the purchase of a hundred-acre tract from Mrs. Mary
E. Johnson for $88,560, and later added still another hundred
acres.

The following month the alderman revealed his spectacular
plans for his new residential suburb. He pictured tired citizens of
the First Ward recuperating on Colorado's green lawns.

Colorado Springs greeted John's new project with enthusiasm
and naively accepted him without investigating the background
of this likeable, exuberant man. Local newspapers were carried
away. The *Gazette* of January 1, 1903, headlined its news,
"Johnson Tract in Ivywild Will Become New Chicago," and
continued:

> The first effort to give Colorado Springs a residence suburb
> along the line of many great cities is to result from transfer of
> the Johnson tract west of Ivywild . . . to be made an attractive
> residence area. It was bought by Black as a representative of
> Alderman John Coughlin of Chicago who is the most promi-
> nent and influential of the three men who are present owners
> of the tract. The alderman was said to be interested in several
> projects of a large character.

The newspaper hailed the project as an indication of how safe
and solid the area was for real-estate development. The ground
was described as "a quarter of a mile wide, a mile long north
and south across Cheyenne Creek Valley, from the top of Broadmoor Hill on the south to a point on high ground north of the
Cheyenne Cañon streetcar line." The article went on to reveal
the plan to bring one of the best landscape gardeners from the
east to lay off the ground, put out the streets and parks, set
out the trees, and put in cement sidewalks. Each lot would carry
an improvement clause and each would assent to Colorado
Springs' liquor prohibition clause, except that the prohibition
clause would not apply to certain groups of lots reserved for the

154

building of a hotel. The transaction was called, "one of the most important deals ever made in the vicinity." The press also hinted that "these were men of money enough to buy whatever fancy dictates." They continued that by this time $105,000 had already been invested and would be a means of bringing hundreds of thousands of dollars more and of persuading prominent families from Chicago to come here.

Paul Borke, a landscape gardener, was called off his work at St. Louis World's Fair to take over the grounds of the new suburb. Borke was famous for his planning of the Japanese village at the fair. With forty assistants he was to landscape John's new project, making use of native shrubs and the artificial lake and the seven springs already on the property. In addition, 6,000 trees were to be planted—walnut, catalpa, spruce, soft maple, and others from Iowa, and some from the south. Offices for the building project were opened up at 19 1/2 East Pikes Peak Avenue where lots were already being grabbed up by would-be members of the new "colony."

Throughout the bubble of excitement over the real-estate boom the local papers no longer referred to John as Bathhouse, but granted him the dignity of his official title. It sounded better in "Li'l Lunnon."

John was intrigued by a bear which he saw on a nearby ranch and with his usual impulsivenes, bought it for his property. Boys, seeing the bear chained along the road, would stop and box with it, and it became something of an attraction to tourists riding to the end of the streetcar line.

The Bath had always loved animals and now that he had such extensive acreage, citizens began to drop off a few stray kittens and to present him with a few pets—first two eagles, then two coyotes, later a deer and a half dozen burros. John Harlan, owner of Pabst Park in Milwaukee, suggested to the Bath that here was a natural location for a "Coney Island in the Wilderness"— and John was off on a new project.

With a beneficent hand John opened his Zoo Park, collecting animals of all kinds over a period of years. According to Wendt and Kogan, Hinky Dink felt that the zoo was definitely deficient —that what was needed was an elephant, and Bath chimed in, "They is two elephants in Lincoln Park eating up the taxpayer's money. One elephant is enough. Maybe I should take the other elephant off the hands of the taxpayers." The smaller of the two Lincoln Park pachyderms, a slightly damaged elephant with a broken trunk, was borrowed for John's Colorado project. Princess Alice, who had caught her trunk in a trap door and torn off the tip and therefore could not meet the esthetic requirements of the more sophisticated easterners, was crated and shipped to Colorado to relieve the burden of the Chicago taxpayers, who were probably uninformed of their new-found economy. Princess Alice became the pride of John's life; affectionate and cheerful, snub-nose Alice followed John wherever he went.

She snapped her chain one day and went looking for John. Alice wandered about in the snow and came down with a cold. Walter Colburn, who, by this time. was manager of the zoo, suggested calling a vet, but John, with bland confidence in his ability as an elephant doctor, refused.

Colburn later described the incident to biographers and others:

> "What do I do when I get a cold?" John asked.—"I take a drink of whiskey. What's good for humans is good for elephants but they need more of it. She needs a quart." Colburn and John pushed it down the throat of squealing Alice. Halfway through she began to gurgle and drink of her own accord. She became lively, squealed, trumpeted and tossed straw over her head, went swaying through the stalls, snorted at the horses and sent workmen scattering. She gamboled in snow at the top of the hill. She became a confirmed alcoholic but from then on Alice drank like a lady and never became intoxicated again. A few dainty gurgles and she would go swaying into the outfield, her poor crippled trunk curled proudly, her little eyes shining, thinking thoughts elephants think when they are particularly happy. (Lords of the Levee.)

The animals were kept comfortable by means of heating stoves. A tragic fire from an overheated stove killed five of the valuable animals at one time.

Alligators were added to the zoo collection to make it one of the largest alligator farms in the country. A family of seals attracted attention, as did Tammany, the largest captive lion in the world. The animals prospered and produced—the mother camel had a baby, and a prize was tentatively offered for the best name suggested for the infant, but before a decision could be reached, John himself had christened the baby Colorado.

John went lavishly crazy over rides and elaborately constructed scenes. He added "The Feeler," "The Lion's Bride," "Pilgrim's Progress," "Igara," and "The Mountain Torrent." "The Feeler" was a ride of a thousand thrills, "The Old Mill" a bower of flowers representing different countries, and "The Igara" a mystic vision. "The Mountain Torrent" featured thousands of gallons of water lighted by colored lights. A miniature railroad wound its way over rustic bridges and through woodlands. "The Under and Over the Sea" was adapted from Jules Verne and involved a boat trip showing the wonders of the ocean. Children loved "The Buster Brown House." John Coughlin announced his decision to run his project as a first class ladies' and children's park—no drinking to be allowed on the grounds (except for Princess Alice) and no liquor sold. One feature called "The Down and Out Club" pictured John D. Rockefeller counting his gold and Chauncey Depew and others resting.

In one summer, John spent $60,000 in adding new attractions. Naturally, the zoo required a new wardrobe for its owner. John flashed the latest style in haberdashery with his specially designed menagerie shirt. The dozen new creations from New York cost John a neat $500, but they were worth it, for the new garments were hand-embroidered, with thirty or forty different kinds of animals in bold relief on each. The bosoms of the shirts contained two hundred and forty pleats. John declared to a local reporter, "As I am going to wear them myself, I don't see that it is anybody's business but my own." It was suggested that he alternate the shirts on various days and hold receptions to suit the proper category; on "monkey day" he could wear his monkey shirt, and in this fashion pass through the entire dozen.

Entrance to John Coughlin's Zoo Park on Cheyenne Road. *Photo courtesy Pioneer Museum, Colorado Springs.*

Lady tourists at the buffalo exhibit. *Photo courtesy Pioneer Museum, Colorado Springs.*

From a journal of a boy of ten comes a child's-eye-view of the old zoo. Landell Bartlett wrote in his journal of 1907 a graphic impression of the wonders to be found in this "Coney Island Wilderness." Under the title of "A Zoo in the West," came a lengthy description of the amusement facilities, the animals, and a choice bit about the day John Coughlin came from Chicago to be with the children on the *Gazette* free day. On this day, children stood in line for blocks to get the free coupons for every ride and concession in the park. The diary was amply illustrated with newspaper pictures of this and the zoo atractions. There was also a picture of burly John, towering over a group of little boys in knee breeches and young girls in white dresses.

Little Lan began:

> The "Zoo" I am talking about is about five miles out of Colorado Springs, Colorado, United States of America. It has more than fifty acres of land shaded by trees. . . . Here is a list of the attractions, not the animals.
> "Buster Brown"
> "Roller Coaster"
> "Under and Over the Sea"
> "Giant Circle Swing"
> "Fun Factory"
> "Refreshment Stands"
> "Rollar (sic) Skating Rink"
> "Merry go round"
> "Chute the Chutes"
> "Bump the Bumps"
> "The Old Mill"
> "Electric Theatre"
> "Penny Slots"
> "Miniature Railway"
> "M'Gunns Animal Arena"
> "Baby House"
> "Shooting Gallery"
> "Boulding (sic) Alley"
> "Cane Gallery"
> "Theater"

In describing "The Buster Brown House," the boy wrote, "You pay your ticket to the man at the side of the door. Then you go through a cavern, very narrow, and only room for single file. An electric light keeps turning on and off so that you get kind of stupid. . ."

In describing the "Under and Over the Sea," the youngster said:

> We walk on sand and the walls glitter in the red light. It seems as though we are travelling through a cave of garnets and rubies.

Young Lan told of John Coughlin's appearance at the zoo on Children's Day:

> The man that owns the zoo is a citizen of Chicago, Illinois, by the name of John Couglin. On Thursday, June 20, he was at the zoo to see all the children. That was *Gazette's* children's day when all are admitted on everything free. Between five thousand and six thousand children were present.

Older visitors were impressed, too, and at a famous barbecue in 1911, some five thousand people were served barbecued beef, mutton, veal, and lamb, and toured the costliest of all the attractions, the bathhouse with its hot and cold plunge. The crowd donned the latest style in swim suits. The plunge was a favorite adult attraction, and was kept brightly lighted at night.

Walter Colburn manned the many spectacular pyrotechnic displays and one local paper commented on a feature attraction illustrated in fireworks, "The Battle of Manila." "The Sinking of the Maine" and "The Fall of Morro Castle" were other spectacular displays touched off by young Colburn.

Although the zoo consistently lost money, Bathhouse shrugged. He was having a good time, and there was more where that came from.

John continued to woo the muse and wrote a poem for the *Colorado Springs Gazette* to welcome reporters to a press convention to be held in the city. The following lines appeared:

ODE TO VISITORS
WELCOME TO THE PRESS
My colleagues of the Press, to you I tip my sombrero,
The freedom of the town is yours.

Roller Coaster. *Photo courtesy Pioneer Museum, Colorado Springs.*

Princess Alice, the "borrowed elephant." *Photo courtesy Pioneer Museum, Colorado Springs.*

161

Thrice welcome to where you go
We're proud to have you in our midst
And hope you'll come again
No fairer spots in all the world
Than "Garden of the Gods" domain.
Yon mount against the azure sky
Appropriately yclept Pikes Peak
To reach its snow capped top with alpine stock
Twould take a week
Old William Tell who roamed the Alps ne'er gazed on
    grander loftier scene,
Than that of Pike's easy ascent of which is via cog ma-
    chine.
Breathe in the ozone, for there's no purer on this mundane
    sphere
That's why I come to Colorado Springs to spend vacation
    every year.
The Switzerland of America it Burton Holmes so aptly
    calls.
No finer scenery anywhere than Cheyenne Mount and
    Seven Falls.
Lest I forget, I call your attention to my wondrous zoo
It lies out here on Cheyenne Road.
A pretty spot indeed to view.
There's birds and animals galore and every pastime
    'neath the sun,
A Coney Island, Luna Park and Dreamland all rolled
    in one.

John believed in the power of advertising and managed to
sneak in a plug for his own property whenever possible.

So captivated by his own muse was he, that John determined
to publish a book of poems and, as a sincere tribute, to dedicate
the volume to his colleague, Alderman Kenna. Poor, defenseless,
little Hinky Dink rose screaming like a wounded tiger. According
to the story which appeared in the *Chicago Tribune,* Kenna was
not slow to act and raged, "Unless he is restrained by order of
the court John is going to publish a book of poems. The title may
be *Ballads of the Bathhouse,* in fulfillment of a threat made by
the poet Laureate of the City Council five years ago." Kenna

declared that if Coughlin dared to do any dedicating to him he would sue for slander and libel.

> I told him, no, that I wouldn't allow my name to be used in the book, and I also served notice on the publisher if that book of poems was dedicated to me I'd never be able to live it down—and the disgrace. I've got troubles enough without that.

"Just you wait until Mike sees the illustrations and he'll jump at the chance," was Coughlin's reply. "Mike, you know, don't understand the literary game. Automobiling is his hobby."

Plowing his fingers through his thick pompadour the bard of Michigan Avenue continued:

> I first thought of getting out a book five years ago but I've been too busy. I have compiled twenty-eight choice selections. It will be profusely illustrated. Yes, profusely. I like to say that word. It makes a fellow think he's got money in his kicks.

Diving through a pile of manuscripts the alderman read a few choice bits:

ODE TO A LOWER BERTH
O lower berth, to thee I sing
Your downy couch is fit for king.
In Morpheus' arms I slumber deep
The train rolls on while I'm asleep.

Across the isle sits Phoebe Snow
All dressed in white
Her face aglow.
I made a mash on Phoebe last night
By softly murmuring, "anthracite."

"I guess that's kind of poor, isn't it?" said the aldermanic bard. "It's what I call good stuff, has red corpuscles,—style is my own. No man can counterfeit it. A lot of my stuff is over people's heads. Other poets have the same faults." John promised that sometime, when he was in the proper frame of mind, he would write a sonnet on plate glass and fire insurance. Meanwhile he turned out such gems as:

163

SHE SLEEPS AT THE SIDE OF THE DRAINAGE CANAL

In her lonely grave she sleeps tonight
At the side of the drainage canal.
Where the whippoorwills call at the twilight hour
They planted my sweetheart Sal.
Just a mile this side of Willow Springs
Not far from the Alton track
There lieth Sal, my dear old Pal,
But these tears won't bring her back.

Lacking any finer feeling from his bosom friend, Hinky Dink, the Bath offered to dedicate his verses to Henry Carrol, precinct captain who retaliated by threatening to challenge John to a duel if he carried out the promised dedication. The poems were published in the *Chicago Tribune's* Sunday supplement in color, "with the picture of the bard strumming a guitar and yodeling from a balcony before his entranced Council Colleagues."

The Bath promised poetically to build a bathhouse on the summit of Pikes Peak, "and run for Mayor of the mountains the middle of next week." He continued:

In the fastness of their reaches
The Yankee eagle screeches
And the Democratic donkey sings, sings, sings;
And the Democratic donkey sings.

His pastoral on maple sugar John considered the best thing he ever wrote. He said of this masterpiece:

It has real poetic feeling, genuine rhythmical muse which cannot be counterfeited. Of all the poets since Chaucer's time not one of them has ever written a line about the sap in the maple. They have handed out the same line of spring poetry year after year about flowers and birds and azure skies but people get tired of that kind of dope. They want something up to date. I'm the boy that can slip it right over the home plate. I thought it was about time some poet got busy on the sap question. On my Colorado ranch I have a sugar bush and just as soon as I get a wire that the sap has started to run I'll pack my grip and bid farewell to Chicago for at least two weeks. My sugar bush out there at Colorado Springs has got anything in Vermont or New Hampshire skinned a block.

164

The poem had all other spring poetry skinned, too. It read:

MAPLE SUGAR MAKING—A PASTORAL

I'm living in hopes that the rays of the sun
Will soon start the sap rising in the maple to run.
You may have your marshmallows and chocolate creams.
But give me the sap when it's boiled and congeals.

There are kisses and bonbons and fudges galore
Piled high on the counter of each candy store,
I care for them not, but I'd go without meals
For the soft maple sap when it's boiled and congeals.

The robins and bock beer will soon pipe their lay.
You can tell by the moon that they're headed this way.
Oh, where are my pails and the sugar to tap.
I want to be in on the "first" run of the sap.

A Chicago newspaper recorded:

The Bard had a habit of arriving in the offices of *The Evening Post* clutching a neat little package tied modestly with baby blue ribbon. Unfolding it, he would offer to read his latest effusion although modesty forbade him praising his own work. He did reveal that the difference between a pastoral poem and the ordinary ode to spring was that the pastoral must have a dash of ginger which only the true poet is capable of slinging into the muse. Anybody can sit down to a typewriter and knock out a spring poem, but only the real poet can put over the pastoral.

It soon became known that John ran both a pick-up and a delivery service on poetry. Jack Lait, a newspaper man to become famous for his exposé of both minor and major crimes, practiced his "peeping tom" techniques on the sensitive would-be poet. John became hoist by his own lariat. Lait published the facts—that John Kelly, another newspaper man, was the true author of the deathless verse. Coughlin screamed, "Nobody writes my stuff. It comes natural to me. I dash it off before I know it." Many years later, in 1932, Kelly acknowledged he was the true bard, but John continued as Poet Lariat, under self-hypnosis.

Bathhouse was in Colorado Springs in April, 1908. He wanted

to inspect the zoo which was opening its season in May, and there were certain preparations to be made for Chicago's First Warders who might be dropping in during the coming political convention in Denver. It would be good to entertain old cronies with western hospitality and to show them some of the country he had adopted.

His "aldermanic pass" made it possible for him to zoom back and forth between his two homes with the greatest of ease; so he buzzed back to Chicago for Easter which was on April 19, that year, and was back in Colorado Springs to speak at the Antlers on April 23.

Rushing in where angels feared, John spoke of a plan for matrimonial bureaus which he thought could best be conducted under government control. The *Colorado Springs Gazette,* April 24, 1908, quoted his speech as follows:

> What we want is a national matrimonial bureau to be supplemented by state bureaus in every state in the Union. The trouble at present is that too many men get into connubial bonds who are not worthy to enter the kingdom and too many men who are worthy are kept out through inherent bashfulness, timidity or something that prevents them from approaching the fair sex. On the other hand, too many women who have no other qualification than that of being good fishers of men win out at the matrimonial bargain counter while their weaker and more modest sisters are left to blush unseen and cast their fragrance on the desert air. Now with properly regulated matrimonial bureaus under government control, all this would be avoided and divorces would become rare as orchids at Christmas. The bureaus could be under the control of officials expert in judgment of human nature and only those who are mentally fitted for each other and compatible in every way would be allowed to wed. The past record of both parties could be scrutinized and a guarantee certificate issued with the license. My scheme is only in its primary stages but the details are a mere matter of proper organization. I would like to see the federal government take up the matter seriously and also to make it a campaign issue.

The banquet audience yawned, applauded, and dismissed the proposal.

July of that year brought the Democratic convention and the

$50,000 special train from Chicago to invade Denver. The First Warders and the Marching Club with other politicians from the Windy City reserved two cars of the train and Hinky Dink kept one for himself. The trip was a lively one. The train load had been well fortified against the trip across the Great American Desert of Kansas by a lavish supply of champagne, whisky, gin, lemons, and all the makings.

Down Denver's Seventeenth Street came the Marching Club, ignoring the catcalls and insults from the opposing faction at the Albany. Straight into the lobby of the Brown Palace they marched, where they engaged in a "battle of music" with other bands in the lobby. The First Warders did themselves proud. Kogan and Wendt in their *Lords of the Levee* reported that hardened miners and cattlemen left screaming for open air, and that Hinky Dink looked over his men with pride, saying, "Not a gink in the crowd that eats with his knife," recalling some conventions when the dinners had looked like "exhibitions of sword swallowing."

The First Ward's private cars were attached to another engine and a telegram was dispatched to Bathhouse to get out the keys to Colorado Springs. The Bath met the train with six automobiles, the mayor and prominent citizens, a band of genuine howling Indians, and a salute from six-shooters. Then followed a trip to the regional beauty spots, complete with eulogy and gestures by John. Then came the picnic at Zoo Park with corned beef and cabbage, supplemented with foamy beer and bubbling champagne. It was a whee of a day for the First Warders, only spoiled by the fact that something had gone wrong in Denver. Hinky Dink's proxy got his orders confused and elected the wrong man.

Back in Chicago, the reformers were edging their way into the spotlight again. The influence which Stead and Gypsy Smith, among other reformers, had sparked at intervals had burned low but had by no means died. When the time drew near for the annual First Ward Ball, every reformer's shoulder was put to the wheel to clean up the traditional orgy. The *Tribune* joined forces with the side of the angels and threatened to print the name of every respectable citizen who attended the ball. Bathhouse was willing to make a few concessions in order to throw some oil on the waters. He said he didn't want any disorderly characters who got loaded somewhere else to come and claim they got it there. He compromised further by announcing that no kids would be allowed at the ball and that preachers could come if they behaved themselves and promised to stick by the rules.

With such a guarantee of orderly conduct, the night of the 1908 First Ward Ball was the biggest brawl ever held. The doors literally burst open from the pressure of the crowd and people were spurted into the streets. Women fainted and were passed over the heads of the crowd. Ladies of the Levee came escorted by the police. White slavers were on hand with the rest of the underworld. Coughlin led the Grand March holding the arms of the Everleigh sisters, dropping their arms finally to direct the band with both hands. The crowd marched twenty-five abreast singing "Hail, Hail, the Gang's All Here." Wendt and Kogan stated that the Everleighs spent at the rate of fifty dollars an hour, that young rakes drank champagne from the "girls'" slippers, and that one hundred extra policemen were paid by the city for extra duty. The next day the police blotter showed they had been more or less on the job. "They made eight arrests. Seven were released without punishment; and one Bernard Dooley was fined twenty-five dollars for trying to enter a building through a rear door. He was sentenced to work it out."

This was the last flamboyant First Ward Ball the city was to know. Gypsy Smith had set the yeast that was fermenting into reform. Stead had tried it in 1893.

One more such ball was attempted but was said to be the saddest and dullest ever seen.

The reformers closed in for the kill. On March 10, Mayor Buss appointed a vice commission of thirty members. They were given $5,000 to do the job. Coughlin and Kenna shrugged, "One single block of Armour Avenue cleaned up more than that on a Saturday night." They ignored the handwriting on the wall and were

168

only faintly concerned when 1,825 operators were arrested and the girls moved off Michigan Avenue.

Bathhouse John found himself confronted with a new problem in the form of Woman Suffragists. In 1914 they picked up the hatchet and indicated him as public target number one. He was opposed by Marian Drake whose campaign cry was, "We're turning the searchlight on the First Ward." The women were determined to make their first vote felt. Coughlin shrugged at the needling feminine thrusts and shook them off as a great dane might ignore an annoying toy terrior. He took the positive approach and declared himself to be in favor of raising teachers' salaries—he protested that he had inherited his money, and resented violently a statement that he had been born in Waukegan, and said that he loved everybody.

On election day, Marian Drake and her women voters marched to the polls, carrying milk and sandwiches to the workers who had previously been nurtured on beer and pretzels.

Coughlin and Kenna got out the vote in their old First Ward fashion. Their men handed out candy kisses to the women and specimen ballots to the voters. Actually, these were regulation ballots, procured in some underhanded manner. The voter would take the marked ballot, retire to the booth, and exchange it for the one issued to him. Dropping in the already marked ballot, he would then return the blank one to the boys, who would pay him for his vote. This would then be marked and ready for the next floater.

Despite his scorn for the weaker sex in politics, Bathhouse had to extend himself to beat "the dame" by a margin of 3,000 votes instead of the original 8,000 which he had anticipated. It was all wrong, and he was tired. He headed back to Colorado Springs and his beloved zoo, and Cheyenne Mountain, and again sharpened his poetry pencil.

In 1916, his Colorado Springs residence burned down. Spontaneous combustion, Walt Colburn always figured. It had been such a nice place, standing almost in the alfalfa patch and right across from the timothy field in a spot which is now about the

169

700 block on Cheyenne Boulevard. As if this were not blow enough, Colorado voted, a few months later, to close all saloons. This Coughlin took as a personal insult and swore that his love for Colorado Springs was over. He closed his zoo and tried to sell it. He was offered a meagre $30,000 for his million dollar investment. A Methodist temperance group made a bid. Coughlin would have none of it. He would rather give it away. He did—to Walter Colburn, the sandy-haired lad who had been a part of John's household, and who had cut his wisdom teeth in the Coughlin regime. To Walt fell the dismal task of dismantling the zoo.

Colburn said, "It was a sad breakup of the zoo when Coughlin declared he would no longer stay in Colorado Springs, nor ever come to the zoo again, because the state had gone dry. He just stepped out . . . and left it to me to dispose of things."

According to Charles Dudley in an account in the *Colorado Springs Gazette and Telegraph* of March 25, 1951:

> . . . the sacred cow was butchered by a local meat packer. The bear was eaten at a restaurant after it had been chained in front for a while. The elephant had already perished in the four-foot snowstorm of 1913 and had been burned in a grave about the size of a cellar at the zoo. Rides and installations were taken down and sold and a local tent and awning man helped Colburn put up tents all over the grounds and he opened the first auto court.

(The only remaining evidence of John's "Dreamland" now is a fragment of the bear cage.)

Tourists poured into the resort city and Colburn's auto court prospered. Business interests objected to the new enterprise, but the tide could not be held back. Soon other and more elaborate auto courts sprang up.

Bad luck seemed to be coming in bunches for John. His greatest tragedy came in 1924, when Mary Coughlin died. She had kept in the background of his political life so much that many had thought the Bath was a bachelor. John, sincerely bereft, told reporters, "We were brought up together. We were, you might say, companions since we were six months old. We were sweethearts all our lives, as children, from the time we could walk. Her home was her life. Her church work and her home were all she cared for."

Six months later Big Jim Colisimo, who was muscling in on Chicago politics and was cashing in on Prohibition opportunities, fell into a Hollywood-type extracurricular romance and was killed. It was an event that shook the underworld and brought mutterings of Mafia, Torrio, and Al Capone into conversation— Al Caponi, also called Alphonse Capone, and sometimes Al Brown, who fronted as a second-hand furniture dealer.

Capone got his start as a signalman whose job it was to lounge against a certain fence at the north end of the district, and, when raiders were spotted, push a nail which operated a warning switch. At twenty-three he was promoted to become Torrio's office manager. This young newcomer to Chicago was without fear or conscience, and took over the center of the stage to create a reign of terror and a bath of blood which left John and Hinky Dink playing the roles of rank amateur comedians. Capone loafed in Hinky Dink's place and finally summoned the two old First Ward leaders to his office. Capone made it clear that he would tolerate the two, left it more or less to them to get out the vote, and gave them the sinister suggestion, "Ya keep ya nose clean, see?" They saw.

Coughlin grew heavier and more ineffectual but he did not realize the changes which had come about. He kept up his reputation for sartorial perfection, and continued to bet on the horses, but with miserable luck. According to biographers he remarked once, "Anyhow it was a great life. I enjoyed every minute of it but Lady Luck played me false."

In his later years John attended the council but he left the big things for the other boys and only advocated piddling measures to hold onto a flagging attention. He suggested U-turn ordinances, tried to fix the length of women's skirts, maintaining that "if they were any shorter they would be a menace to health and any longer would destroy an element of civic beauty." He advocated separate streetcars for women so that they would not be crowded out of their seats by tired working men, and he put up a hopeless battle to prevent Chicago females from wearing knickers. The council smiled behind their hands, gave him a dinner, dubbed him "Knight of the Bath," and remembered lessons of political maneuvering which many of them had learned at his knee, but pushed him aside when the big issues came up. He still continued to dress in his ornate plumage and to rise and spout poetry on every occasion when permitted. The council gave him the half-attention reserved for those who are growing senile.

On the street, the underprivileged and the old pals still approached him for jobs, money, and favors, and he would reach for his thinning wallet, or refer them to his farm or send them to the county for help.

In the same room where Al Capone was said to have held forth, in the Lexington Hotel, Coughlin finally took to his bed for the last months of his life. The steam was turned up hotter than it had been in the Turkish bath, but John, who had always worn two suits of underwear, found that he could not be warm again. Horse trainers and bums and an occasional alderman came to visit him, and even Carter Harrison dropped in.

On November 8, 1938, John Coughlin died, a poor man with debts of $56,000 which his estate could only partially satisfy. The city hall was draped in his honor. Black and purple crepe was placed over the empty council seat and a vase of roses placed on his desk. John would have liked it that way. He liked flowers. Mary had had them painted on his first political spittoon.

The ghouls reached for John's empty chair and the party recalled Hinky Dink to take his place. Hinky Dink, retired and tired, and in no need of money, took John's place reluctantly, only because the party needed him to keep it from the Nitti crowd, the current underworld threat.

In Colorado Springs, the Zoo Park along Cheyenne Creek was November cold and quiet where John had spent his happiest vacations. Walt Colburn mourned a good and generous friend and benefactor. "Li'l Lunnon" remembered and sighed and half forgot.

172

The wave of time has almost covered John's behemoth footprints along Cheyenne Road, and an attractive housing development called Three Eagles has erased the old home site.

Down by the creek there is still a tangled jungle area and a broken cage. The little lake is called Viper's Pond now by young boys who hunt frogs there.

The ghost who haunts this place is genial, and warm, and loves people, and animals, and even that "Hog butcher for the world."

He beckons small boys over no trespassing signs and with a Sandburgian gesture, "counts his money and throws it away."

The lake is smaller now from time and silt, and sometimes the evening reflection is more colorful than the sunset it reflects. Could be.

SOURCES

A *Critical Anthology, Modern American Poetry*, Louis Untermeyer, Harcourt, Brace and Company, Inc., New York, N.Y., 1936
Colorado Springs Evening Mail, 1901 (various issues)
Colorado Springs Telegraph, July 20, 1902, July 5, 1903, July 22, 1903
Colorado Springs Gazette, 1901, 1902, 1903, 1908, 1909, 1910, 1911, 1912, 1913, 1915, 1916, August 20, 1950, March 25, 1951
Journal of Landell Bartlett
interviews with
Walter Colburn
I. B. Bruce, Chief of Police, Colorado Springs
Landell Bartlett
Pioneer Museum of Colorado Springs, Colo.

Nikola Tesla,

The Man Who Lived Upstairs

> "He lives life up in the top of his
> head where ideas are born and
> up there he has plenty of room
> . . . " Arthur Brisbane

The year was 1899 and the Pikes Peak community was buzzing
with comments and questions about the mysterious structure
that was taking fantastic shape on what was Nob Hill at that
time. Old Mr. Dozier, the contractor, was building it and maybe
he knew what he was doing. (The city directory located the
structure on North Foote, a mile east of the postoffice. One old-
timer recalls it as being on Hancock. Another remembers it in
the vicinity of Bijou and Swope. One says it was on Iowa. Most
people have forgotten entirely.)

As it was being built, it looked as though it might be round, or
octagonal, or maybe square. The tower at one end impressed
everybody. There was a question whether a floor was to be put
in. It seemed to be a half-breed combination of barn and but-
tressed castle complete with eighty-foot tower and a two hundred
foot mast which held a copper ball three feet in diameter. This
was wired down into the mysterious depths. The roof slanted to
form the buttresses. It was an architectural enigma, as much a
puzzle to the man on the street as was the mystic wraith who
lived there.

People saw Nikola Tesla come and go, a very thin man, over
six feet tall, weighing less than one hundred fifty pounds, with
fine delicate features, black hair and mustache, big hands and
clear gray eyes. Tesla felt gray eyes were indicative of intellect.
He spoke perfect English with a slight foreign accent. He was

immaculate in his dress and conducted himself with dignity and reticence. He was not rude but he had no time for the ladies of "Li'l Lunnon"—nor anywhere else. Tesla was not unfriendly nor inhospitable, but there was definitely an air of "do not disturb" about him. After a while as the weird tales grew about what went on inside his laboratory walls, the average citizen gave up and decided it was beyond him anyway.

Most people were afraid to get near the structure which housed macabre experiments. The inventor, too, was not without his fears. He was at home with lightning bolts, but Colorado's mountains left him shaken, and sometimes when a friend took him driving on the high and narrow roads, he hung his long, scrawny legs over the edge of the pony cart, ready to jump at any moment. He was always relieved to get back to the safe confines of his laboratory.

Perhaps the twenty men who had been the select guests of Leonard E. Curtis at the dinner on May 27, 1899, at the El Paso Club were the only ones who had the slightest idea of Tesla's plans for high altitude experimentation with lightning and its scientific significance. Not one of these men was aware of the greatness of the genius who stood before them and whose mind harbored the embryo truths and principles which would be employed in mass communication (particularly in the fields of radio and television) and whose "Tesla coil" was to become important in industrial history. It was impossible for them to know that his findings would become forerunners in the development of unborn atomic energy or that the discoveries to be made on Nob Hill would be valid long after the discoverer was half-forgotten. Least of all did they realize that Tesla's most important discovery would be made in the local laboratory.

The *Colorado Springs Gazette* reported the banquet and mentioned the wonderful possibilities of wireless telegraphy and transmission of power. The reporter covering the assignment spoke highly of Tesla and his place in the scientific world and of his air of humility and modesty. Governor Charles S. Thomas, an honor guest of the evening, expressed his pleasure in the occasion.

Laboratory of Nikola Tesla in Colorado Springs. The building in the background is the Union Printers Home which is a few blocks to the east. *Sketch by Lois Wilcox from an old photograph.*

Nikola Tesla. *From Yale School of Engineering. Photo courtesy Denver Public Library, Western Collection.*

176

A reporter from another paper declared that the evening had taken on an "empyrean" quality—that Tesla had been as "the man in the midst of fire; . . . half spirit and half bird and all wonder and wild desire."

Desire Stanton recalled that Zebulon Pike had been an important discoverer in this region early in the 19th century and that with the advent of Tesla, another discoverer had come to camp at the foot of Pikes Peak. The article ventured to state that Tesla was "armed with a more mighty key to electrical science than that of Poor Richard." The article also asserted:

> Nikola Tesla, the Servian scientist, whose electrical discoveries are not of one nation, but the pride of the world has taken up his abode in Colorado Springs where he will remain for some time conducting experiments in the medium of light, air and perpetual sunshine.

Nikola Tesla's story began in 1857 when he was born in Smiljan, Austria-Hungary. His fortunate heritage was his intellectual background. The family was a representative one, generously sprinkled with members of the clergy and army officers. His father was a clergyman in the Serbian Orthodox Church. His mother, although uneducated, was of natural intelligence, clever at devices, and of inventive nature.

Nikola's education consisted of public school in Gospich and higher schooling in Croatia. His father had been opposed to Nikola's seeking more education because he thought the boy was too frail for the discipline of further schooling. However, following a siege of cholera at which time the boy seemed to lose the will to live, the father withdrew his objection to school and gave his promise that Nikola might contine his studies. Nikola seemed to regain health and energy almost immediately. So followed the completion of his education in the Polytechnic School in Gratz. In Prague he studied languages in order to master further engineering.

From the beginning the boy was certain of his destiny—that he was born to the high calling of inventive science. No monk could have had a more dedicated sense of direction, and he assumed the celibacy and privations demanded by the strictest orders. Women had no place in his life—they were sensual pleasure and would have proved a stumbling block in his certain path, and he could afford neither the luxury nor the time-consuming distraction of a normal family life. He was a born genius with all the eccentricities caused by his off-center make-up. He seemed to be possessed of the gift of knowledge of all scientific truth in the manner in which the saints are granted heavenly visions. The proof of natural laws seemed unnecessary for him except as a requirement for communication with his less perceptive colleagues. He possessed the mathematical orderly mind and the strange power to see all phases of a problem solved without any need for computation.

To Paris he went to enter the profession of electrical engineer. All his gifts worked together. His inventive talents were employed in telephonic achievements and work with the rotating field principle. He was anxious to come to America where the doors of opportunity seemed wide open and his immediate employment by Edison was both a benefit and a stimulus. With his tendency to be a lone wolf, Tesla began to be impatient to carry out his own ideas. For a brief time he joined a company to make and sell one of his inventions, arc lighting, but he was no promoter and he fretted under administrative requirements. Machinery at Niagara Falls came to bear the Tesla name, and he continued with world recognition and fame. He became a citizen of the United States in 1889.

There were several distinct reasons for Tesla's coming to Colorado Springs. The climate and the altitude were decisive factors in his choice. He had his experimental eye on the top of Pikes Peak, too. The rare storms that abounded in this high country were the media with which he wished to prove some truths he already knew. Rumor had it that he had been offered free electricity with which to conduct his experiments in Colorado Springs. This was another important deciding factor. He, alone, knew the magnitude of his dreams.

As though the gods, themselves, were jealous of his power and probing, the laboratory was damaged by lightning soon after it was built. Tesla was not wholly unprepared, for it struck at the exact moment that he predicted it would. The first bolt had actually hit ten miles away. Tesla was not satisfied to be limited to celestial lightning but attempted to duplicate it by his own methods. Colorado Springs did not soon forget the commotion caused by this experiment. Tesla described it in this way:

> . . . To carry the problems on which I was working farther, I had to master electrical pressures of at least 50,000,000 volts and electrical discharges were necessary for some purposes measuring at least 50 or 100 feet.
>
> The results I attained were far beyond any I had expected to reach. One of the first observations I made in Colorado was of great scientific importance, and confirmatory of a result I had already obtained in New York. I refer to my discovery of the stationary waves in the earth. The significance of this phenomenon has not yet been grasped by technical men but virtually amounts to a positive proof that with proper apparatus such as I have perfected, a wireless transmission of signals to any point on the globe is practicable.
>
> . . . in perfecting my apparatus I encountered at first great difficulties. I had a few narrow escapes from sudden sparks jumping out to great distance and a number of times my laboratory caught fire, but I carried all the work through without a serious mishap. I gradually learned how to confine electrical currents of pressure of 50,000,000 volts to produce electrical movements up to 110,000 horsepower, and I succeeded in obtaining electrical discharges measuring from end to end, 100 feet and more. These results, were however, rendered more valuable by the fact that they opened up still greater possibilities for the future.

It was not the scientific significance of this experiment that impressed "Li'l Lunnon," however, at the time. Tesla's contrived holocaust produced thunder that was heard in Cripple Creek, fifteen miles over the mountains. Tesla stood outside his laboratory, properly attired in honor of the event. He wore a cutaway coat and black derby hat, and he stood an inch taller because of the rubber soles and insulating heels on his shoes. He watched his homemade storm with glee. Suddenly it stopped. Tesla screamed at his assistat who he thought had closed the switch. The bewildered assistant protested. By calling the power company, the scientist learned that his synthetic storm had knocked out the power lines of the entire city.

Tesla had poured so much power into the earth with his experiments that several hundred times the amount usually contained in a single electrical stroke had been discharged in an hour.

Tesla felt the patriotic obligation to turn his discoveries to government use although he realized the dual nature of his findings and hoped that they would lead to the emancipation of the human race rather than its eradication. He was unable to control the final direction of his discoveries once the power was relinquished from his hands.

In 1901 Tesla told a reporter from the *Philadelphia Inquirer* that he regarded his latest results concerning stationary electrical waves in the earth as the most important he had ever attained. The reporter wrote:

> Briefly, Telsa has been able to note novel manifestation of energy which he knows is not of solar or terrestial origin, and being neither, he concluded that it must emanate from one of the planets.

The reporter then described the Colorado Springs experiments and quoted Mr. Tesla:

> I set out to carry on my experiments along three different lines: first to ascertain the best conditions for transmitting power without wires; second, to develop apparatus for the transmission of messages across the Atlantic and Pacific oceans, on which problem I have been engaged for eight years, and third to work on another problem which involves a still greater mastery of electrical forces and which, with my present knowledge I consider of still greater importance than even the transmission of power without wires, and which I shall make known in due course.
>
> It was in investigating feeble electrical actions transmitted through the earth that I made some observations which are to me most gratifying. Chief among these are certain feeble

electrical actions which I could barely note occurred, and which by their character unmistakably showed that they were neither of solar origin nor produced by any causes known to me on the globe. What could they be? . . . I have incessantly thought of this for months, until I finally arrived at the conviction a machine which will without the least doubt be fully competent to communicate with the planet Mars.

All this talk of Mars drew fire and criticism and ridicule. Professor Holden, formerly director of the Lick Observatory, was one who pooh-poohed Tesla's claims. He attacked Tesla's "guesses" and extravagant imagination. He predicted that Tesla had made an error and that he could not back up his "guesses" with proof. He also revealed a bit of pique in that Tesla had not shown his apparatus to other experimenters.

A Colorado Springs editorial writer rushed to Tesla's defense, declaring that Colorado Springs people felt very kindly toward Nikola Tesla. The editorial had the implication that "Li'l Lunnon" was discreetly tittering over the crack-pot idea. He said:

If there are people in Mars, they certainly showed most excellent taste in choosing Colorado Springs as the particular point on the earth's surface with which to open communication. In fact we may feel assured that if the mystical one, two, three, which Tesla says may have impulsed from Mars, should be translated from the planetary code, it would read, "How is the weather in Colorado Springs?" Or something equally localized.

In direct rebuttal to Holden's criticism, the same reporter said:

Frankly, we prefer the Tesla "guess" to that of Holden. It is a good rule in inventional science when you're going to tell one, tell a good one, and men have become great by observing the rule.

The man in the moon is gone and even H. G. Wells cannot bring him back, but we refuse to give up Mars. If the selection of Colorado Springs as a point of superior knowledge where Martian signals would be most likely to be noticed and understood is not a sign of superior intelligence, what more could be expected? For the pres-

181

sent, we stand by Tesla, and we have no doubt that ere long he will not only catch the repetition of his one-two-three message, but he will be able to announce to the Martians the quotations and sales of the Colorado Springs Mining Stock Exchange.

So while Tesla wrestled with the mysteries of the universe, little writers played with words.

It was Tesla's plan, as a result of his Colorado experiments, to erect two terminal stations for communication with the planets. One was to be set up in London and one in New York, with huge oscillators (such as the one used in Colorado) at the top of the high towers and with disks in balloons to catch the strata of rarified air. Messages were to be flashed around the world at a little more than letter postage. Tesla realized he would need a receiver on the objective star, and the inhabitant of the other planet should know "enough to take the message."

The *Denver Republican* quoted Tesla as saying:

> I would send light to whole cities and give to mere machines all the motions of intelligence. Men of science have found it difficult to believe me. I gave a demonstration of one experiment which is the most beautiful I have ever tried. . . I had a boat without a crew or captain controlled merely by the force of my intelligence . . . it seemed to be instinct with life . . . it was governed simply by electrical waves striking upon a machine. . .
>
> My idea is that people are simply automata governed by transmission of circumstance surrounding them upon the eye. This is the greatest idea of the age.

Tesla had the gift of diversified direction of mental effort and many experiments were being carried on simultaneously. One of the most amazing and amusing of his experiences came as a result of his study of mechanical vibrations during which he made discoveries which led to his construction of an "apartment-size" earthquake machine which he gave a try-out in metropolitan New York. The result was that in an area of a dozen thickly populated square blocks, windows began to break, plumbing pipes disintegrated, and plaster began to fall in the police department

182

quarters. The police rushed to Tesla's laboratory because experience had taught them that various phenomena had been produced from that source. Here they found Tesla smashing a machine which had reacted beyond his expectations and which had frightened him with the powers which he had unleashed.

When he reviewed the incident later, in the thirties, he explained that so powerful were the effects of the telegeodynamic oscillator that a tiny machine so small he could fit it in his pocket and which required no more that 2.5 horsepower, had power to wreck such structures as the Empire State Building and reduce it to rubble within twelve to thirteen minutes. ("And the walls came tumbling down!")

Already to the credit of this labyrinthine genius were patents dealing with "direct current, motor and generator controls, arc lights, polyphase currents, electric currents, electric transmission of power, dynamos, motors, transformers, circuits and systems insulation, wireless systems, radio telegraphy, radio mechanics, methods of tuning and selection, detectors, steam turbines, pumps, speedometers, patents dealing with airplanes, mechanical oscillators, and thermomagnetic motors."

Strangely enough, Tesla was completely unrealistic and his make-up had none of the qualities of the promotor. In fact, he definitely realized that his calling was that of discovery and not of development. Others stepped in where he left off, made practical use of his revolutionary achievements, converted them into commercial use, and were awarded the fame and wealth that could have belonged to Tesla.

But Tesla was not particularly concerned. He was aware of his niche and far too busy to concern himself with matters outside it. His genius naturally caused him to be oblivious to the desires which motivated the ordinary person. Hence he lived in another orbit, lonely and eccentric. His eccentricities bordered on the neurotic. He had a very definite germ phobia. He washed his hands incessantly. He was said to use a towel only once (eighteen towels a day were put in his hotel room), to throw away handkerchiefs and collars after one use, and to discard gloves after a week's wear.

He usually dined alone. Tesla would have liked to have been social and there were periods when he had allowed himself the luxury of entertaining friends at dinner and on such occasions had even enjoyed preparing elaborate meals for their pleasure. But all this took time from the important things and he was acutely aware of the destiny which he had to fulfill and which was limitless in scope but circumscribed by time. He acknowledged no supreme being nor spiritual after-life nor religious convictions. Human emotions he considered but another form of power which could be controlled and he preferred to allocate procreation to lesser human creatures who could not achieve the intellectual heights on which he dwelt. He had his own theories about mental telepathy which he felt could be explained by scientific formulae.

He believed that there was unleashed power in human energy and remembered strange experiences as a child which resulted in his conclusions. He recalled:

A long time ago when I was a boy, I was afflicted with a singular trouble which seems to have been due to an extraordinary excitability of the retina. It was the appearance of images which by their persistence, marred the vision of real objects and interfered with thought. When a word was said to me, the image of the object which it designated would appear vividly before my eyes and many times it was impossible for me to tell whether the object I saw was real or not. This caused me great discomfort and anxiety and I tried to free myself of the spell. But for a long time I tried in vain, and it was not, as I still clearly recollect until I was about twelve years old that I succeeded for the first time by an effort of the will in banishing an image which presented itself. My happiness will never be complete as it was then, but fortunately, (as I thought at the time) the old trouble returned and with it my anxiety. Gradually the desire arose in me to find out every time what caused the image to appear and the satisfaction of the desire became a necessity. My mind became automatic as it were. . . It was not long before I was aware that also all my movements were prompted in the same way and so searching, observing and verifying continuously, year after year, I have by every thought and every act of mine demonstrated, and so daily, to my absolute satisfaction that I am an automaton. . . . I remember only one or two cases in all my life in which I was unable to locate a first impression which prompted a movement or thought or even a dream.

There were times when Tesla described man as being only an automaton, a mere "meat machine" as he called it—then there were other periods when he seemed to waver in this conception of human life. At such times he considered man not an ordinary mass of spinning atoms and molecules, but he acknowledged that man possessed certain higher qualities by reason of the creative principle of life.

Tesla seemed driven by a frantic energy and considered sleep an unnecessary luxury. He felt that two hours was sufficient for him and smiled at Edison's need for four! He even hinted that Edison might have fudged with a few catnaps. He credited his remarkable abilities to inheritance from his mother and always sensed a psychic bond with her which was revealed clearly to him by a telegraphic phenomenon at the moment of her death. He tried to explain the strange event by natural means.

The manner of the genius was noticeably humble and unassuming. Yet, his countenance bore the mark of one who was dedicated.

Arthur Brisbane said of him:

His face cannot be studied and judged like the faces of other men, for he is not a worker in practical fields. He lives life up in the top of his head where ideas are born and up there he has plenty of room . . . . He stoops— most men do when they have no peacock blood. . . in them. And he differs from most men who are written and talked about in the fact that he has something to tell.

Tesla was the first and probably the only scientist who was ever known to have turned down the Nobel Prize for physics. It was a high honor and a world acclaim. This was in 1912 when he was in desperate need of money. Here because of his scientific, orderly mind he protested the award which was to have

185

been given jointly to him and to Thomas Edison. Tesla felt that since Edison was an inventor and he, Tesla, was a discoverer, they could not be paired. Tesla held inventors to be persons of commercial motives, and he could not reconcile the association of the two. It was probably in some measure a matter of meticulous vocabulary or perhaps semantics.

There was one time when Tesla did consent to accept the Edison medal, a coveted award in the scientific field. Tesla was groomed for the occasion in full dress. In the course of festivities, just before the presentation was to be made and Tesla was to speak, he disappeared. By merest coincidence, his close friend, Behrend, recalled seeing Tesla slip a small package of bird seed in his pocket before leaving the hotel. Rushing down to a nearby plaza, Behrend found the scientist feeding his pigeons. The birds were perched on his head and shoulders and formed a "mosaic pattern of color." With an aura of St. Francis surrounding him, Tesla was completely absorbed. Behrend slowed his pace so as not to frighten the birds and approached Tesla gently to lead him back to the world.

Pigeons had a strange part in the life of Tesla. The birds represented a facet of his nature which few knew existed. Through his exhausting drives, Tesla had managed to sublimate the normal human affections. Love could be suppressed but not eliminated. This disruptive power only gained momentum by its repression. It was like one of his steam experiments, but this was one force which Tesla failed to understand. Every man has his Achilles heel. One day a pigeon found the vulnerable spot in Tesla's heavy plated armor, and such a love poured forth that he was helpless. To this gentle bird, a symbol of love, he gave all his pent-up affection. It was in 1921 that this pigeon became ill, and Tesla knew that she was going to die. Again he associated the eye with all knowledge and felt that the bird's eye was overwhelmingly brighter than any of his electrical experiments. With the approach of death for something he loved, he was aware of this dark force over which he had no control. He stayed away from work to care for the bird and savor the last

186

sweetness of his love. When the bird died, Tesla became addicted to solitary night walks. Some said, "He is thinking of his discoveries," but there were others who knew that he spent his lonely walks coaxing the sleeping pigeons of the streets from their rest. With a plaintive, strange call, he awoke the birds who came at all hours to answer his bidding.

With the death of his beloved bird, something vanished from his life. The vital force of love overwhelmed him as it has lesser mortals and he finally recognized the truth that without it there is no creative meaning. Did he toy with the theories of reincarnation as he sought for comfort? Later he said, "I have fed pigeons for years . . . for after all . . . who can tell?"

In 1924, on May 30, the *Colorado Springs Gazette* carried headlines that brought back memories to residents who had all but forgotten the mysterious stranger of the early part of the century. Large print declared:

TESLA DISCOVERED DEATH RAY IN EXPERIMENTS HE MADE HERE. BUDDING ELECTRICAL WIZARD BUILT LABORATORY ON NOB HILL IN 1899 AND MAINTAINED BAFFLING SECRECY ABOUT WORK. NOW SCIENTISTS ARE DEVELOPING NEW WEAPON.

The article went on to recall Tesla's Colorado laboratory and the dark, slim foreigner who worked there. The article declared that Tesla's discoveries had led to the development of an invisible ray, capable of halting automobiles and stalling airplanes in midflight. The ray was said to be the result of Tesla's Colorado Springs activities. It had been offered to the United States Army and it was said that the use of it had caused French airplanes to descend over Bavaria the previous summer.

Old timers who read the article remembered the litigation between Carl Duffner, who claimed that he had been an unpaid caretaker for Tesla, and Tesla, who claimed Duffner was not a caretaker for the laboratory. It had always been the little people who nipped at his heels. Some remembered that after two years of haggling, the court had awarded Duffner judgment against Tesla, yet the city directory listed Duffner as a resident of Victor during one of the years that he claimed to be taking care of the laboratory. One person remembered seeing the laboratory in a state of neglect. This might have been Tesla's reasons for fighting the issue. It seemed strange, for Tesla was ordinarily a willing spender for service.

Some recalled vaguely that J. P. Morgan had given him $125,-000 when he returned to the east to continue his experiments there and thought again of the $30,000 that John Jacob Astor had put up for the construction of the old laboratory in the nineties. A very few remembered that when the property on Nob Hill had been sold the weird structure had been torn down and the lumber sold to C. E. Maddox who used it to build his home in Ivywild, and that the piping had been sold to the old St. John Plumbing Company.

Police Chief Hugh D. Harper who read the article recalled the time when he was a streetcar motorman and used to drive past the old laboratory. He said it was about two hundred feet east of Hancock Avenue. The chief remarked, "I guess we all thought him crazy."

Manly D. Ormes, librarian for Colorado College said, "while Tesla had a national reputation at the time he was here, he was generally regarded as a visionary." Mr. Ormes added, ". . . it now appears that the people may have been mistaken."

With the turn of the forties, Nikola Tesla was an old man living in a New York hotel room. With his years, his eccentricities increased and his star waned; his health decreased and his patents were carried out by younger men. The world seemed to forget and he was only concerned with the pigeons that lit upon his window sill and came into his room. The hotel management asked him to cease feeding the birds or to move, so he moved to another hotel and kept on feeding pigeons. He was found dead in his room by a maid who grew concerned and ignored the *DO NOT DISTURB* sign for the first time and the last time. It was January 7, 1943, when Tesla died as he had lived—alone. Funeral services were held in the Cathedral of St. John the Divine. Many of his ideas and formulae had been carried in his retentive mind and possibly were images on his retina, but an unseeing world knew no way to decode his mysteries and so buried them with him.

An Associated Press dispatch from New York carried a Tesla story, telling of the mysterious barn-like structure on Nob Hill in Colorado Springs, where he had carried on experiments. They mentioned him as a prophet without honor in those days. Scientific societies declared him (overlooking Edison) "next only to Benjamin Franklin." They concluded the story in these words:

> Tesla is dead, but radio is commonplace today, and television, according to disciples of the scientist who did his research work in Colorado Springs, will be commonplace tomorrow.

With the perspective of death, the world began to see the giant who had been too close to them to be appreciated. This intellectual genius had not resented their yappings and their blindness. So firmly was he convinced of his own calling and purpose, that he did not expect to be accepted, even by his own colleagues.

He said, once, "the scientific man does not aim at an immediate result. He does not expect that his advanced ideas will be readily taken up. His work is like that of the planter—for the future. His duty is to lay the foundation for those who are to come, and point the way. He lives and labors and hopes with the poet who says,

> Lo! these trees, but bare poles seeming,
> Yet will yield both fruit and shelter!

(from Goethe's "Hope" translated by William Gibson)

SOURCES

Prodigal Genius, Nikola Tesla, John J. O'Neill, Ives Washburn Inc., New York, N.Y., 1944

The Colorado, Frank Waters, Rinehart & Company, Inc., New York, N. Y., 1946

Mountain Sunshine, vol. 1, no. 1, page 33 (July-August, 1899)

Colorado Springs Gazette, Jan. 9, 1901, page 7, col. 6
March 10, 1906, page 5, col. 6
May 27, 1899, L. E. Curtis gives dinner
May 30, 1924, page 1, col. 3-4
May 31, 1924, page 18, col. 3
May 18, 1899, page 5, col. 3
April 6, 1899, page 3, col. 1
November 19, 1905, page 1, col. 1
January 9, 1905, page 7, col. 6-7-8
March 9, 1905, page 4, col. 2
October 30, 1903, page 1, col. 7
July 2, 1904, page 5, col. 3-4
September 6, 1905, page 5, col. 1-2
Century, Vol. 60, pp. 175-221, June 1900.
Facts, May 27, 1899
Interviews with
Mrs. William Tudor
Simon Halle
Charles Dudley
Earl Boatright
Gene Bacon
Julie Hoefer

Les Girls,

They Wore a Yellow Ribbon

With the uncanny instinct of the Capistrano swallows, the soiled doves alighted in the western mining towns as soon as the prospectors' tents were pitched. Theirs was the oldest profession in the world. Love was a salable commodity; giving it away was a luxury which only led to trouble, sometimes to gunfire. Through the hands of these women went many of the early fortunes of the raw mining camps.

With the first strike of pay dirt came the gartered girls to ply their trade behind cotton-stuffed keyholes and covered transoms. Their arrival was considered an omen of prosperity, a sure sign that the camp was to grow into a permanent settlement. A sharp distinction was made between the women of the west— between the fancy woman with her ostrich feathers and yellow ribbon, and the sunbonneted, respectable wife.

There were two opinions of these *filles de joie*. Most men were inclined to have a sentimental tolerance for all womankind, but even so, their attitude toward the Magdalenes was mixed with scorn and abuse, even while patronizing the establishments. The western man shared the problems of any lonely emigrant whose need was to remember, or to forget, or just to seek release. Added to this was the longing for a pleasant atmosphere and the warmth of a woman, counterfeit though it might be.

There was less tolerance in the attitude of the sunbonneted wife who faced the constant competition. She failed to see justice in a code which enforced a Spartan self-denial and the deprivation of family needs on one woman while the hard-won earnings were spent to buy ruffled garters for a painted hussy. To the family

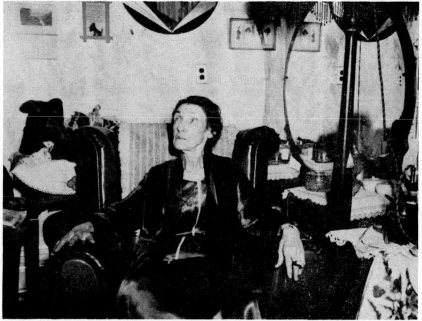

Laura Evans in her "house" in Salida. *Photo courtesy Denver Public Library, Western Collection.*

Myers Avenue, Cripple Creek. *Photo by Horace S. Poley, courtesy Denver Public Library, Western Collection.*

woman, these easy virtue lassies were a threat to the very foundations of her home. There was no ground for compromise. She had a natural envy of the clothes the girls wore, and the red-plush furnishings of their houses contrasted too graphically with her bare-floored home lined with newspapers.

There were many reasons for the girls who followed the flame: environmental and personality factors must, of course, have furnished some background for their choice of occupation. In the overwhelming majority of cases the underlying cause was probably a rebellion against poverty. Another factor may have been a first mistake which left an indelible brand in an unforgiving era. Or perhaps there was a delusion that the occupation offered a chance for easy, glittering, fast money. Many times there was rebellion against a rigid, stifling home. And sometimes, simply, the devil tormented the flesh. Once the choice was made, there was no turning back; all ties were cut and the girl was isolated from her family and from a great part of life, without the protection of the law.

The smart ones were those who eventually took over the management of the house and let their girls work for them. The madams were the majority stockholders in a thriving business venture.

Most of these women have long been forgotten. There was a quality of anonymity and impermanence about their very existence. The men who were their lovers by night failed to recognize them by day, and the guest books were incomplete. And each inmate of a house changed her name almost with the frequency and rapidity with which she shed her clothes. Usually the basic reason was to prevent being traced by families and friends back home.

Since the transactions were of a private matter, there are few old-timers who cared to reminisce about the girls on the line. A few of the women, however, were so flamboyant that they have become legendary.

One of the most flaming of the scarlet women to descend upon Colorado's camps was Laura Evans. When she died, in

Salida, in 1953, the *Denver Post* of April 9 carried a story only a few would admit to remembering. The paper described the services:

> Recalcitrant nature could have provided better fittings Wednesday afternoon when Laura Evans was put into the grave.
> Squalls of white obscured the mountains, even the Snow Angel on the side of Mount Shavano. The wind whistled through the pinons, rocked and tilted the lavender casket and its frail burden on the straps of the lowering carriage.
> Someone murmured:
> "This day's like Laura. Sunshine. A little rain. Sunshine, gusts and a little snow. Then more sun."
> So maybe it was all right.
> There was both tempest and beguiling calm in Laura, the Leadville belle of the gaudy years on Fryer Hill, the last of the famed madams of Colorado.

It was from Denver's Market Street that the seventeen-year-old Laura with the "brunet voice" graduated to Leadville where the silver was pouring out of the mines in millions. The pockets of careless miners spilled coins when they flung their clothes over the backs of the chairs, but, unlike others of her kind, Laura left the silver where it fell. She had been a St. Louis woman, vital, vigorous, and determined upon two things, a good time and plenty of money to indulge her tastes. Unhampered by a conscience, Laura was full of daring, gall, and wiles. "On the surface she was tougher than hard rock. Underneath she had a heart of butter." The heart of butter, or of gold, was standard equipment for the fancy woman and was more often fancy than fact. It is known, however, that Laura was a soft touch, "that during her lifetime she 'loaned' without thought of recompense sum after sum to friends and strangers who were 'on their uppers.' . . . To her known honesty, prospectors entrusted boodles of money."

Laura was flamboyant, without fears or inhibitions, and learned early in the game that "it pays to advertise." She kept her name in the foreground by her ebullient escapades which were the talk of the towns. Soon she was known from coast

194

to coast, partly for her beauty and personality, but in large measure for the antics in which she indulged.

Leadville never forgot two of her forays. Once she couldn't resist bribing a circus worker to lend her and a friend a pair of brightly gilded Roman chariots, with the circus' best teams hitched up in Roman style. Down Harrison Street the race was staged, the one respectable avenue where the girls were forbidden to promenade. Laura and her girl friend raced with frantic speed, banging on the gongs at the front of the chariots and scattering kids, dogs, clergymen, and sunbonneted housewives in all directions. The loss of a chariot wheel on turning a corner too sharply ended Laura's brief career as a female Ben Hur and threw her into the arms of the law. Arrest followed quickly, but reprieve was soon at hand.

The incident did nothing to quell Laura's enthusiasm for speed, horses, or exhibitionism. For her next wild flight she chose as her stage setting the famous Ice Palace, constructed painstakingly by the proud citizens of Leadville, in 1896. For this demonstration, Laura chose a steed named Broken Tail Charlie, and with him hitched to a phaeton on runners, plunged straight into the elaborate Norman structure, the citizens' pride, leaving a trail of destruction in her wake as she tore through the displays and only came to a halt when Broken Tail Charlie decided he had had enough, broke loose, headed for his own barn, and left Laura stranded in the debris.

Not content with holding the reins on horses, Laura highlighted her career when one of Colorado's wealthiest men squired her into the Vendome Hotel and piloted her toward the elevator. Laura insisted on running the elevator herself, with the result that she got it stuck between floors, and then, with her customary tendency toward overdoing things, ran it upstairs so fast that it nearly went on out the roof. Her abilities did not extend to horseflesh or mechanical contrivances.

One of the most incongruous friendships of Laura's career was her acceptance by Augusta Tabor, the straitlaced, New

England first wife of the silver king. Possibly Augusta preferred an honest professional to one who only professed honesty.

Laura had implicit faith in her own ability to perform feats outside the scope of her chosen profession. On one occasion she offered to mind the store while Mrs. Tabor did the washing. Laura had had no training in good housekeeping, but she did have a weakness for thick steaks. To oblige the customers in the Tabor store, Laura cut her slices "as thick as an axe handle," making about four steaks out of one leg of beef. Augusta, her New England frugality outraged, screamed, "Laura, what have you done to my leg?" Laura was simply out of her element. Augusta should have recognized that her flashy friend's abilities did not extend to storekeeping.

Tired of following the gold camps, and realizing the advantages of being self-employed, young Laura transferred her talents to Salida where she opened elaborate houses patronized by the well-to-do tycoons, and any others who could afford the price. She became an economic figure to be reckoned with and was in the same financial bracket as the wealthy mine owners of Leadville, Salida, Central City, Cripple Creek, Blackhawk, and Georgetown.

Laura's "pocket money" she carried in a silk purse on her left leg. Her girls "wore silk garters embellished with ten dollar gold pieces, locked on their thighs with gold lock and chain." Laura's girls were the prettiest in the west, and, quick to sense the importance of a good investment, she "outfitted them in the prettiest silks and boarded them in the plushest rooms" in her houses which were "models of Victorian perfection." Her velvet-draped parlors created a feeling of quality. With her warmth and generosity, she had the love and loyalty of all the brothel beauties in her employ. Although Laura prided herself on her graduation from the ranks, she remained available—for a price. To the last, she persisted in rolling her own cigarettes.

When Laura Evans died in 1953 she was still surrounded by the rococo decor which had been so in keeping with her flamboyant career. Bead-fringed lamps ornamented the tables. On her four-poster velvet-canopied bed were sitting her empty-faced dolls.

The feeling at Laura's passing was not particularly one of loss of an individual but a knowledge that the end of an era had come. The memories which her death evoked were of a certain unrepentent devilishness which only death could stop. Death took her for her last ride, probably her only slow one, and she no longer held the reins.

Many years before, in that fly-by-night world, Laura Evans' early exit from Denver had left no gap. Her place was soon filled. The early history of the city had centered its area of vice on Holladay Street, named for the stagecoach king, Ben Holladay, who became more and more irritated at seeing his name associated with the dens of iniquity. Changing the name of a street wasn't as easy as discarding one's own name, but at the breaking point, Ben Holladay petitioned the city council to erase him from the street maps and the name was changed to Market Street.

Here the shining lights of the red-light district were Mattie Silks, Jennie Rogers, Blanche Brown, and Ella Wellington. Their "ads" were to be found in Denver's *Red Book,* a guide to the "pleasure palaces." So openly did the line flaunt its wares that the waves of reform began to gather, while the underworld rocked with raucous laughter and utter unconcern. The tides of change gathered force, however, until finally they could no longer be ignored.

One of the first attempts to make sin less obvious and therefore less profitable was an order to remove the garish signs advertising, all too graphically, the pleasures to be found within. The madams retaliated with what might be called "the epitome of direct or laundromat advertising"; they stated succinctly ... "Men Taken in and Done For."

It could not be said that the girls and their employers were entirely uncooperative with the officials. When the demand came that prostitutes label themselves by means of yellow ribbons in their hair, they more than complied by appearing completely garbed in yellow, from parasol to shoes, creating such a golden haze that "the street looked like a sea of demented sunflowers."

Reform was not necessary in "Li'l Lunnon"; righteousness was built into the very foundations. Therefore the dubious necesity of providing the illicit pleasures fell to the adjacent area of Colorado City. As early as December 26, 1872, the Colorado Springs paper *Out West* gasped the first gasp of dismay and alarm at the fact that the neighboring city to the west was "harboring an elephant in their midst in the shape of a dance house and common brothel." The better portion of the citizens were quick to beseech the town trustees to abate the nuisance. From the rarefied air of Colorado Springs came the query, "How a place which aspires to be the permanent seat of a growing county can indulge hope under such circumstances is beyond our calculations and the sooner such dens of iniquity are abolished the better." Thus the tone was set quite early, with vice rampant a few blocks west, and Colorado Springs sitting demurely looking on "and partaking of the benefits of the mess . . . shuddering with hands over eyes, but peeping between fingers."

"Old Town" pandered to the gay youth and some not so gay —and some not so young. On West Colorado Avenue were twenty-six or twenty-seven saloons in one small area, all vying for trade. Most of them were on the south side of the street, which made for an easily definable dividing line. No lady walked on that side. The red-light district was mainly quartered on Washington Street (now Cucharras) about the same length as the saloon district, mostly from the 2400 to the 2600 blocks, but spilling over somewhat for another two blocks west. At that time the concentration of brothels was heaviest between what was then Sixth and Seventh Streets (now 26th and 27th; formerly, the city limits were at 20th Street and all ensuing streets were numbered from the first).

Mamie Majors, Laura Bell, and Minnie Smith, the most popular of the madams, and their girls walked sedately to the corner

Colorado City, 1860. *Photo courtesy Denver Public Library, Western Collection.*

Holladay Street, Denver, latter part of 19th century. *Photo courtesy Denver Public Library, Western Collection.*

199

drug stores and bought their magazines. One old timer recalls that they did not dress garishly, as might be supposed, but dressed and behaved like ladies, "in fact, more like ladies than did the flappers of the later twenties." The girls did not solicit on the streets but kept fairly close to their own quarters.

Local papers openly proclaimed that the brothels had paid police protection, but it was vehemently denied. The facts came out, finally, and the community learned that a semi-monthly fine or tribute was paid to the officers. "Each house is assessed so much per inmate and payment gives them two weeks' immunity." It was common talk that one chief of police always received a gift of silverware from the madams as a Christmas bonus, but usually returned it.

A lady known as Lou (Eaton) came to Colorado City about 1887, but became plain Minnie Smith when she established herself in "Old Town." An article in the *Colorado Springs Gazette* for March 9, 1924, recalled her establishment and something of Minnie herself:

> She bought one of the largest old time houses about 20 feet from the street, with a fence with a gate about it. She was a woman in the middle thirties then, a slender little woman, not good looking and a vixen when aroused. . . It was said that she came from Buena Vista and had been known in various mining camps of the state.

Minnie became more well known for her flaming temper than for the decor of her house. She was in trouble a great deal. The article went on to state how "On one occasion she beat up a lawyer of the town with the butt of a gun and had to face assault charges, barely escaping the worse one of murder, saved when he recovered."

In spite of her rough temper and crude exterior, Minnie, of course, had the traditional heart of gold. Among the notables at Colorado City were Bob Ford, Soapy Smith, and Bruce Younger of the notorious Missouri bandit family. When Bruce was killed in a spectacular tragedy, Minnie donated grave space in Evergreen Cemetery beside the body of her first husband, Royser.

Minnie had some real competition. Laura Bell held forth in Trilby House on Washington Avenue, in an ornate atmosphere replete with ballroom, costly furniture, and liveried servants. Laura was often accompanied by her niece, "Little Laura," whom she was educating. They were both killed many years later in an automobile accident with their friend, Dusty McCarty, owner of the Tenderfoot Saloon.

With the silver strike in the San Juans the girls followed the miners to the mushrooming camp of Creede, Minnie Smith in the vanguard. It was like a gathering of the clan, in 1892, as the scum gathered in the wildest of the wild towns. Control of Creede was divided between Soapy Smith and Minnie Smith, with Minnie dominating the upper part of town where Nat Creede's log house stood, and Soapy ruling the lower part. Bob Ford's headquarters were in the saloon near the triangle.

In an article in the *Colorado Springs Gazette* H. S. Rogers told of the fate of Minnie: "When Creede's glittering bubble burst, it threw the component part that was Minnie Smith into the lap of Cripple Creek, but she was not distinguished there. Her star was waning . . . she had come down to a mere rooming house landlady." She must have looked with envy at Lola Livingston, madam of the Mikado House, Hazel Vernon, owner of The Homestead with its entourage of such beauties as Grace Carlisle and Pearl De Vere. And there was French Blanche, who had followed the soldiers to Africa in the Boer War and was almost legendary for her beauty.

But the most envied one of all was Pearl De Vere in her Paris gowns. She could set her sights at the woman-hating Stratton, and get results. Pearl made a striking figure riding side-saddle, like the other ladies, on a horse named She Devil. But she was most beautiful the night she danced at The Homestead, "wearing a new eight hundred dollar ball gown of shell-pink chiffon encrusted with sequins and seed pearls and sent direct from Paris." On that same night, Pearl killed herself by taking an overdose of morphine. She was buried in the pink chiffon gown in a service which brought on one of Cripple

Creek's sentimental binges. The Elks band, followed by the girls from the houses (and watched from behind the curtains by the respectable), traipsed mournfully to Mount Pisgah cemetery where the popular song, "Goodby, Little Girl, Goodby" took the place of the usual hymn. The services were brief. The Pearl De Veres are soon forgotten. The band is said to have left the cemetery in double time, playing Cripple Creek's own tune, "There'll Be a Hot Time in the Old Town Tonight." Mourning was forgotten and business was as usual on the line.

French Blanche knew triumph and tragedy, too. She had been brought to the district, it is said, by one who had seen her photograph and was so impressed by her beauty that he sent money all the way to Africa to pay her passage to the gold camp. She was set up in an establishment at the thriving stage stop at Midway. It was said that a jealous wife put an end to Blanche's gay life by throwing acid in the girl's face. Blanche is reported to have married later. She died in November, 1959, after a long illness.

Minnie Smith, after her quieter years in the Cripple Creek area, took the familiar route of an overdose of morphine. H. S. Rogers said: "At the age of forty-five her candle had burned from both ends, and vanished at the middle . . ." There wasn't much to administer of Minnie's estate, but "ample opportunity was hers to have amassed one for she moved where fortune danced in and out of men's hands every hour in the day," Rogers said.

Respectable citizens of Colorado Springs acted as her pall-bearers—many others were at the funeral.

Back in Minnie's old territory, the noteworthy citizens were still deploring the adjacent "cesspool of sin" that was Colorado City. It took the suicide of a young blade to spark the inevitable reform. Tucker Holland had been for some time intimate with Dollie Worling and had even been living at her house. There was the complication of a divorced husband and the fact that Dollie's affections seemed to waver between the two. On a night in 1908, young Holland and his brother had gone out to buy sandwiches for Dollie and her girls. On their return they learned that Tucker had been supplanted by the ex-husband. The young man's clothes were brought to him and handed out the door by one of the girls, with the instructions to spend the night somewhere else. The youth was heard to remark, "This is the end of me."

The next morning he returned and was cordially received. Dollie went to her bedroom window and saw a newsboy pointing a toy gun at her poodle dog. (The poodle was the stamp of her profession; no respectable woman would own one.) She called to Tucker that the boy was going to shoot her dog.

"Here's for me, too," was the answer, as he shot himself. Dollie grabbed the gun and turned it on herself, saying, "If he is dead, I die, too," but the girls rushed in and prevented her suicide.

The trial which ensued was the means of rocking the tidal wave of reform. The evidence of bribery and collusion with the police stirred the civic conscience to the depths and the outcry went up for the closing of the euphemistically termed "clubs."

The council meeting which followed was more of a political brawl than a moral clean up. Some argued for preserving the district intact, saying that otherwise the women would be scattered all over the area, and besides, the city needed the money. Judge Cunningham replied that the licensing of disorderly houses was against the laws of the state and the nation and that, "If the women of the red-light district are doing a legitimate part of the world's work, let us take them into our own homes and let them eat from our tables with the rest of the families."

The annexation of "Old Town" had long been a political football and the clean up campaign added fuel to that fire. General Palmer offered to hire a group of the unemployed west side men and pay them good wages if they would cease opposition to the annexation of Colorado City.

On February 3, 1908, a local paper headlined, "Clean Sweep Made, Red Light District Thing of the Past."

The houses were dark and the women had been ordered to move on. There is a legend that they were taken in a group to a section north of town, pointed toward Denver, and told to move on, and that the little stream bed which marked their point of exit thus received its name of "Dirty Woman Creek."

A year later residents were surprised to find that the clean up campaign had not been entirely successful. A fire purged what man had overlooked. The newspaper declared a $40,000 loss of nine houses in the red-light district, believed to have been in operation. Among them were listed The Stone Front, operated by John Boyd, The Three Deuces, in charge of Anna Wilson, The Red Light, owned by a resident of Los Angeles, The El Paso and The Mansions, cared for by Bessie Paxton, and The Trilby, operated by Laura Bell.

The blaze of the fire, fanned by a high wind, could be seen for miles around. Police Chief Wolfe was afraid the entire city would be ignited and called for help from Colorado Springs. Firemen were praised for their heroic efforts which finally put an end to the conflagration at dawn. The mayor, when reached by reporters, was vague as to whether the district would be rebuilt as it had been.

Eventually, vice was pushed a few blocks farther north, beyond the corporate limits of the town and a newly established incorporated area of Ramona came into being. The *Gazette* of October 7, 1913, described Ramona as being "wet and how." The new town rivaled Colorado City in "gaity and bacchanalian delights." It was doomed to a short life of four years and died with the birth of state-wide prohibition. Ramona vanished. The last memory of the old days on the west side was gone.

Cripple Creek's heyday, too, was on the wane. A young writer came from the east to write of Colorado Springs and the neighboring gold camp. He enjoyed the cosmopolitan atmosphere of "Li'l Lunnon" with its polo, its charming architecture and good tea. The only fly he could find in the ointment was the surplus of writers of original poetry, a fault which continues to exist.

Young Julian Street went up to Cripple Creek on the Short

Line, but the altitude was tiring. He made a rather hurried and breathless survey of the town, which he later described inaccurately as "above timberline and above cat line." He spent the preponderance of his one-hour tour on Myers Avenue, the redlight district, where he made a few observations of its decrepit inhabitants. Here he found

> . . . a row of tiny one story houses crowded close together in a block. Instead of numbers there were names of Clara, Louise, Lina, etc., on the doors . . . . From one of the shacks a man left without looking at me. . . . There was an old woman in a white linen skirt and a middy blouse who looked grotesque for her years . . . .

Street's only interview was with Madam Leo, "Leo, the Lion." In her establishment, a calendar from a French painting hung on the wall, portraying Cupid kissing a filmily dressed Psyche. "That's me," said Madam Leo, "that's me, when I was young." Street's sketchy visit and subsequent article failed to include the Shakespeare Club or the churches of the little mining town. The irate citizens rewarded the author of the *Colliers* article by changing the name of Myers Avenue to Julian Street.

In Cripple Creek today The Homestead stands alone on Myers Avenue. It is furnished with the gilt of the gaudy days and even the "fainting" couch, which was used for the more delicate ladies, is in its niche in the corner.

But the scarlet days are a memory and their demise was probably effected by many circumstances. Prohibition changed the environ and vice became an expensive luxury. The crib girls were supplanted by the call girls. Sin took on an aura of mink and diamonds.

Woman suffrage put power in the hands of the emancipated sex. They employed it as a lethal weapon. The changing attitudes toward sexual mores raised the blinds.

There are a few of the "scarlet ladies" of the old districts left. Some have married into homes of wealth where the past is not mentioned. Some who were less successful at covering their trails have not been accepted into polite company. A number of

Laura Evans' girls have become movie stars or married into positions of society and wealth. Laura "protected their purple pasts, as she did her own true name."

Some, then, have covered their pasts meticulously with a blanket of respectability and legitimate business. One of these each year attends the pioneer celebrations of her community, poses for her picture, unsuspectingly, and half-believes that no one remembers. They say she cries a great deal now, but her tears are not of regret. She is old and weak and she hasn't been well. Her eyes are empty of all emotion and full of meaningless tears.

SOURCES

Cripple Creek Days, Mabel Barbee Lee, Doubleday & Co., Garden City, New York, 1958

Money Mountain, Marshall Sprague, Little, Brown and Co., Boston, Mass., 1953

Julia Bulette and Other Red Light Ladies, Hillyer Best, Western Printing and Publishing Co., Sparks, Nevada, 1959

Wildest of the West, Forbes Parkhill, Sage Books, Denver, Colo., 1957 ed.

The Fabulous Cripple Creek District, George Bowman, Fred Johnson and George Bowman, 1958

Denver Post, April 9, 1953, two articles by Earl Pomeroy

Rocky Mountain News, April 12, 1953, article by Pasquale Marranzino

Colorado Springs Gazette, March 9, 1924, article by H. S. Rogers, "Go Back Thirty Years with H. S. Rogers, Some Recollections of Yesterday—a Bit of Comment Today"
    January 20, 21, 23, 29, 1908
    February 3, 13, 1908
    April 8, 1917
    March 9, 1924
    January 10, 12, 1909

Out West, December 26, 1872

Colorado City Iris, January 15, 1909
    May 15, 1908

"Three Plats of Colorado City," Lorene Englert, paper for Historical Society of the Pikes Peak Region.

and interviews with
George Bowman of Cripple Creek
Mr. and Mrs. George Cross of Colorado Springs
Mrs. Etta Fisher of Colorado Springs
correspondence with
Mrs. A. C. Denman of Victor
Mr. and Mrs. Fred Mentzer, Cripple Creek.

Winfield Scott Stratton,

White-Collared Carpenter

In 1872, the little colony on Fountain Creek was suffering growing pains when Winfield Scott Stratton pulled in from the east with his carpenter tools and three hundred dollars. He was a tall, thin young wisp of a man of twenty-four. Neatly clad in his customary white collar and white shirt, he felt confident both of his ability and of the opportunities in the mushrooming community. He noted the portable houses which had been shipped in from Chicago as a stop-gap until more permanent structures could be established.

With his friends, Joseph Donovan and J. E. Eaton, who had preceded him to Colorado Springs, he went to find another acquaintance by the name of James Raymond, whom they had known in Lincoln, Nebraska. Raymond had set up his carpenter shop on Pikes Peak Avenue and had known the town since its very beginnings. In fact, his first glimpse of Pikes Peak Avenue and Tejon Streets, the future hub of the city, had been the sight of a span of mules plowing up the ground. Raymond not only gave Stratton his first job in Colorado Springs, but also offered him the added hospitality of sharing his shavings-filled mattress.

Stratton had come originaly from Jeffersonville, Indiana, where he had been born on July 22, 1848. He was the only surviving son in the family of Myron Stratton where daughters already numbered eight. It was a respectable family with industry, thrift, and honesty as basic traits and traditions. The father was a solid citizen, shouldering his civic responsibilities by serving for eighteen years on the town council. He was highly esteemed for his integrity, intelligence, and religious faith. The mother, of German descent, employed her native frugality to keep her large family neat and clean and well fed. The father was a hard working and competent carpenter in the boatbuilding firm of Logan and Stratton.

It is logical to presume that the sensitive young boy, Winfield, was overpowered and overruled by the petticoat majority which held sway at home.

He was given the best education the town could offer, the public school and also the private school of C. Leonhard. Stratton's skill in drawing was noted very early. He worked first for his father in boatbuilding and then apprenticed himself for three years to a carpenter and mechanical draftsman, Christian Heine. The young man always went to work in his white shirt and collar. On the surface he was mild, retiring, and thoughtful and somewhat of a dreamer.

There are accounts which say his quiet manners concealed a violent temper which at times erupted with volcanic intensity. A young stepmother may have led to dissentions between the boy and his father or perhaps it was just time to leave the nest. The constant shift of population to the west had caught Stratton in its tide and with a five hundred dollar nest egg from his father he set out. First it was Sioux City—then to Lincoln, Nebraska, where he plied his trade. He seemed an incongruous figure in his white shirt and white collar among other carpenters in blue shirts and denim. Here he met Joe Donovan, Edwin J. Eaton, and James D. Raymond, and the four spent hours after work talking of news of the west and the opportunities it must offer for ambitious men.

One by one these young men packed their gear and set out for the west. First Raymond struck out with the news of the first stake driven in Colorado Springs. Then Donovan straggled after. Eaton held out until spring, when he finally succumbed to the lure of the life of a cowboy. Only Stratton remained tethered by a good job and two pieces of property that had to be turned into cash before he joined his friends.

It was August before the four gathered together in Raymond's carpenter shop in Colorado Springs.

Winfield Scott Stratton. From William N. Byers, *Encyclopedia of Biography of Colorado, Chicago, 1901. Courtesy Denver Public Library, Western Collection.*

From the moment Stratton arrived in the colony, he had faith in the future of the town and soon invested in a lot, in half interest with Raymond. By spring he had bought out Raymond's interest and built a small shack on the back of the lot. He accepted his civic responsibilities by becoming a member of the volunteer fire department. On December 2, 1873, he opened his first bank account in the Springs. The record of that first small bank account was to have repercussions years after his death.

"At this period," Frank Waters has said, "he was three things, he never was afterward: he was hungry, sociable, and interested in carpentry."

The local paper on May 24th bore an ad for

GRANNIS AND STRATTON
CONTRACTORS, CARPENTERS AND BUILDERS
PIKES PEAK AVENUE AND NEVADA AVENUE
COLORADO SPRINGS, COLORADO
CONTRACTS TAKEN AND DESIGNS FURNISHED

Busy as he was with the new partnership, by November, 1873, he was involved with the construction of his new home on Tejon Street. During the period of his parnership with Grannis, he helped to construct the house on the "red lot" on the northwest corner of Weber and Kiowa. This house was later purchased by W. S. Jackson and eventually became the home of Helen Hunt Jackson. It was to house three generations of one of the "first" families of "Li'l Lunnon."

The partnership with Grannis was a thriving venture, but domestic difficulties brought an end to the firm of Grannis and Stratton, when, in a burst of chivalry, Stratton raised a ladder to Mrs. Grannis' bedroom and assisted her to run away from the cruelty of her husband's drunken tantrums. The partnership had served to further Stratton's reputation as a competent architect and builder. Stratton received most of the pending business deals of the dissolved firm.

By the last of November he was partner with J. D. Rogers, according to the *Colorado Springs Weekly Gazette*. At this time Stratton was enjoying a social whirl and participating in civic responsibilities. Once, when serving on the jury, he took a firm stand in opposition to the whisky ring when two violators of the temperance clause appeared in court. He and Rogers heartily endorsed the Temperance ticket.

In 1874, Joseph Dozier took over Stratton's partnership to share with Rogers and to release Stratton for a new venture in the mining region of the San Juans. Stratton was warned that he would lose his shirt in this gamble. He did.

That same year he came back broke to sell the shop for a thousand dollars to Dozier. The gold fever had hit him, and for the next seventeen years he outdid Jacob in his period of servitude for a half-promised reward. When money ran low, he sharpened his carpenter tools long enough to finance his next venture. During these years he tramped the state and prospected in Chalk Creek, Del Norte, Leadville, Creede, Tincup, Breckenridge, and the Wet Mountain Valley.

In 1876, Stratton obliged D. K. Lee, a friend whose social calendar was a bit involved. Lee had promised to take two young ladies to the same dance on the same night, and he implored Stratton to do him the favor of escorting a Miss Shields while he took Miss Zeurah Stewart. From that time the four went out together occasionally. Lee, observing Miss Shields more carefully, decided he had made the wrong choice and married her. On July 26, 1876, the seventeen-year-old Zeurah Stewart, who had been Lee's former girl friend, married Winfield Scott Stratton in a ceremony performed by the Reverend H. B. Gage of the Presbyterian church in Colorado Springs.

The marriage was tempestuous from the very beginning. Stratton took his wife to her Illinois home shortly after they were married and left her with her parents to await the birth of her child who was born six months from the date of their marriage. Zeurah never returned to Colorado Springs and Stratton never reconciled himself to his son and when speaking of him denied the relationship. On January 25, 1879, Stratton was granted a divorce on the grounds of desertion.

Meanwhile Stratton dabbled in inventions. An item in the *Colorado Springs Gazette* on February 1, 1879, declared:

> We called yesterday at the carpenter shop of S. E. Session and were there shown an ingenious bracket saw, invented and manufactured by Mr. W. S. Stratton. It is made upon the cam principle and is capable of turning out excellent work rapidly. It is well worth looking at.

Leadville caught the carpenter-prospector's eye in 1880, but with his consistent failure, he was unlucky. The nearest he came to a silver strike was the commission he was given by Tabor to construct a huge silver dollar on top of the Tabor Bank of Leadville.

He returned periodically to Colorado Springs with empty pockets to make new business alliances, all of which were short-lived. One of these was with F. A. Weston, a well known contractor who advertised Stratton as a capable workman. Their office was opposite the new opera house. They figured in the construction of several of the most solidly built residences of the city.

Every spring, with the thaw of the creeks, Stratton experienced the insatiable urge to chase the rainbow again. He was practical and intelligent enough to realize that he was wasting his time in futile pursuit unless he had a maximum of technical knowledge. In 1885, he enrolled in Colorado College to take a course in assaying.

In that same year, his father died leaving the son a small bequest. Stratton immediately sunk his inheritance in the prospect holes of the Ouray district.

In 1891, he entered a grubstake agreement with Leslie Popejoy to search for cryolite. It was in July of that year that Stratton found himself camped in the Cripple Creek hills. It had been a futile two month's search for cryolite during which time he had never ceased to looked for gold. He had listened to Crazy Bob Womack, but he had seen little evidence of the metal and it was still a concensus of opinion that a sheep pasture was no place to look for gold. It was on the night of July 3, 1891, that the forty-three-year-old Stratton was sitting by a dying campfire. That night he received a vision or a dream which he never denied. It was as though a revelation had burst upon him and he knew with absolute certainty that on the south slope of Battle Mountain was the lode that was to bring him fabulous wealth. He had seen his future in one bright moment. Early in the morning, the sun found him already in the brier patch by the altered dyke. He was staking out his claim on the Independence and the Washington.

He bought Popejoy's interest in the claim for "the price of his grubstake which was two hundred and seventy-five dollars with interest." In exchange Stratton was given an unwritten agreement conveying all interest in the claims to him. It made him the greatest mining king of Colorado. He outdid Tabor and Walsh and all the ones that previously he had eyed with envy.

Bob Schwarz, a Swiss cobbler who had always custom-made Stratton's boots and who had been one of his best friends, was rewarded by being placed in charge of all his mining properties plus his chore of making Stratton's boots. In this latter task he was indispensable.

Stratton had frequented the parlor houses of Cripple Creek as many a lonely miner had done. Now, he had the girls come to him in the small frame house he built for himself a few steps below the Independence. His taste became discriminating and he would have nothing but the cream of the brothels. Pearl De Vere with her love of Paris gowns became one of his favorites. A million dollars a year put him in a position to dictate his tastes. It also made him the vulnerable target for every conniving female who might feather her nest. He was also a soft touch for every beggar and prospector who might be down on his luck at the moment. It became Stratton's custom to supply the restaurants with meal tickets to hand out to those who were hungry.

Legends began to grow—especially since Stratton did not fit the accepted pattern. He could afford to indulge his whims and his taste for Kentucky bourbon. A story grew, that at one time

he had taken Lola Livingston, a madam of Cripple Creek's
Mikado House, to the Brown Palace. Some said the desk clerk
would not allow them to register. Some said Stratton threw
champagne bottles down the center stair-well of the hotel. It was
reported that he forthwith bought the hotel and fired the manager, who was N. Maxcy Tabor, the son of H. A. W. and
Augusta, Tabor's first wife. This is a very controversial story.
Years later, a newspaper of 1907 listed the Brown Palace as
being in the possession of the Stratton estate and said that a
change of management would soon be announced.

On October 13, 1909, the *Colorado Springs Gazette* related
this summary of the old controversial story. (Young Tabor's
name was spelled both Maxcy and Maxey.)

> MAXCY TABOR'S LEASE EXPIRED OCTOBER 31.
> STRATTON TRUSTEES TO DIRECT BROWN PALACE
> HOTEL. OWNED BY THE STRATTON ESTATE.
> The history of the Brown Palace has been marked with bitter-
> ness from the beginning . . . There has always been dis-
> agreement between owners and manager.
> In 1892 Maxey Tabor became manager and soon there-
> after the late W. S. Stratton who was heavily interested in the
> property conceived a dislike to him with the request that
> Tabor was requested to resign. Tabor felt that the mining
> magnate was unfair and taking advantage of a lease that
> still had some time to run refused to step out. Balked at
> this, Stratton set out to acquire full control of the hotel with
> the intention of ousting Tabor, but died soon after he had be-
> come the majority stockholder and while Tabor's lease still
> had some time to run.
>   . . . Tabor tried to get money to buy the property from
> the Stratton estate but was unsuccessful.

Shortly after the Brown Palace escapade of the gay nineties,
many other wild stories of equal eccentricity popped up. Stratton was credited with giving all the laundresses in Colorado
Springs, bicycles, so that they might ride home after a hard
day's work. He felt that these girls were too poor to ride the
streetcars. Many could not understand how a Mason of his
standing could give donations to Father Volpe in Cripple Creek,

but Stratton declared he was sure every cent he gave to the priest would be used to alleviate the suffering in the district. His donations to the simple faiths such as the Salvation Army, and to Father Uzzell's church in Denver, bespoke the simplicity of his creed. He was known to resent the stained-glassed, high-steepled churches.

Yet, there is an amusing anecdote told of a time when he attended the church service of the Grace Episcopal congregation in Colorado Springs. This was the fashionable church home of many of the north-end millionaires. The story goes that on one Sunday one of the more prominent "Li'l Lunnoners," a pillar of the church and leader in the community, sailed down the aisle to her customary pew. Arriving a bit late that morning, she was appalled to find Stratton already seated in her pew! She sat down gingerly for a few moments and squirmed uncomfortably. Then, taking out her pencil and paper she dashed off a note and handed it to the intruder. It said, "I occupy this pew every Sunday, and I give the church a thousand dollars a year for the privilege." Mr. Stratton glanced at her note and added on the bottom, "And damned well worth it, too!"

Other stories centering around Stratton told of his love of music and his wish to have all the music he wanted, someday. An insight into his character that revealed a kindness for animals and a certain bit of sentiment was disclosed by the pansy bed that bloomed over the grave of his old pet dog. And then, there was always the story of Stratton's hiding five-dollar bills under certain household objects to see if the housekeeper dusted properly. There was no end to the talk of his peculiarities.

Up in Cripple Creek the panhandling became too much for him and he decided to move back over the hill to Colorado Springs where the majority of mine owners had established their residences. He was expected to follow the pattern and make his home on fashionable Wood Avenue or Cascade or somewhere in the north end, but instead he purchased the comfortable Weber Street home which he had previously built for Dr. Beverly Tucker. It was hardly a fashionable north-end location, yet it was a good house and in a very good neighborhood. It was not far from the William Jacksons. He bought back his old carpenter shop which he had formerly sold to Joseph Dozier. The old place had a sentimental meaning for him. He remodeled, and furnished a suite of offices, and bought a carriage and a chestnut team. Aside from that he made no splash.

Despite his newly established offices, he was more often to be found on sunny days sitting on the horse trough in front of the First National Bank building. He always wore a Stetson hat. His shiny new boots were still made by his friend Schwarz. These boots were a fetish to Stratton and it was said that Schwarz continued to make them but that "he never licked them."

To his secretary, Charles Ramsay, Stratton gave the concise but simple directions, "I have a very few instructions to give you, in fact only this—When bills are presented, if correct, pay them at once—these people may need their money."

Panhandling was by no means eliminated with his change of residence. If possible it became only a more highly organized effort. Stratton was known to have set up a few old prospectors with rigs and horses to ply the tourist trade when a vein ran out.

In 1894 he extended his real estate holdings by purchasing the De Coursey Corner which was located on the southwest corner of Pikes Peak and Nevada Avenues. It was said to be the largest strip of land owned by one man in the business center and as important a real-estate deal as was ever made in the area. The *Gazette* boasted:

> Stratton is more heavily interested in the ownership of Cripple Creek mines than any other man and is amply able to buy the best real estate in any town in the United States, and the fact that he places his investments in Colorado Springs speaks volumes for the town. It has been said that Stratton has it in his power to do for Colorado Springs what Tabor did for Denver. It is safe to assume that others will follow his lead.

217

The articles estimated the cost for the property at about $50,000 and interested citizens wondered what he would do with the ground. Those who had been doubtful what benefit would be derived from the Cripple Creek mines began to realize the situation. Later Stratton turned over land at the opposite corner to the government at half-cost for the construction of a new postoffice building.

More and more as the tourist drivers pointed out the millionaire, he began to withdraw to the privacy of his own home and the protection of his office door. Even there he was besieged by a horde of people, and in the group, one day, came the most disturbing visitor of all, a dark-eyed young man, tall and slim. He introduced himself to Ramsay as Isaac Harry Stratton. Stratton granted his son a reluctant and brief interview. When the office door closed on the boy, Stratton sent for his lawyer whom he instructed to make arrangements for the payment of $100 per month for the young man's education at the University of Illinois, with the stipulation that he should not return to Colorado. There is some evidence, however, that the boy did return and that he stayed at the ranch home of his father's oldest friend, Joseph Donovan, but that he did not see his father alive again. The visit so upset Stratton that he became violently ill and took to his bed.

A trip to California was prescribed by his physician, Dr. D. H. Rice, and a private car, "Wanderer," was engaged.

Just the day before Stratton left, his big chestnut team created a commotion on Pikes Peak Avenue by attempting to run away. The *Colorado Springs Gazette* described the excitement:

> They came down the avenue at a terrific rate and the driver was an expert evidently and managed to turn them up Cascade without accident and then they were given rein until they had exhausted themselves. In the carriage was Stratton's sister, her young daughter and two other ladies and they all had presence of mind to sit quietly throughout the trying ordeal. It is stated that Mr. Stratton awarded Johnnie Leversedge, his driver, by a handsome check for $1000 for sticking to them as he did.

The year of 1896 marked an election fever, with Stratton making the biggest election bet of the year if not the biggest ever made. The *Colorado Springs Gazette* of Thursday, October 29, 1896, reported:

> Yesterday afternoon, Mr. W. S. Stratton of this city was talking to a number of citizens most of whom are supporters of Major McKinley and they got to bantering one another for bets. Mr. Stratton made the offer to bet one hundred thousand dollars against three hundred thousand dollars that Bryan would be elected. He agreed that if he won he would give the money to the Colorado Springs Free Reading Room and Library Association. If the other side wins, they, of course may keep their money.
>
> Mr. Stratton was asked about the matter last evening and made the following statement. He said, "I made the offer and I mean it. The money must be in the bank and there will be no 'Jaw bone talk' about it. I understand that the men to whom it was made are going to try to raise the money tomorrow. I did not make the offer because of any information that I have on the election, but I had a feeling that Bryan is going to win. I am deeply interested in seeing Bryan elected. I realize that the maintenance of the gold standard would perhaps be best for me, individually, but I believe that free silver is the best thing for the working masses of this country. It is because I have a great respect for the intelligence and patriotism of the working people and believe that they will see their duty and interest at the polls is for free silver that I am willing to make such an offer."

His lawyers shrewdly advised him to require that the money for the bet be put up in Colorado Springs in order not to be done out of it because of New York laws on betting.

Although he was definitely *nouveau riche,* he possessed none of the gauche qualities usually attributed to that group. He was quiet and reticent and "a man of wide clear information and extensive reading, a man whose opinion on books was discriminating and sound. . . . He has given away fully a quarter million dollars. . . . If he is a fool, he has unquestionably to be a fool in his own way." So commented the *Colorado Springs Gazette.*

His tendency to reticence was further indicated in an article in the *Evening Telegraph* which appeared on August 19, 1897. The author of the article was Charles Stokes Wayne, and as he described the various masquerades and representations which would be portrayed in the coming Flower Festival, he said:

> It is just possible that Mr. W. S. Stratton whose pockets are bursting with the coin of the realm, will not attend the ball. He has a way of keeping in the background whenever there is a display of a public nature and I can hardly conceive of him making an exception of this affair. If, however, he should go, I should look to finding him as a living representative of the Almighty dollar. . . . If Mr. Stratton would make a point of keeping both hands on the dollar edge, it is altogether reasonable to expect how many people would have an inkling, at least, whose face is hidden behind the mask.

It was eight years after the discovery of the Independence that Stratton allowed a report of the mine to appear in the *Gazette*. The article described his current mining area as being one hundred and fifty acres lying below the Portland and with the Strong mine on the west. It also declared the net profits to have been $2,300,000 and the gross take to have been $4,000,000.

Business drew Stratton to England in 1899. His physician went with him. The mining magnate was very ill. "Li'l Lunnon" was startled when they received the news that he had sold the Independence for $10,000,000. Money failed to satisfy a sudden loneliness and he wired Schwarz to join him. They toured Europe seeking the healing waters of Carlsbad for sugar diabetes and liver trouble and stomach disorders. Stratton delighted Schwarz with a visit to his sister in Constance, Switzerland, and before leaving, Stratton gave the sister twenty thousand American dollars and bought her a good home.

He returned to Colorado to find Anna, his housekeeper, in an upheaval of decorating and took up residence in the Brown Palace Hotel in Denver, until things were back to normal again in the Weber Street house. Meanwhile, he called Anna frequently, admonishing her not to let anyone in the house—particularly not his son!

In 1901 he purchased land in the Ivywild section and made plans for Stratton Park and a residence area. This included part of the Foster ranch. He expressed renewed faith in the future of Colorado Springs. He had invested heavily in the streetcar system and he continued to extend the lines. At one time he planned to run the streetcar line straight north on Tejon Street and he requested permission from Colorado College to lay the line through the campus but he was refused. Instead, General Palmer's generous donation made possible the construction of Palmer Hall directly across the line of the proposed streetcar route. It had been Stratton's intention to bequeathe $250,000 to Colorado College. The necessity of putting out $25,000 for a four block detour around the campus caused him to change his mind. He reflected that, "Colleges breed lawyers." He struck the Colorado College clause from his will.

There were other difficulties. In Manitou, a landowner demanded an exorbitant price for a streetcar right of way across his property. It was suggested to Stratton that he lay the rails across this land and let the court assess the damage. Stratton said, "I could do that because I am a rich man and he is a poor man—but that would not make it right." He paid the price that was demanded.

One of his most generous gestures to the city had been the gift of the new building for the Colorado Springs Mining Stock Exchange. To do honor to the occasion, the representative business and professional men of the city determined to pay homage to Stratton with one of the most lavish banquets ever held in the city. About a hundred and sixty prominent citizens attended the eight o'clock dinner at the Antlers on January 15, 1902. According to the *Gazette*:

> The tables were decorated in red and green, arranged in four rows, extending the length of the room, with one table connecting them at the west end of the room. This table was reserved for the most conspicuous guests of the evening, including the guest, Mr. Stratton, who, however, was unable to attend. Although his absence made the function

resemble the play of *Hamlet* with Hamlet left out, the expressions of high esteem which were indulged in by every speaker of the evening, the personal praise and laudation of him in whose honor it was held, was perhaps more free and eloquent with Mr. Stratton absent than if the sentiments of those who paid tribute to his worth had been restrained through fear of bringing embarrassment to Mr. Stratton, present . . .

It broke up a short time after midnight and all the guests departed with a sense of an evening enjoyably and profitably spent. Following is the menu which was served in faultless style:

MENU

Queen Olives

Radishes   Celery

Salted Nuts

Consomme a L' Antlers

Lobster a la Newburg

Small Tenderloin a L' Independence   Green Peas in Butter

Imperial Punch

Roast Quails on Toast

Salad Rachel

Biscuits Tortoni   Assorted Cakes

Fruit

Coffee   Cognac and Liqueur

Cigars and Cigarettes

Champagnes

Cazanove

Vintage of 1893

Heidsieck and Company

Monopole.

Perhaps Stratton failed to appear at the dinner because he couldn't wear his boots, and, of course, he couldn't eat any of the food, and sitting through sixteen speeches even in one's own honor might have been something of an ordeal. He seemed to prefer staying home with his extensive library and his Kentucky bourbon.

He disliked crowds. He preferred an occasional lady friend from Denver to spend the week-end, and he enjoyed a few close

associates such as young Verner Z. Reed and old Bob Schwarz—
"good old Bob who never licked his boots."

For months Stratton drank in the solitude of his library to
dull the pain and drown the loneliness. He was slowly losing
ground.

The *Gazette* of September 11, 1902, reported that Stratton
was in a stupor and that his physician had remained at his
bedside all night. His sister, Mrs. Cobb, had arrived from
California. Donovan sent off a wire to young Stratton, informing
him of his father's condition. A few days later Stratton's death
was announced.

Death came on the 14th of September on a Sunday night.
Old Bob Schwarz was at his bedside holding his hand. Quiet
came to the house on Weber Street but no black crepe was hung.
Stratton's favorite flower, red, red roses—tied with purple ribbon,
made an effort to brighten rather than sadden the house. Young
Harry Stratton who had come in answer to Donovan's telegram
was permitted to view the body but not allowed to stay in the
house.

The common knowledge of Winfield Stratton's love of roses
caused the supply of Denver, Colorado Springs, and Pueblo
greenhouses to be exhausted and it was necessary to import
them from Chicago.

Nellie Walker, a well-known sculptor and artist, arrived to
make a death mask of Stratton's face. She had been commissioned to design a monument in his honor.

The local paper carried the announcement that on September
17, Stratton's body would lie in state in the Mining Exchange
Building where all might call to pay their respects to the community figure. Ten men from the staff of the street railway
system were chosen to be the guard of honor. The building was
to be decorated with a profusion of living potted plants and
bright flowers. There were to be no symbols of mourning.
Stratton had always deplored funereal trappings.

The funeral service was held at ten o'clock in the morning at
his Weber Street home and was private with only a few close

friends and associates and his immediate family in attendance.

It was an Episcopal service with the Reverend Benjamin Brewster in charge. The Elks lodge quartette sang "De Profundis." This was followed by the Lord's Prayer and prayers from the Episcopal service. The old hymn "Lead, Kindly Light" was in itself a penitential prayer for one who, "was not always thus, nor prayed that Thou, wouldst lead me on." The minister seemed aware of Stratton's human frailties but emphasized the point that his good works had weighed heavily in the balance. He quoted the words of Dr. William Henry Channing which Stratton had kept framed on his wall and the spirit of which had motivated him. The Reverend Brewster read:

> To live content with small means; to seek elegance rather than luxury, and refinement rather than fashion; to be worthy, not respectable; to study hard, think quietly, to talk gently, act frankly; to listen to the stars and birds, . . . to bear all cheerfully, to do all bravely, await occasions, hurry never; in a word, to let the spiritual, unbidden and unconscious, grow up through the common.
> This is to be my symphony.

At two o'clock the funeral cortege started for Evergreen Cemetery. Every streetcar on the system stopped and remained stationary for five minutes as the hearse left the house. When the procession reached the cemetery plot, one hundred and eighty Masons, with their white-gloved hands crossed, formed a double line to make an aisle to the grave. Through this aisle the casket was carried. All evidence of the freshly dug earth was hidden as Stratton would have liked. His body was placed beside the grave of Mrs. Anna Chamberlin, his sister. Hundreds of curious bystanders milled around the place, sometimes disturbing the Masonic services. Finally the crowd dispersed and only an armed guard remained to give evidence of the importance of the figure buried there.

The newspaper accounts declared that his wealth had brought him no happiness except as he could give it to others—that his death at the age of fifty-four had only emphasized that money could not purchase a single hour of life, free air or sunshine, health and human love, that are the common heritage of mankind. They continued:

> Stratton left a permanent mark on this city to be long remembered, not for what he had but for what he has done. He had said, "I like to do these things. I have no great income from my money as I have invested it, but if I should find another bonanza I would do it all over again."

Long before the body was lowered into the grave, speculation ran rampant as to what disposition had been made of the vast holdings. An inventory of his personal property revealed some curious things. His jewels consisted of, "two ordinary watches, a watch fob and two pearl shirt studs." His personal property included two old sway-backed horses, Sorrel and Baldy, of no value at all, that he had pensioned out to pasture on the Bates ranch. This small item recalled to many the severe winter when Stratton had purchased a lavish supply of bird seed for the stranded, hungry, horned larks which had invaded the town in one of the Colorado Springs "unusual" weather storms. And some remembered the pansy bed of the old dog, Dick's, grave.

Up in Cripple Creek, they were awaiting the reading of the will with anticipation, convinced that the town would soon have its new library and nearby Victor would have a playground for the children. In Colorado Springs, the churches and Colorado College were convinced that the will would add substantial amounts to their endowments. The Masons hoped for a new temple, and the city needed a new public library. Even the man on the street hoped.

Bewilderment, chagrin, and righteous anger followed the reading of the will. It was announced that the bulk of the estate, amounting to more than $6,000,000, had been left as a memorial to his father, Myron Stratton. It was to finance a home for the aged and worthy poor and orphans of the county. It was to be handled by a board of trustees in sympathy with the will and committed not to contest it.

"Li'l Lunnon" was horrified at the prospect of a poorhouse in plain sight of the Antlers Hotel. One irate citizen voiced the views of many when he said, "The moral effect upon Colorado Springs, may well appall the thinking citizen. . . . The rag-tag and bobtail from the ends of the earth will arrive to take up residence here and acquire a home."

In the will, for the first time, Stratton acknowledged the relationship with his son and bequeathed him $50,000— "with the reservation that if he contests the will it reverts to the estate."

To his nephew, Carl Chamberlin, he willed his household and personal effects. To his nieces and other nephews he left $50,000 each. To his old friend Byron Logan, the son of his father's old partner, he left $10,000. To the Deaf and Blind School, he willed $25,000 in trust, the interest to be given annually to students for excellence in work or demeanor or both. This was in addition to the $100 a year which he had previously given the Institute.

The will was the topic of all conversation in Colorado Springs for some time. Opinions varied as to the fairness of it. No one was happy about it. Those who had received grants tended to be disgruntled over the amount. Those overlooked were smarting under what they felt to be injustice. They changed their former opinion of the character of the man, accordingly. Only a few who knew they wouldn't be included were smiling because the mighty had fallen.

Within four days after the publication of the will, headlines declared that young Stratton,

> . . . has obtained council to conduct litigation as a result of the nature of the last will and testament of W. S. Stratton. Young Harry has been employed in a bank in Pasadena but determined to make his home in Colorado Springs until proper settlement could be made. He declared that it wasn't the money itself in which he was interested but that he wished his deceased mother's name to be cleared of implications.

The public of Colorado Springs was sympathetic with young Stratton because a poorhouse was the last thing they wanted.

Others watched the outcome of the suit with avid interest because on the verdict they would base their own decisions on the practicability of bucking the issue.

Harry took a job as cashier with Shields-Morley Grocery Company. He called his old friend Donovan as a chief witness in the court proceedings. It was said that Donovan had been almost a father to the boy. However, there were 160 witnesses summoned to testify before a jury of laboring men, one of whom was a Negro. After a month of litigation young Stratton received $350,000 in a compromise. By the time he paid his attorneys he had some $235,000 left and was considering purchasing an interest in the grocery company for which he worked.

Harry's wife became ill, and they were planning a few weeks trip to Oshkosh. Just before they were to board the train, Donovan had a summons served on young Stratton, claiming that there had been an agreement that Donovan was to advance the money and secure witnesses in return for which he was to be paid ten per cent of the money received in the will contest. Donovan maintained that he was out $500 for his time and other services.

The success of the son's suit unleashed the hungry hounds who snarled and joined the fighting pack to gnaw at the golden bone.

In one day there were thirty-five suits filed and dismissed against the estate. Little people who wouldn't have faced Stratton alive evidenced no fear of the dead. One remembered when a child had stumbled into an open prospect hole, probably Stratton's, and demanded justice in the form of cash.

A young woman found some penciled notes which she claimed contained a promise from Stratton to give her father 40,000 shares in the Portland mine. Her father had left her $100,000 but she felt that something was due to her from the Stratton estate.

Leslie Popejoy felt that more was due him for grubstaking Stratton although he had evidenced no feeling of injustice when Stratton was alive. Death seemed to lend perspective to this debt.

227

A sister sued for interest which she felt should have been paid on her share.

The Venture Company of England sued saying that Stratton had salted the Independence.

Newspapers thriving on the sensational value of the suits began to bring out scandalous attacks on the deceased man's character. The *Denver Post* for October 13, 1902, contained an account by Richard Work of Jeffersonville, Indiana. Excerpts from this lurid article show some of the accusations. In parenthesis are the conflicting facts of the case:

> Twenty years ago Win Stratton was a blear-eyed sot in this city, and his haunts were the barrel-houses and his friends were the seedy garbed wrecks on the whiskey reefs.
>
> *(Stratton had left home thirty-seven years before this account.)*
>
> When he was nearly forty years old he was penniless, friendless, seedy, poorly educated, cast off by his family, and apparently on the road to a pauper's grave.
>
> *(He was not cast off by his family, but given a small nest egg to establish himself. He had the average education of a young man in his community.)*
>
> No one had the slightest idea that this miserable creature would amass a fortune. It was one of the most improbable and impossible things to be thought of. He was born in Jeffersonville and lived the greater part of his life there.
>
> *(He lived the first seventeen years there!)*
>
> His father, Myron Stratton, was once a prosperous shipbuilder, but his business dwindled away and finally he had nothing but a small carpenter shop. The writer attended school within a stone's throw of the shop and remembers it well. The shop was not worth more than $10 or $12 and one might have thrown a brick through it almost anyplace.
>
> *(Myron Stratton was able upon his death to leave a small bequest to his son.)*
>
> It was here that Win Stratton learned to use a hammer and saw. He never was much of a carpenter.

(Many of the houses he constructed in Colorado Springs are still standing and one of these houses has sheltered three generations of the same family.)

. . . his parents attended the fashionable Presbyterian church.

(It was the less fashionable Christian Church.)

. . . but Win Stratton probably never saw the inside of the church.

(Stratton was always a student of the Bible and was a contributor to many faiths and was known to have attended church on occasion.)

I remember well the last time I ever saw him. It was the last day he spent in Jeffersonville before starting West to seek his fortune . . . It was at his old resort, the saloon.

(Work was a child of ten at the time. What was he doing in the saloon?)

He had on a slouch hat with grease spots on it. The front was flopped down over his eyes. . . He wore no collar . . . his trousers were brown jeans turned up a trifle.

(Even as a young man, Stratton was noted for his neat, clean appearance, and particularly for his white collar.)

The next morning Stratton went to his father . . . and asked him for two dollars. The father was angry and during the quarrel that ensued he knocked the father down and blacked his eye.

(The father gave him a nest egg when Winfield determined to go and left him an inheritance when he died and Winfield Stratton left the bulk of his estate as a memorial to his father.)

Finally he landed in Denver. Years passed . . . There came the startling information that Winfield Scott Stratton, formerly a poor carpenter of Jeffersonville, Indiana, had found enough gold to make the Monte Cristo look like very small potatoes . . . . His loving sister, who suddenly awoke to the fact that she had always just doted on him boarded the train and went at once to Denver. At the time Stratton was boarding at a big hotel . . .

(He was living in a small house near the Independence in Cripple Creek.)

. . . Stratton got to thinking about the old home place and decided to revisit it. He remained just one hour.

(Stratton never did return to his old home.)

James Parker, a resident of Jeffersonville, replied in an article in the *Colorado Springs Gazette* of October 20, 1902, and countered the bitter accusations of Work, stating:

> The early life of W. S. Stratton was not one of poverty and want but was a life of moderate circumstance fraught with industry and perseverance . . . he was prosperous at his trade and owned property in Colorado Springs, and consequently could not have been on the "road to a pauper's grave." The claim of absolute perfection has never been made for W. S. Stratton, but few there are whose vices are so overbalanced by virtues.

The same day, an issue of the *Denver Post* dated October 13, 1902, bore a heart-rending story by Polly Pry about the unjust treatment of young Stratton, opening with an error in his name, calling Harry, "Isaiah Harry Stratton." His name was Isaac Harry. She recounted an interview with the young man. He was supposed to have told the true story of his mother and Stratton. He said:

> In 1875 . . . the mother's family came to Colorado Springs . . . There in the fall of 1876 my mother met Mr. Stratton. The next March my grandmother died suddenly of heart trouble and Mr. Stewart, (stepfather of Zeurah), wanted to return to Illinois. On this account my mother and Stratton were married immediately, a few days after her mother's death.
>
> *(Actually, records show that Stratton and Miss Stewart were married not in the spring but on July 26, 1876.)*
>
> . . . after they were married about nine months, he one day ordered her to pack up her clothes . . . he took her next day to the train and they went to Danville, Illinois, . . . and there he left her alone without means and without friends.

(Others say he took Zeurah after two months of marriage—and left her with her family.)

Three weeks later at Cabery, Illinois, in the house of the stepfather, I was born.

(Isaac Harry Stratton was born in January, 1877.)

Polly Pry pried with more questions which she reported with Stratton's answers.

"Your mother married again?"
"Yes, . . . yes, but I would rather not talk of that. She married for a home for me. . . and. . . and. . ."
"She was not happy?"
"No, she was very wretched, and I. . . I. . . have known what it was to be hated by a stepfather and repudiated by my father—and to see my mother die of a broken heart."

Polly said, "the young face turned towards the dazzling sky was very pale and the voice trembled, 'Do you wonder that I insist upon my right to a just inheritance?'" Polly then declared that young Stratton vowed to her that if he won his suit, the poor would not suffer! She continued to paint the dramatic picture and said,

Looking at his old, young face, where sorrow has already laid her withering finger, and pain and humiliation and shame have written their ineradicable lines—I felt that "the sick and the helpless" would not fare badly at the hand of the boy who had known the sting of poverty and drank (sic) of the cup of grief and so I said, "No, I believe you will do what is right."

We talked a little while about himself and his future, and he denied that he had any thought of marrige or had made any plans for the future.

(He had a wife and was considering buying an interest in a large concern in Colorado Springs.)

Polly went on to state:

His eyes are as blue and as clear as a child's . . .

(They were said by those who knew him to be black.)

231

Polly concluded:

> I cannot help but believe that the claim of I. Harry Stratton
> is a just and right one. Mayhap on the theory that "to he
> who suffers much, much shall be given."

> *(Polly was a little mixed on her grammar and scripture, too,
> at this point.)*

So ran the gossip and the courts kept in session.

Over a period of years, twelve women recalled that they had
been married to Stratton. One of them claimed that she had
been married to him in Texas on or about January 1, 1874.
Unfortunately, the courthouse records and all records in that
county had been destroyed by fire. The attorneys for the estate
hired Burns Detectives who gained the confidence of the woman
and found that she was conniving with her witnesses to collect.
It was further proved when the case came to trial that Stratton
could not possibly have been in Texas on that date because of
the deposit date, with his signature, on his first small bank
account in Colorado Springs at that time, and the testimony of
Joseph Dozier and William S. Jackson and Irving Howbert that
Stratton had been in the city then. There was no train service to
Texas and it would have been a physical impossibility for him
to have been there.

As late as 1916, a Rose Ellen Stratton of Kansas City happened to remember that she was Stratton's sister. Up to that
time she had been in a mental institution and had been incapable
of filing. She claimed the entire estate as the only living heir
and stoutly insisted that Stratton was insane at the time he made
his will. And so it went over the long period of years. It is
ironic that considering Stratton's aversion to lawyers, they fat-
tened themselves on the litigations. Yet, it was through the
asuteness of one of these lawyers that the estate was saved at
all to carry out the terms of the will. Dave Strickler earned that
honor.

Every suit delayed the building of the Myron Stratton Home
so that nine years after Stratton's death, it existed only in the will

of the man who planned it. The trustees had increased the value of the estate through wise investments and the streetcars were running at a profit despite the innumerable free passes that were handed out. These passes became the target for criticism at the hands of the *Colorado Springs Gazette* and Judge Robert Kerr, who insisted that the free transportation was robbing the estate of thousands of dollars a year. It seemed that the trustees had presented these favors, not in the pattern of Stratton, who gave the bicycles to the laundry girls who didn't have the carfare, but instead the passes had been presented to the doctor, merchant, lawyer, and chief—and tax assessor and their ilk. Little wonder in the next election, the Stratton estate opposed Judge Kerr.

It was on December 18, 1913, with no fanfare and no addresses of welcome, three old men moved in as the first residents of the Myron Stratton Home.

Today, the trees have grown around the neat cottages of the elder residents of the Stratton Home. The young people who live in dormitories take the bus to school and they dress in clothes of their own choosing. They share the fun and activities in Colorado Springs public schools. A college education awaits any of these children who show aptitude. The older people sun themselves on the porches and make out their individual grocery orders to fill their needs of butter, eggs, and fresh meat, and even the little luxuries that make all the difference. Religious opportunities are open for all without restriction to creed, but imposed on no one. All rest secure in the knowledge that medical attention and nursing care will be available for all their needs.

The community of Colorado Springs, now, points with pride to the Myron Stratton Home as a unique and successful experiment in living.

About two hundred residents usually form the population of the pretty home south of the city. A little less than half of them are children who live in dormitories. There is no stigma attached to being a resident, and the only obligation placed upon the children is that of living up to the best of their potentialities and thus making the home a living monument. Founder's Day, on July 22, used to be an occasion for remembering and rededicating, but recent years have brought some changes and Founder's Day is just another day. Education for the children is not restricted to the three R's. Dancing instruction has been included. Self respect is instilled along with Stratton's belief that honest labor is worthy of a white collar.

Dr. E. J. Brady, an early superintendent of the home, said of Stratton:

> He gave the labor of his years for the creation of the noblest charity of modern times. Yet, like other great men, he was little understood and little appreciated by those who were his contemporaries. No one realized then, the great knowledge he had of the social conditions over which we as individuals have little or no control. He had that rare insight into human psychology which is so infrequently expressed by one without the opportunity for education. He possessed the ability of entering into the lives of others; an ability to work out human relationships for humanity as well as for himself. He fearlessly planned, outlined the use of his great fortune without any attempt to evade responsibility, utilizing his own self-reliance and independence to insure its success.

Independence was perhaps the keyword to the enigmatic character of Winfield Scott Stratton. He was independent in his thinking, his convictions, behavior patterns, and ideals. He was a man of achievement, yet there was an element of dream woven into his makeup. Even his great mine was located by a dream and labeled Independence. It may not have been purely indicative of the date. Independence is the quality which is instilled into the young people of the Myron Stratton Home as they are trained to stand on their own two feet and look the world in the eye and make their own strikes.

SOURCES

Midas of the Rockies, The Story of Stratton and Cripple Creek, by Frank Waters, Sage Books, Denver, 1937-1949

Money Mountain, Marshall Sprague, Little, Brown and Co., Boston, Mass., 1953

Cripple Creek Days, Mabel Barbee Lee, Doubleday and Co., Inc., Garden City, N.Y., 1958

Guide to Colorado Ghost Towns and Mining Camps, Perry Eberhart, Sage Books, Denver, 1959

The Book of Colorado Springs, Manly D. Ormes and Eleanor Ormes, Dentan Printing Co., Colorado Springs, 1953

Colorado Springs Gazette, excerpts 1873 through 1926

Denver Post, October 13, 1902.

Empire Magazine, Denver Post, "Story of the Empire's Foremost Humanitarian" by Byron Akers, 1946

"King of Cripple Creek," *True Magazine*, by Marshall Sprague. March, 1953

Interview with
Kenneth Brown
Mrs. J. F. Bischof

Wings over Chalk Creek

Sometimes the west is cruel country. The beginnings were hard; sometimes the cruelty carries over into the present to complete the circle. Often over the mountains one sees vultures circling, waiting for something to die. Patient and inexorable, they glide and wait for the last breath to expire, when they may circle down in safety to gorge themselves on what remains. Such an atmosphere of morbid expectancy hovers over the Chalk Cliffs, and the odor of decay seeps out of the padlocked building that was once the old Home Comfort Hotel. Something of the past is dying. All that is left is a little huddled figure that lies in a nearby hospital.

The end of the story of the Stark family is made up of rumor and conjecture, bits and scraps of personal knowledge, reminiscences from faded memories stitched into a patchwork which must of necessity bear the personal touch and the hand-stitched seam.

With our first acquaintance with the little town of St. Elmo, many years ago, there was no imminent aspect of death, only the feeling of a village gone to sleep. The fishing was good up at Grizzly Lake; there were even bigger fish in Pomeroy and Hancock, and St. Elmo was the logical place to rent a cabin. We would enter the old Stark store, buy our bits of supplies, and ask for the cabin directly across Main Street next door to the City Hall and the jail. Buckthorn bushes grew up by the steps of the cabin; the chipmunks scampered in front of our feet. Going through the two bedrooms, papered with Victorian wallpaper and furnished with sagging beds, we would deposit our supplies on the kitchen table, in front of the wood stove. Tony Stark would invariably remark, "I'll bring the wood."

Early photograph in St. Elmo area, by Roy Stark. Second from left is likely Annabelle Stark. *Photo courtesy Ted Jacobs.*

Stark store and Home Comfort Hotel, St. Elmo.

If it was growing dark we would light the coal oil lamps and build the fire.

The night came early because the surrounding mountains cut off the sun. We spent many an evening across the street in the Stark store around the pot-bellied stove with Roy and Tony and old Mrs. Stark. The old shepherd dog dozed in front of the fire, nearly blind, his eyes having been scarred in close combat with a cat.

Roy and Tony told us the story of the old town and how it got its name from a now out-moded best seller, *St. Elmo* by Augusta Evans Wilson of Columbus, Georgia. The town had first been named Forest City, but when a community in California made first claim to the name it was legally changed in 1881 when the Colorado town was incorporated. The Starks told us that the miners used to bring their dust from the Mary Murphy mine and put it in the store safe. They related how the Mary Murphy got its name, recalling the mine owner's illness and subsequent recovery through the efforts of a nurse. In gratitude, the mine owner had given the mine her name. The Stark brothers also impressed us with the legendary miracle quality of that mine by which it continued to produce when all the others in the district had faded out. They told of the way the old toll roads used to wind over the passes to Leadville and Gunnison and Tincup, to Ashcroft and Aspen. They showed us the old schoolhouse, no longer in use. It was cheaper, they said, to take the few children left to board in Buena Vista and attend school there, than to hire a teacher now. The school had been used for church services by both Bishop Machebeuf and the Methodist Father Dyer.

Mrs. Stark, the mother, did not contribute anything to the conversation. Roy said, "Mother could tell you a lot, but she isn't able."

Once during that early period Roy sent a most welcome card to one of us in the hospital. It was a picture post card of a snow scene at St. Elmo and it arrived after a long period of fever—even the sight of that pictured snow was cooling and refreshing. When the nurse asked that day what we would like for dinner, for the first time in weeks we recalled something that would taste good—and asked for trout, remembering St. Elmo and its deep, trout-filled lakes and icy streams.

News came to us, in May, 1943, that Roy had died and shortly after that his mother, too, was dead. With these two deaths change began in St. Elmo. When we went back again there was another member of the family whom we hadn't met before. Annabelle Stark Ward had come back to the home place and was living there with her brother, Tony. Roy's capable management was noticeably lacking. Tony was definitely shaken by the death of his brother, and he implied that Roy had been a victim of modern medicine, but didn't care to discuss the details. There was a decline in the appearance of the cabins and the store, and the two occupants bore the stamp of eccentricity. The eccentricities increased with the years, until casual visitors were no longer welcome. Annabelle posted herself on the porch of the store clad in a long black coat, high topped shoes, and a man's felt hat. (Later she added still another hat on top of the original one.) Pretending to sweep the porch, she kept an owl-like vigilance on everyone who walked the street. Her head seemed to pivot completely around to observe every movement of the stranger, and if he dared to show a camera she was inclined to threaten him with a gun and run him out of town. Pictures were obtained only under difficulty and with subterfuge. An antique dealer, intrigued by the rumor that Miss Annabelle had hidden stores of cut glass and old buttons, on their original cards, went to talk to her. But the Starks were no longer anxious to sell anything. This particular day was one of Annabelle's bad ones—she made no attempt to hide her hostility and made it clear that she had nothing at all to sell.

The antique dealer asked, "Do you have any picture post cards of the place?"

Miss Annie shook her head. She said, "We used to carry them but we don't any more. People just kept buying them so we don't bother with them now."

So the store grew more cluttered. Although Tony was the postmaster, letters were allowed to accumulate and dust gathered on them as they poked out of their pigeonholes. It behooved the camper not to forget essentials because the stock in the store became more and more depleted, and what the owners had was in a jumbled mess and individual items were difficult to find. One unused cabin was filled to overflowing with discarded claim shovels picked up around the abandoned mines and appropriated by Tony, but to what purpose no one knew.

The years crept on, but Tony and Miss Annie took little notice of the passage of time while the accumulation of old newspapers grew higher, the tin cans piled up in the kitchen, and the paths between the boxes grew narrower—and life closed in.

An occasional curious writer tried to find a story in the lives of the peculiar pair, but encountered only frustration, closed doors, conflicting accounts, and active hostility. Legends began to mushroom around the two strange figures who made no effort to help people to clarify the truth. The two Starks usually seemed unaware of what was happening to them, but once Annabelle remarked to a writer, "I don't know why I stay here. I came to take care of my brothers when they were sick and I stayed and now I'm covered with cat hair and I'm beginning to be just like them. I don't know why I stay."

So the time went on with Annabelle and Tony making uneventful trips to Nathrop or Salida, with supplies as the excuse, starting down their mountain late in the afternoon, usually around four o'clock when it was already beginning to grow dark, and it was dangerously dark when they returned around midnight. On their last such trip together in 1958 Tony failed to negotiate a familiar turn and they were discovered by a miner, trapped under their old car in the cold night. It was luck that the miner had happened down from his mountainside at that particular moment and could help them back to the store.

Shortly after, we again knocked on the locked door of the Home Comfort. Miss Annie appeared, wearing two hats and the same old black coat. We inquired about Tony and were told he was too ill to see anyone. We were not invited in. The chipmunks scampered about the porch, fat and well-fed. They were her special charges, as were her old dog and the numerous cats.

The next news was that both brother and sister had been taken to Salida to the hospital, that the store was padlocked, and that there would be an auction of its contents. Antique dealers pricked up their ears. But this auction failed to materialize, for some reason. It seems that everyone has an eye on the Starks' possessions and perhaps our wish is the most foolish of all because we want nothing of any intrinsic value—unless there is a value in sentiment. We thought of only two objects we would like to have out of that cluttered supply—the old bread board Mrs. Stark used when she baked the continual supply of bread for the laborers who cleared the snow from the Alpine Tunnel, and a cracked teapot of no value whatsoever.

The next information was that Tony had been transferred to the State Hospital in Pueblo where he died of double pneumonia (and possible malnutrition) on June 7, 1958—the third member of the family to die on the seventh day of the month.

And so the story stood for over a year with the tangled rumors piquing our curiosity. Yet we did nothing. We, too, stood at a standstill until a jeep excursion took us again over to St. Elmo. The same blue sign in front of the Home Comfort Hotel swung in the breeze and boasted, "Commercial messages sent to any place in the world." The sun shone in the same warm manner, but things were *not* the same. The chipmunks still scurried on the old board walk, but they were thinner now without Miss Annie to feed them. The grizzled-gray little dog had moved across the street where an efficient curio store manager fed him. No one forbade us to take pictures. We missed the black-clad figure with owl-eyed vigilance, and some of the flavor was gone. Anyone could take pictures now.

We glimpsed the end of the story. We thought we saw a vulture perched on a nearby limb. We felt that perhaps time was running out for St. Elmo, Miss Annie—and us.

241

We chose a bright day in December to tie up a few threads. We only succeeded in unraveling more.

By this time, the legends had grown, the truth was buried even deeper, and the Stark story was as cluttered as their store. There was a sense of apprehension and waiting, and the smell of decay and death, and an ominous rustle of wings, and a circling shadow on the snow.

We went to old timers, historians, newspapers, mortuaries, and legal advisors, to piece together a crazy-quilt story that is full of holes, drab in spots, bright in others, but with dark ugly patches as spotted as old Mrs. Stark's skirt.

From these people we gleaned old stories of the past, such as the days when St. Elmo was the crossroads of the trails leading to the mining camps across the Continental Divide, when it was the largest town at the junction of five gulches, the freighting center for Gunnison and Aspen and its trails choked with traffic. One man recounted that when he asked for a private room in the town's only hotel, he was offered a bed with a chalk mark around it for his private suite. During the boom years the town grew to 1500 and 2000; there were five hotels and a jewelry store and a newspaper called first the *St. Elmo Rustler* and later the *St. Elmo Mountaineer*. At Grizzly Gulch they were putting out the *Chrysolite Bugle*. The Mary Murphy Silver Cornet Band was tootling away and "did just splendid" at the Fourth of July celebration, 1885. Anton and Anna Stark were on hand to see the scrub horse races, the striking-match races, and the slow jack race. The first church services were held in a bunkhouse to which a high-backed rocker was brought to serve as the bishop's chair. After the schoolhouse was built in 1882, both Father Dyer and Bishop Machebeuf held services there. The Starks were on hand for Catholic services in the little school, and Mrs. Stark kept a small home altar in her bedroom.

On Saturday nights the miners held their rendezvous up and down the street in front of the Starks' Home Comfort Hotel and sometimes ended the night in the jail across the street behind the City Hall.

In 1890 a fire took its toll of St. Elmo, as it did in many of the mining towns.

Some who live near the Chalk Cliff area still remember a Dickensian character who used to have a cabin ten or fifteen miles up the neighboring Cottonwood Pass—Sam Denny, a Confederate war veteran who could neither read nor write and who squatted on a claim and lived there for thirty or thirty-five years. A hay meadow supported a cow or two, and all summer he picked the wild raspberries and made gallons and gallons of red raspberry jam. Visitors passing by his cabin would call to him, saying, "Sam, how are you?"

Invariably the stock question would bring the stock reply, "I'm all ready to go into a box." The next moment he would inquire, "Have you got a newspaper?" Upon this, he would expect the visitor to read the paper to him from cover to cover. In lieu of his inability to write and consequently to record, Sam relied on a remarkable memory with which he could recall the year, the day, and even the hour of most any event he cared to remember.

But it was the Stark family uppermost in the minds of those familiar with St. Elmo and its background. The Starks had arrived in St. Elmo in the early 1880's. Of German descent, Mrs. Anna A. Stark was born January 11, 1858, in Munjar, Kansas. Her three children were Anthony, born in Hays City, Kansas, March 8, 1881; Annabelle, born about 1879 or 1880, place unknown; and Roy, born January 15, 1888, in Glenwood Springs, Colorado. Little is known of Anton Stark except that he was little, ineffectual, and affable. His only claim to masculine superiority was his mustache. Despite the fact that his wife was small, almost Oriental in stature, she was the dominating factor in the family. Her coloring was almost Russian. She has been called "the brains of the outfit." She was peppery, domineering, dictatorial, and "a little spitfire." Periodically she ran Anton out of town, but he drifted back. Family troubles did not end even when both his legs were amputated. Mrs. Stark ruled her children with the same firm hand and was known to have whipped them all, even after they were grown. Quite early, little Annabelle decided that she didn't want a marriage like her mother's. Mrs. Stark had already decided that none of her children would ever marry. She provided for her family and tried to furnish all three with an education. It was said by some that all the children attended Catholic schools in Denver, and letters discovered since tend to verify this.

Mrs. Stark remained in St. Elmo and ran the Home Comfort Hotel where she advertised "all the comforts of home given to commercial men, strictly first class, best meals, comfortable clean beds, telephone and telegraph communication is also available to its guests." Those who remember staying at the hotel claim her advertising did not overrate her accommodations, that the rooms were clean and comfortable and the meals were exceptional. It is said that she baked bread during the snow slides on the Alpine Tunnel, sometimes working all night to feed the workers on the railroad. One visitor to the Home Comfort recalled Mrs. Stark's wonderful biscuits and her unusual method of mixing them. She kept a black iron kettle full of flour ready. This flour she hollowed out into a well into which she poured the sour milk and other ingredients, gradually working in just enough flour by intuition to make her famous biscuits which she browned by a split-wood fire and which she served piping hot with wild honey from the valley.

Friends recall young Miss Annabelle about 1906 when she was a telegrapher for the Colorado and Southern Railway and when her fingers flew over the keys and when she was "the most beautiful girl in Chaffee County" with her wavy brown hair, blue-gray eyes, Dresden complexion, and neat, trim figure. All the boys were quite aware of Annabelle. Her life had been separated from St. Elmo for a period. She had incurred the awesome wrath of her mother by marrying outside the church, a railroad worker and member of the Masonic order, named Ward. Part of Annabelle's married life was spent in Denver and in Trinidad. She is said still to own a house in Trinidad.

After the death of her husband, about 1918, Annabelle sold insurance in the Chalk Creek area, and one old schoolmate recalled the time she dropped into his store to sell him some insurance. She was clad in a neat black suit and was wearing patent leather pumps. "She was pretty."

Roy and Tony stayed on in the little town to look after their mother. For years, Roy was postmaster of St. Elmo and Tony was his assistant. On the surface, everything was well in the Stark family, with only occasional outbursts of temper. The boys were good to their mother. They took her into Salida for the winter. They saw that she got to mass at St. Joseph's Catholic Church each Sunday. Roy frequently went to Denver "on business." There were different interpretations in the valley as to Roy's business. There are some who say Roy was secretly married and had a wife and daughter living in Denver and that he visited them frequently. There are others who say he might have had a daughter, but he didn't have a wife. Roy was known to be a friend of Bonfils of the *Denver Post* and as a very competent photographer, Roy frequently sold pictures to the *Post* and to magazines. It was said also that Roy would never have dared to reveal his marital status to his mother—or she would have whipped him!

With the decline of the mining interests in the Chalk Creek area, much of the property in the valley was defaulted for taxes, and the Starks were credited with acquiring all sorts of claims and real estate by tax default. Roy was the businessman who kept an eye on all available resources. Disgruntled onlookers who did not want the property themselves, more or less resented the pyramiding acquisitions of the Stark family, particularly since the Starks were not always cordial to their neighbors. True, Roy was genial enough, perhaps a little too friendly to be trusted, according to some. Tony was a sinister figure, with a mysterious shadow about him and a furtive air. Mrs. Stark was becoming increasingly careless in her dress. She was acquiring the eccentricities which were to become the trademark of the family. One friend recalls the picture Mrs. Stark made when she crossed the footbridge over Chalk Creek, below the house, wearing her old black skirt and with a heavy cape thrown over her head. She steadied herself by means of a shepherd's crook which gave her a peasant's appearance. Mrs. Stark was growing feeble and frail, but clung to her despotic rule with an iron hand. On one occasion, it is said, when Roy headed for an extracurricular pleasure trip in the spring when a man's fancy led him to imbibe a little too much and he returned home in less than sober condition, his little old mother was furious. Rumor has it that the old lady and Tony threw Roy in the creek. Fact or fiction, Roy fell ill with pneumonia. Here again, legend has grown and fiction cannot possibly be separated from fact. It is known that a doctor was called in only a few hours before Roy's death which occurred at midnight on Friday, May 7, 1943. He had been ill for several days with double pneumonia. The fact that the funeral wasn't held until ten days later leads one to conjecture and adds spice to the stories which have grown up around the peculiarities of the remaining members of the family. One report states that for all that time the mother and Tony refused to believe that Roy was really dead, and that they surrounded him with hot water bottles and stuck him with needles to arouse him. Another said that Tony accused the doctor of giving his brother a pill which had caused him to choke to death. Be that as it may, after a time the odor of death forced them to call in the coroner, but even then the two insisted that Brother was sleeping and could not be disturbed, and they requested the coroner to stick Roy with a needle, which he refused to do.

Only two months later to the day, Mrs. Stark died, July 7, 1943. It was generally understood that the bulk of her property would go to a Catholic charity, but her estate and that of her husband, to date, have never been settled.

Sometime in the interim Miss Annie came back and took the place by the fire which had just been vacated by her mother, and the neighbors reported that she grew as queer as the rest of them. It became an effort even to get down the mountain for the winter and easier for the two remaining to hibernate with the chipmunks in St. Elmo, but spring and the fishermen and the photographers roused them periodically from their lethargy. In the meanwhile, a more or less apathetic neighborhood vouched for Annie's increasing peculiarities, but marveled at the keen vigilance with which she kept her old purse with her wherever she went. They speculated on what it might contain.

After the mother's death, nothing was thrown out. The piles of newspapers mounted the walls and little lanes and paths wove in and out of the house. Bits of decaying food were stuffed into the cracks of the walls. Miss Annie smoked continuously, and some marveled that a second St. Elmo fire did not break out, with cigarettes dropped so carelessly and the old papers piled so close to the stove. Sympathetic visitors plied the two Starks with clothing and gifts which were never unwrapped, but were simply added to the accumulated stacks. Groceries were bought and piled in heaps, unopened, while the two were slowly starving from lack of proper food. Still Miss Annie fed the chipmunks and they grew fat while Annie and Tony grew weaker and queerer with each passing day.

Following the aforementioned accident in 1958, neighbors called the authorities who arrived to take the pair to the hospital. The condition which met them when they opened the door was one of indescribable filth, odor, and decay. The pair were found in their beds with their clothes on. The old hat which Miss Annie kept on her head even in sleep was hopelessly entangled with her hair, which had grown into it. The men lifted the two high over the mountains of debris around their beds and took them into Salida. Here their hitherto simple lives became entangled with legal proceedings. It did not take authorities long to determine by medical examinations that both belonged in a mental institution, but it was decided that Annie was too weak to be moved. Tony was transferred to the Pueblo hospital where he died three weeks later, June 7, 1958, and he was buried in Salida's Fairview Cemetery on June 11. Pallbearers were Robert Rush, attorney; Raymond Drain, Anthony Twist, Todd Cook, Thomas Miller of St. Elmo, and Ted Jacobs. Mass was held at St. Joseph's Church, the Reverend Maurice Gallagher celebrant, and with a children's choir participating. Attending the funeral mass were

247

A. B. Leiker, a cousin from Hays City, Kansas, and his daughter, Therese.

A conservator was appointed for Tony's estate, which has not yet been settled. With the bills for Annie's hospitalization mounting, the conservator requested permission of the court to sell some of the property from the store and permission was granted, but later, other lawyers petitioned to have the decision reversed so that now the matter rests in files of the Colorado Supreme Court. There is a rumor that a sizeable offer was made by some Oklahoma business men for Tony's interest, and for a time it looked as though the estate might be sold to satisfy financial obligations.

Those in authority say there was no money available for expenses except about $800 found in Tony's shoe. There are rumors that Annie's old black purse held $2100 and numerous uncashed pension checks (from the pension of her deceased husband) at the time of the accident. Others say the amount was $1700, and there are a few who say there was nothing—and a very few who say they don't know.

Annie was not left alone in her illness. According to authorities, an acquaintance came forward and paid her bills and brought her clean clothes to wear in the hospital. Although Annabelle was at first declared mentally incompetent by medical examiners, a petition was initiated later to restore her to reason. This petition was passed by medical authority. Apparently, the December day in 1959 when we called on Miss Annie at the hospital was not one of her better ones. She was totally unaware of everything and could only make irrelevant comments and throat noises. She stared at us blankly and could recall nothing of her life, or St. Elmo, did not remember where she went to school, or if she had ever gone. The names of her brothers brought no glimmer of recognition. She fingered the covers over her pink outing flannel nightgown. Her hair was clean, cut, and inclined to wave a little, and iron gray. Her eyes were blank of expression but were a gray-blue. Her skin still had a Dresden quality and some of her features a sculptured look. Her tongue

248

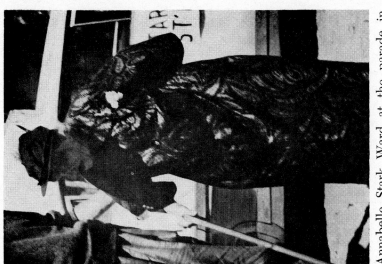

Annabelle Stark Ward at the parade in Buena Vista, 1959. *Photo courtesy George Douthit.*

Annabelle Stark Ward closing the door on an intruder. *Photo courtesy George Douthit.*

249

rolled aimlessly in her toothless mouth. The attendant in charge stated that Mrs. Ward was much as usual, that she only talks to herself and then is incoherent and inclined just to make noises. Friends continue to leave gifts and she seems at first to get infuriated, and then to be pleased. We took cameras into the hospital intending to take a picture, but seeing that defenseless old woman, weak and unaware of what was going on, we laid the cameras aside. It hardly seemed sporting when she was so helpless.

Annabelle must have been better on an earlier occasion because a friend had taken her in a car to the parade in Buena Vista. Since the restoration to sanity Miss Annie has been able to make a will. The name of the beneficiary is naturally not publicly known. This will was said to have been witnessed by a priest and two others. Everything has been done legally.

At St. Elmo a big padlock is on the door of the Home Comfort Hotel and store. It was said that the store contained valuable newspapers with every edition of the *Denver Post* which was ever printed, that there were antiques of cut glass and china and buttons, still on the cards, that there were uncashed checks and money, and unopened letters. Others in authority say the newspapers were of no value at all and have been destroyed and that what little was found in money was turned over to the court and that there were no antiques other than cheap hotel china. No one is supposed to have gone into the place until the authorities took charge, and yet it is said that Annabelle's marriage certificate appeared somehow out on the dump, and there are those who vow that old currency of large denominations turned up in the area in strange places, and that furniture was sold in Colorado Springs that had belonged in St. Elmo.

Once Miss Annie asked for her mother's altar figures, but apparently forgot her request as soon as it was made and they are still in her old home. Anyway, they are only cheap tin, covered with gilt, and not valuable, as many had imagined.

With the dwindling days of Annabelle Ward, the last of the Stark family, with whom St. Elmo has always been identified,

an era is drawing to a close. The few interested people are concerned mostly with what will happen to the estate.

So Miss Annie lies quietly in her hospital bed, unaware of
what is going on. Some say she is more aware than you think,
though how that can be determined is a moot question.

But here and there an old timer remembers when she was
"the most beautiful girl in Chaffee County" and an occasional
one grieves over inexorable change and there is one over Tincup
Pass who says, "Little Annie Stark, she was such a pretty little
girl."

St. Elmo will never be the same without the Stark family.
There is an ominous rustle of wings in the wind as the big black
birds glide down over the valley.

POSTSCRIPT TO WINGS OVER CHALK CREEK

The inevitable "seven" did not overlook Miss Annie. She could
postpone but not evade the inevitable seventh of the month.
It was on April 7, 1960, that her condition became worse and
she was transferred from the nursing home to the Salida Hospital.
Annabelle Stark Ward died on April 25, 1960. The cause of her
death was recorded as arteriosclerotic heart disease. She was in
her eighties.

Reports come now that there is some confusion concerning
her will. Relatives are said to be contesting it. The decision
regarding the property at St. Elmo is likely to be long delayed by
litigation. The old store is boarded shut. Miss Annie's little dog
seems contented and is cared for by neighbors. The chipmunks
no longer look expectantly for crumbs.

The talons of the black birds grow increasingly defined as they
make their final swoop.

SOURCES

Digging Gold Among the Rockies, C. Thomas Ingham, Philadelphia, Pa., 1888

Stampede to Timberline, Muriel Sibell Wolle, University of Colorado, Boulder, Colorado, 1949

Bonanza Trail, Muriel Sibell Wolle, Indiana University Press, Bloomington, Indiana, 1953

Chalk Creek to the Past, copyright Don Smith, 1959

Colorado's Century of Cities, Don and Jean Griswold, copyright Griswold, Mazulla, 1958

Salida Daily Mail, May 7, 1943

Salida Daily Mail, July 8, 1943

Salida Mountain Mail, June 12, 1943

Rocky Mountain News, article by Jack Foster, June 12, 1958

and interviews and correspondence with

Tony and Roy Stark, and Annabelle Ward of St. Elmo

Mrs. Frank Fielding of Nathrop

Mrs. Ella Carson of Buena Vista

Judge Harry McGinnis of Salida

Ted Jacobs of Salida

Joe Stewart of Stewart's Mortuary, Salida

Mr. and Mrs. R. F. Dickinson of Salida

Lowery Englebright of Tincup

Steve Frazee of Salida

Al Armstrong

Mr. and Mrs. Murneane of Salida

Mrs. Lily Williams of Orland, California

George Douthit of Colorado Springs

Dr. R. A. Hoover of Salida

Mrs. Thomas Miller of St. Elmo

Edna McKeage

and others

Sky Pilots over the Rockies

There are many and varied approaches to deity. The rough paths of those who travel the road to glory often intersect. So it was with the "itinerant three" in Colorado. Although their ideas were divergent, their goals were convergent. Despite irreconcilable creeds, they had in common an unwavering faith, both in their church and the territory, a burning zeal, an organizational ability, a stubborn determination, and all the requisites of the frontiersman.

On snowshoes, by muleback, and by buggy, "Father" John Dyer, the Reverend Sheldon Jackson, and Bishop Joseph Machebeuf all came to be indentified with the foundations of religion in the raw Colorado territory. They were easily recognized, each with his characteristic mode of travel.

Individual as were their creeds, so must be their stories

First of the trio into the territory came Father Machebeuf in 1860. Born in France, August 11, 1812, Projectus Joseph Machebeuf came to America at the age of twenty-seven. His early church career was established in Ohio and led to Canada, New Mexico, Utah, and eventually to his becoming the first Bishop of Denver. His immediate concept of America was of the vastness of his field. He came to an early recognition of the impossible scope of his problems but he said, "Help me to thank God that I have more work than I can do."

In New Orleans, en route to New Mexico, Father Machebeuf joined Father Lamy, Vicar Apostolic of New Mexico. There was bitterness and opposition to foreigners in the southwest, but Father Machebeuf won his new people with love. He felt an affinity for them because his language and theirs had similar undertones. He was so strongly identified with the Mexican

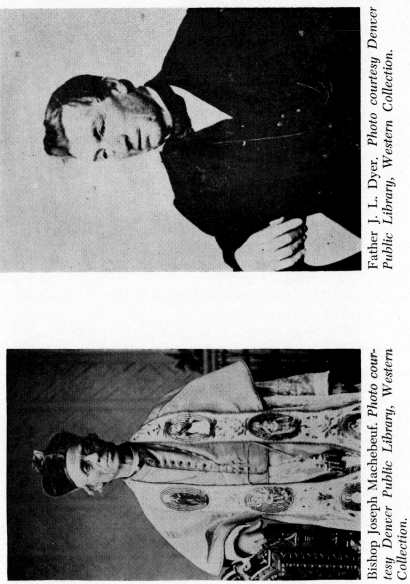

Father J. L. Dyer. *Photo courtesy Denver Public Library, Western Collection.*

Bishop Joseph Machebeuf. *Photo courtesy Denver Public Library, Western Collection.*

people and their historic church that he came to be a large figure in Willa Cather's *Death Comes for the Archbishop*. There followed a near decade with Father Machebeuf as the shepherd of a scattered flock. He left his mark indelibly upon the New Mexican scene. With the rush to the gold fields, came the call to every faith, and Father Machebeuf was chosen for the Pikes Peak country. With Reverend John Raverdy, selected for his youth, good health, and persevering qualities, in 1860 the priest made his way to the old parish at Conejos in the San Luis Valley. At Pueblo they found the Mexican families were seeing a priest for the first time. Marriages were blessed and children baptized. In Colorado City they met their first gold seekers. The pair set up their tent and offered the clean oblation for the first time in the history of the American settlement of Colorado. In Denver they selected a vacant lot, counted their flock of fewer than ten Catholic families and eyed the three thousand souls obviously unsaved.

There were foundations already laid for a church, but work had stopped for lack of funds and leadership. Father Machebeuf supplied both, and dipped into his own pocket to assist toward the completion of a building. The plain structure, 30x46, had a roof in time for Christmas mass and the canvas kept out the wind from the windows and mellowed the light. Christmas greens hid the rough walls and added decoration. Father Machebeuf added a wooden shed, 12x30, for the parish house.

In this territory he was elevated to bishop and there were some who felt he was not qualified for the position. They felt that they had "lost a missionary and had not gained a bishop." And certainly he was, to the day of his death, the missionary at heart. His early church expansion extended to Arapahoe City, Golden City, and Central City. He crossed all the ranges, for his territory reached to Santa Fe. He made frequent trips to New Mexico to pick up materials for the sacraments and even went into Mormon territory in Utah.

Every community retains certain anecdotes of the valiant missionary. In Central City they recall that he performed the marriage ceremony for the first white woman who had entered the district. He was not averse to using the facilities of any building in order to bring spiritual benefits to his people, but he demanded that his congregation accept their obligations and establish their own churches within a reasonable time. On one such occasion, in Central City, when the people seemed lackadaisically willing to continue in borrowed quarters, he decided on drastic action and at the close of the mass he ordered the doors locked and the keys he placed in his vestments. He declared firmly that no one would be allowed to leave the building until the question of the church was settled. A "free will" offering was taken and pledges were made.

People in many of the towns always recognized him by his little old square buggy that came bumping over the hill. Besides its fiery little priest, it contained the portable altar and the sacred symbols of the church. In St. Elmo, the bishop held service in a bunkhouse, using a high-backed chair, and when the schoolhouse was built in 1882 the services were transferred there. When he could not make the trip over the hill, Mother Stark said her prayers before the little altar in her bedroom.

Father Machebeuf inaugurated the Manitou Mission in Colorado City in the home of John Langmayer. In 1873, a service was held in Colorado Springs in the Reading Room and a church building was soon erected on the corner of Sawatch and Rio Grande. The name was St. Anne's, but in 1887 was changed to St. Mary's.

There was a wiriness about this little figure and an irresistible attraction because of his constant alertness and unwavering dedication. Willa Cather said of her Father Joseph Valliant:

> . . . one of the first things a stranger decided upon meeting Father Joseph was that the Lord had made few uglier men. He was short, skinny, bowlegged from a life on horseback, and his countenance had little to recommend it but kindliness and vivacity. He looked old. ["Machebeuf was gray before he was sixty and in early years as wrinkled as a man of eighty."] His skin was hardened and seamed by exposure to weather in a bitter climate, his neck scrawny and wrink-

led like an old man's. A bold, blunt-tipped nose, positive
chin, a very large mouth, the lips thick and succulent but
never loose, never relaxed, always stiffened by effort or working with excitement. His hair, sunburned to the shade of dry
hay, had originally been tow-colored. . . . There was noth-
in his outer case to suggest the fierceness and fortitude
and fire of the man . . . everybody believed in Father Valliant
—homely, real, persistent, with the driving power of a dozen
men in his poorly-built body.

This was a perfect description of Father Machebeuf.

He often claimed, "Providence has always given me strength
in proportion to my work." It was a standing joke that he would
never die in bed. He was a human dynamo, constantly on the
move, all energy, activity, and business. He knew full well the
meaning of righteous indignation. There was no vengeful feeling
in his make-up but justice was tempered with kindness. His education was adequate but not profound. He felt more at home
with the poor and humble. He dreaded society and pompous
people. He knew his theology and could preach a good, practical
sermon. He spoke and wrote English well, but felt more at home
in Spanish or his native French. He had the simple approach
his people needed. Not the least of his accomplishments, he
could fry a good steak on a campfire.

Bishop Machebeuf did not delve in politics, but he openly
attacked women's suffrage, and deplored "short-haired women
and long-haired men."

He felt the importance of education for the young people in
the new Territory and schools within his church jurisdiction were
of prime importance to him.

Among the Bishop's accomplishments in his lifetime were his
financial investments, made not for his own gain, but for his
church. He was not always successful and he was a miserable
bookkeeper. He could have amassed a personal fortune, but he
"had too much prudence to indulge in needless waste and too
little reckless daring to be a speculator." He came to Denver
without a church or a roof over his own head. When he died,
biographers said, ". . . the diocese of Denver could name 64

257

priests, 102 churches and chapels, nine academies, one college, one orphanage, one house of refuge, ten hospitals and over three thousand children in Catholic Schools."

In his declining years a series of accidents dogged at his heels and one by one took their toll of his failing energy. A broken leg slowed his speed and made him lame. A broken wheel on his buggy caused still another injury; a fall on the rocks near Lake City and a severe accident when a wagon wheel caught on the Denver streetcar tracks, all conspired to defeat the wiry little priest. Time and again, the flaming sword obstructed the path of a prophet who was loath to accept the order to halt.

Bishop Machebeuf took refuge in his last illness at St. Vincent's Orphanage in Denver, one of the many organizations which he had founded. Here he received the last sacraments from Bishop Matz and the final blessing of the church was given. He died on July 10, 1889.

The valiant priest had become so much a part of the church scene that it was as if a landmark had fallen. He had truly earned the title, "The Apostle of Colorado."

John L. Dyer was born the same year as Bishop Machebeuf, on March 16, 1812, in Ohio. His was the Methodist camp-meeting conversion and he was never ordained. Dyer was a layman, but he counted his authority from God. He was a little late getting started and seemed forever to have to make up for the delay. He must have felt akin to Job, for sorrow and misfortune were his constant companions. He knew the loss of a wife and baby, and the crippling of a favorite son. Tragedy did not defeat him, but only served to slow him down. He knew that his true mission was in the raw country to the west. His son, Joshua, accompanied him to Minnesota, where they sampled the hardships of circuit riding.

Father Dyer said, "I made up my mind to see Pikes Peak." At the age of forty-nine, with only $14.75 in his pockets, he set out with full trust that the Lord would provide. He rested briefly in Denver, having walked from Omaha, Nebraska. Denver, he described as

> being nearly all on the west side, only a few brick houses on Blake Street; and Wm. N. Byers, *[Rocky Mountain News]* on neither side, as his building was in the middle of Cherry Creek, attached to the lower side of the bridge.

Going on toward the mountains, Reverend Dyer followed the excitement to the Phillips Lode at Buckskin Joe. Here he found that sermons were scarce. Only one regular service had been held, and Brother Howbert had selected a shady spot outdoors for a service, with logs for seats. He asked for those to come forward and join the church, "to form a class," but since no one volunteered, John Dyer, himself, came forward and joined all over again. He said:

> As no move was made, I arose, and said I had often beat up for volunteers, and always felt like joining over again, and now was my time. . . .

More than twenty others followed his example. This formed the first class high up in the mountains. The once-a-week stage to Denver from Buckskin Joe sold its tickets for ten dollars each way. Ten dollars was hard to come by, so Father Dyer hit upon the rough economy of saving his ten by walking the hundred miles in two days and a half. He felt if you can't make it you have to save it.

Father Dyer dressed the part of a miner for these treks into Denver. On one occasion he took an unobtrusive back seat in the Denver service where Colonel J. M. Chivington was preaching, "in his military suit, with belt, bowie knife and revolver." Dyer's presence was soon noted and he was called forth to preach. He led a prayer, and declared, "It was always best for me to whet my own scythe. I will say nothing about the effort, only that I forgot about the poor clothes."

In his own mountain territory Dyer made the rounds of the gulches and mining camps, interrupting the card games to announce that preaching would be held at his cabin, couldn't they cease their games for a few minutes? His cabin he considered the

Father Dyer's Church at Breckenridge.

Presbyterian Church, Lake City.

best place to hold meetings. The interior decoration consisted of gunny sacks for carpeting and two copies of the *Northwestern Christian Advocate* on the table. His early circuit covered two-week appointments in such areas as Park City and Breckenridge.

Winter brought necessity for the contrivance of a pair of skis which he called snowshoes, Norwegian style, nine to eleven feet in length, with which he forever after was identified.

The scanty collections in the plate had to be eked out by whatever means were at hand. Father Dyer became a mailman, express agent, salesman for the *Rocky Mountain News*, and part-time prospector, in addition to his pastoral duties. One time he attempted to deliver a sack of flour to a customer for a small fee and since there was no horse available at the moment, the ingenious preacher fastened a pack saddle on a cow. But the cow rebelled and the flour was scattered to the wind, whereupon Father Dyer decided to dispense only the spiritual bread of the Gospels and leave the daily bread delivery to others.

War brought increasing disasters to his family. Joshua, the oldest son, was a Civil War prisoner in Andersonville; the youngest came back from the war minus a foot.

In New Mexico, Father Dyer held the first Protestant church service on the Maxwell Land Grant. Here he was invading the territory of Father Machebeuf, but Dyer felt that it was good for the Catholics to have a little competition and quoted St. Paul's advice, "to provoke each other to love and good works." He had a healthy respect for the powers of the Catholic Church and for Father Machebeuf in particular. Dyer's ready wit was brought into play when he commented that Machebeuf,

> . . . our old priest and bishop of the Roman Catholic Church . . . was considered a great worker, and can be compared with Brother Harwood in making proselytes. Brother Harwood had the advantage, for he had a good wife to help him.

The congregation at Colorado City determined to build a church but were unable to complete the building in time for a conference which was held in June, 1867. So tents were pitched, and what was perhaps the first camp-meeting in Colorado was organized on the grounds. The entire group went to see the sights in the Garden of the Gods: ". . . it was a scene such as no Methodist conference had ever seen before."

In any part of his territory where no church building was available, Father Dyer would preach in the street, in saloons, gambling houses, and wherever he could gather a crowd. He would fearlessly proclaim the truth, and at the close of the service some self-appointed steward would pass the "hat" among the "boys." Once, at Hitchcock's store in Fairplay, he requested the owner to remove the sign advertising "Good Whiskey" and the manager replied that he would be glad to cooperate, since they were out of that kind of whisky anyway.

Father Dyer had been a widower for more than twenty years, but in November, 1870, he married Mrs. Lucinda Ranking of Douglas County. He said, "Since I could almost keep myself, I thought it was a poor woman who could not help a little." But he found what a man of his age should have known anyway, that two cannot live as cheaply as one—and his financial problems grew.

Dyer's greatest test of faith came following the murder of his lame son, Judge Elias Dyer, in Granite, Colorado, in 1875. Father Dyer was convinced that he knew who the murderers were but could get no one to assist him in seeking justice. His personal conflict was one of "alternate flashes of revenge and forgiveness." It was only in his late years that he was able to reconcile himself to allocating vengeance to the hands of the Lord, albeit somewhat grudgingly.

He took a popular and realistic view of the Indian, that he needed to be subdued and ruled by fear, and thought that easterners in their safe confines regarded the welfare of the "filthiest red-skin" as being of more importance than the well being of a decent white man.

At the age of sixty-seven he was put in charge of the Breckenridge area and still covered much of the territory on his snowshoes. Here he built a church, himself, almost single-handed.

It still stands and is called "Father Dyer's Church." Here he was constantly nagged by the lower element who persisted in stealing or "borrowing" the church organ for their dancing, and dancing to the Methodist circuit skier was an instrument of the devil and a sure road to damnation.

For a time Father Dyer lived in Denver at 712 Glenarm, and even attempted farming a little, but he was still clinging to the small, mushrooming mountain churches. He had preached in more new towns than any other man in Colorado, dead or alive, and he maintained his faith in the future of the territory to the very last. He said:

> All that the towns and cities, from Greeley to Trinidad, have to do, when they get hard up is to look to the mountains, for there the treasures are abundant and unfailing. Colorado, from north to south, from east to west, has seen her darkest days, and the Barren Plains are beginning to rejoice and blossom as the rose.

John Dyer died 1901.

In Breckenridge today, the townspeople point to the landmark of the little white steepled church and remember the genial circuit rider who built it in 1879. In summer, the services are held early, the town's women bring their mountain flowers to place back of the crude wooden cross, and Father Dyer looks on from the sidewall portrait. The services are held early so that the minister may go to Leadville to preach the eleven o'clock sermon as was the pattern of Father Dyer. He uses a car to make the trip on the paved highway.

Announcement is also made that with the coming of cold weather, the services at Breckenridge will be held in the early afternoon. It is too difficult to reach the church on icy early mornings and it is necessary to get home before the evening dark and cold set in. The residents no longer travel by snowshoe.

As soon as smoke began to fan out of Colorado chimneys, Sheldon Jackson was on hand to organize a church. This young zealot was supposedly under the direction of the Presbyterian

Sheldon Jackson Memorial Chapel, Fairplay.

Sheldon Jackson. *Photo courtesy Presbyterian Historical Society.*

Mission Board, but the board couldn't keep up with him. By the time they had ordered him to a new territory, the chances were he had been there, performed his services, and headed for greener pastures, leaving a trail of new Presbyterian churches in his wake. It was disconcerting to the board, but they were too far away and too entangled in formality; besides, this man seemed particularly capable of solving his own problems in the manner in which frontier matters had to be settled. The current was swift, and there was no time to write home for help.

The background of this earnest Presbyterian was a distinguished one. He was born May 18, 1834, in Minneville, New York, and was dedicated from the first by his parents, "as surely as Samuel was dedicated by Hannah." There was never any question in his mind, nor in his parents' minds but that he had been given to the Lord. His education was a matter of compulsion with his family, and he was graduated from Union College and Princeton Theological School. He was a sober-minded young man who gave close attention to his duties. His was no camp-meeting conversion, but his faith was a matter of ever-presence and as closely allied to living as breathing. He could not recall a time when he did not believe in Jesus and seek to honor Him. Jackson's main purpose in life was to win souls. He was licensed to preach in 1857, in Albany, New York.

Sheldon Jackson's first mission work was with the Choctaw Indians in October, 1858, and gradually his movement was to the west with the moving population. So the year of 1870 found him in charge of a vast territory as Superintendent of Missions from Mexico to Canada, Nevada to Nebraska. He established the *Rocky Mountain Presbyterian* in Denver, then a town of 4000. His first tour brought him to Colorado City, where he canvassed house to house for Presbyterians and tried to obtain a Methodist building for a meeting. A Mr. Irvin offered the use of his house twenty-five miles away, for services. The church was organized with five members, and four years later transferred its membership to Colorado Springs. The present membership of that congregation is close to 3000 members.

The Jackson family home was established in Denver for eleven years, but Sheldon Jackson was seldom in it. Doors were open to visitors and Mrs. Jackson presided as the capable hostess. On occasion she filled in as a teacher, such times as she wasn't washing, ironing, cooking, cleaning, mending, and changing the sheets in the guest room.

In 1871, Jackson organized the Synod of Colorado. Operating out of Denver, he went to such places as Gregory Gulch, George-town, Blackhawk, Idaho Springs, Golden, and Greeley. In Greeley, the thrifty, intelligent moral tone was perfect soil for Presbyterian seed. There, too, he built a lasting and influential church. Although the family home was established in Denver, the death of a baby daughter revealed the secret that "back home" meant east, and he took the child there for burial.

The roving Presbyterian took the stagecoach to Fairplay in 1872, where he organized a small group of Christian people and where he organized the church which is now called "The Sheldon Jackson Memorial Chapel." The one-room frame building was dedicated in 1874.

Jackson played an active part in the founding of the Presbyterian Church at Lake City, the first church on the Western Slope, which was dedicated November 19, 1876, five months to the day from the time of organization. Jackson accompanied the Reverend George Darley to Ouray for the founding of the second church on the Western Slope, in 1877. Darley said of him, "Sheldon Jackson never growled no matter how hard the trip. He had pluck."

In his book, *Pioneering in the San Juans,* George Darley tells about the great gift of the bell to the Lake City church. He wrote:

> After our church was built in Lake City, it being the first one on the Pacific slope in Colorado, saint and sinner expressed themselves as being very proud of it . . . . Still, one important thing was lacking. Nowhere in Colorado, west of the Sierra Madre range of mountains, was there a bell of any kind for public use larger than a dinner bell. One day, to my great joy, Mr. Theodore Little, Jr., informed me that his father . . .

had a bell for our church and would "pay the freight." When a man said, "pay the freight" in those days, it often meant a great deal more than the first cost. The bell was freighted in a wagon across two great mountain ranges —the Sangre de Cristo and the Sierra Madre—also over the Continental Divide. The bell was presented to our church in 1877.

In telling about freighting charges Darley maintained that in some areas even needles cost ten times what they did "back east because freight was so high."

He went on to maintain, "The Presbyterians built the first and second churches on the Pacific Slope in Colorado."

It may have been the knowledge of Mrs. Jackson's ability as a help-meet that made her husband aware of the latent power of women in church affairs. He increased their interest by organizing ladies' boards of missions.

Through the columns of *Rocky Mountain Presbyterian*, Jackson was able to reach a large group of interested individuals.

Tradition has always delegated a hand in hand relationship of the Presbyterian clergy with education. Jackson realized the necessity of this association and the fact that sometimes the school had to come first. At one time, he requested from his board a teacher to go into the homes of the Indians and to open up the way for the ministers. The reply of his board was that they did not have a cent to devote to employing missionary teachers, but they added, "We can send you a preacher, though," to which he wrote back, "They won't come to hear a preacher, send us a teacher."

The Presbyterian women formed a group to work for funds for just this kind of thing.

Jackson, like Dyer and Machebeuf, fell in love with Colorado and had unbounded faith in its future. He conducted several tours of notable men and women to show them the condition of the region and a fertile field for his church. No detail was too small for the attention of his orderly Presbyterian mind, and no number of converts too small for a nucleus of a new church. In Idaho Springs his congregation was founded with thirteen members; in Colorado Springs, eight; and in Golden, only four. In Missoula, Montana, he reached a new low—and in this case there were only two gathered together, a freighter named Cunningham who was there for a one night stand and was made the ruling elder, and a Methodist woman who had quarreled with her pastor and was in bad repute with the Methodist community. The freighter left town the next morning after unloading his freight, and never went near the Presbyterian Church of Missoula again. Needless to say, the church died aborning, but was later reorganized in 1876.

Such energy could not be confined within narrow boundaries. The story of Jackson is not complete without recalling his government appointment as Superintendent of Education in Alaska, in 1885. He is best remembered there for introducing Siberian reindeer for food, and it is recalled that he went to Lapland and Norway to purchase reindeer for the herd.

In all his varied experiences, Jackson, too, was remembered for his unconventional modes of transportation. His one million miles of journeying includes such facilities as

> . . . the neighbor's wagon or cutter, by rail, stagecoach, buckboard, army ambulance, lumber wagon, mule team, oxcart, bronco, reindeer sledge, freight, construction train, steamship, dugout, launch, canoe, revenue cutter, war vessel, schooner, and cattle ship.

When all these failed he resorted to shank's mare. If a stagecoach or horse failed to carry him into the mountains, he relied on the sure-footed burro. He said, "We hired our passage into Ouray on the same kind of animal that the Savior made His triumphal entry into Jerusalem."

Sheldon Jackson died in 1908, "the greatest little man in America," a true "pioneer of the cross."

SOURCES

Pioneering in the San Juans, George Darley, Fleming H. Revell Co., New York, N.Y., 1899

Life of Bishop Machebeuf, W. J. Howlett, Register College of Journalism, Denver, Colorado, 1954

The Snowshoe Itinerant, John L. Dyer, Cranston & Stowe, Cincinnati, Ohio, 1890

They Seek a Country, The American Presbyterians, E. Gaius Jackson, Slosser, Macmillan Company, New York, N. Y., 1955

Presbyterian Panorama, Board of Christian Education, Clifford M. Drury, PHD, Presbyterian Church in U. S. of America, Philadelphia, Pa., 1952

The Big Divide, David Lavender, Doubleday & Co., Garden City, N. Y., 1948

Death Comes for the Archbishop, Willa Cather, Alfred A. Knopf, New York, N.Y., 1926

Colorado, American Guide Series, Hastings House, New York, N. Y., 1941

Guide to the Colorado Ghost Towns and Mining Camps, Perry Eberhart, Sage Books, Denver, Colorado, 1959

Stampede to Timberline, Muriel Sibell Wolle, University of Colorado, Boulder, Colorado, 1949

Tales of the Colorado Pioneers, Alice Polk Hill, Pierson & Gardner, Denver, Colorado, 1884

Colorado Magazine, J. N. Hillhouse, "The Sheldon Jackson Memorial Church at Fairplay," Vol. 23, Sept., 1946, page 5

Colorado Springs Gazette, January 3, 1874

and interviews with

June Pauline Smith

Mrs. C. E. Stock

Jean Strang

Horsefeathers and Applesauce,
The Story of Bishop Frank Hamilton Rice

"Horsefeathers and applesauce," thought Bishop Frank Hamilton Rice, "one of the biggest problems in the world is man's inability to say no," and the bishop came to this conclusion long before *Oklahoma* made a hit of "I'm Just a Gal That Cain't Say No." "The trouble," he decided, "is that people need help to say no. Let's form a club, with a dollar membership which will give them something tangible to show they have the right to say it. Besides, we need the dollars!" It wasn't a bad gimmick, but you wouldn't understand the situation at all unless you knew the bishop personally.

It was in the "Bible-belt" in 1881 that Frank Rice was born in the Presbyterian parsonage and by all the rules of that era should have grown up a conservative member of his denomination. Somehow his genes were confused. About the only qualification which he was destined to retain of that staunch denomination was a certain Scotch tenacity for his own convictions. He was a serious boy and it is said that "in his youth he was tortured with what he felt were pious frauds. He cried, prayed, and cursed over questions until he was seventeen." Then he set out, without the company of Sancho Panza, to try to right the world.

Already he began to stray from home base by looking with an eye toward the Methodist ministry rather than his own. "He came to college with a conservative world view, but he was shocked by the teaching he received in the Epworth University of Oklahoma City." Natural rebellion and empty pockets caused him to leave school and to enter the loan and insurance business. Later, taking a position as a parole clerk in the Oklahoma State Penitentiary, Rice laid foundations for early insight into the problems of the unfortunate and the underprivileged. During a prison break he became a human shield for the convicts. The incident whetted an insatiable appetite for the white light of publicity which was to be his beacon to the day of his death.

Frank Hamilton Rice, Bishop of the Liberal Church. *Photo courtesy of Ira J. Taylor Library, Iliff School of Theology.*

Denver beckoned in 1915, where he again sought publicity, this time as a solicitor for the Colorado Prison Association. His arrival was unheralded, but Denver soon became aware that a Don Quixote had come to tilt their windmills and their mores. Stuffed shirts were due to be unstuffed. Well defined patterns were headed for change, insult, and explosion. Rice became employed as editor of *Colorado Manufacturer and Consumer*. He settled his family in a modest house, put the letter from the church, back home, into the Trinity Methodist Episcopal Church, which was routine procedure enough. Here he laid claim to the largest boys' Sunday School class in Denver and accepted his neighborhood responsibility as a scoutmaster. So far all was well in the accepted pattern —but not for long.

Later, the family moved to South Denver, transferring their church membership to the Grant Avenue Methodist Episcopal Church where he again accepted responsibility by becoming sponsor of the Epworth League, solid and respectable. On occasion he satisfied that gnawing hunger to hear his own voice by appearing in the pulpit to speak on church advertising as a means of increasing church influence. Record does not say, but it is safe to guess, he undoubtedly exceeded his time limit, but was probably forgiven because of his innate fire which, up until this time, had been construed as enthusiasm.

Then came the moment, during the absence of the pastor, when he could not resist the urge to light a fuse by suggesting that the church sponsor weekly dances for young people, as a means of combatting the influence of the public dance hall. Teen-age record hops had not been conceived at that time, particularly not under the sponsorship of the church. This was Rice's first windmill. It fell on him.

The next Sunday, the minister threatened to resign if the hypnotized congregation followed the piper's tune, and Rice was given the invitation to relinquish his sponsorship of the League. Like Socrates, he was accused of corrupting youth. He was as annoying as the classic gadfly. Poison might have been considered, but it belonged to an outmoded era and the means would have to be less literal than hemlock.

Rice was not easily defeated and brought the matter to the status of a public debate. His opposition was to come from the Ministerial Alliance. The Rev. James E. Davis of the Central Christian Church opposed Mr. Rice. Arrangements were: if the Alliance won, the offering was to be used in an effort to improve conditions with reference to public dances and Rice was to stop his agitation. If Rice won, church dances were to be allowed. There is no reliable record as to how the referees were to be chosen. Rice was defeated. Whether the decision was honest or not, no one knows. Rice did not stop his agitation according to agreement, but carried his story to the printed page and local papers made the most of it. He advertised in the *Denver Post* and published a dance edition of *Go To Church* publication. Several thousand were circulated in the city. He was relieved of his publishing position with the *Ministerial and Church Directory* and forbidden the use of names of members of the Alliance. One could hardly call this the birth of a crusader, but he had certainly reached the adolescent stage of rebellion. Crusading became his central motivation.

From here on Rice's career took on color and fire, sometimes reeking of brimstone. Never one to hide his light under a bushel, he began building bonfires and they were visible for distances and at times warming and, again, destructive.

Realizing he was in no sense orthodox in either belief or behavior, Rice became aware of his necessary separation from the orthodox church. He had no sympathy for red-tape, or for any form without meaning. He stripped everything to the core and operated with a broadax rather than a scalpel. To many people, upon first scrutiny, he appeared a buffoon. Upon closer examination, one could see that he employed every bit of ridicule, imitation, and caricature in his power to show up the insincerity of outward forms. He cracked the shells and examined the kernels for worms. He was merciless toward the powerful and merciful toward the helpless. He was often wrong and more often damnably right, both of which were uncomfortable and unforgiveable.

With these convictions, on May 22, 1922, Rice filed an application for the incorporation of the "Big Church, Inc." with the Secretary of State. This was refused because of legal excuses.

273

The purpose of the organization was "to live successfully, to meet economic and religious conditions of the age." Members were to be encouraged to take daily baths, favor the regular use of beer, rum, alcohol, brandy, whisky, gin, ale, porter, wine, malt and other compounds which are good for health, sustaining, and beverage for purpose as sacraments.

This time Rice transferred his membership to the Grace Methodist Episcopal Church. Now he felt called upon to espouse the unpopular cause of labor unions. He was invited to speak before the Denver Trades and Labor Assembly. In choosing his subject he abandoned Prudence in favor of Publicity by announcing that his subject would be "Rational Sex Ethics." The storm of protest whirled his windmills even faster. It was voted that Rice should never again be granted the privilege of the floor in that assembly.

Three factors and a possible fourth now drove him into his next move. His taste for publicity, his economic straits, his intense resentment of opposition from organized churches, and a sincere desire to help the downtrodden all combined to crystallize his determination to form his own church. The Liberal Church was incorporated on February 23, 1923.

The unsuspecting officials allowed him to incorporate both a church and a university and granted him all the power invested in the two. The church was incorporated under the laws of eleven states. Any authority not included in the legal document he assumed, by divine right, as coming from God himself. Had the state legislators realized what a buggy ride they were slated for, they would have found some loophole to have stopped him. As it was, they were committed—and the rest of the committing was done by Rice.

(Services were held in ensuing years in Liberal Howe Hall, on California Street, and in the Windsor Hotel; then he moved to 1438 Sixteenth Street, the basement of the Inter-Ocean Hotel; the final meeting place was Labor Hall in the Loop Building, 1450 Lawrence Street.)

He called a meeting of the board and had himself elevated to Bishop of the church. At a public ceremony the following Sunday, he had himself consecrated and began the work of the church

274

which he carried on for twenty-two years. He dreamed of a large following of the unchurched and of a building to be erected at South Logan and Virginia Streets, where religion and science might meet and be taught. But this dream was never to be realized. His beginnings were in the slums and his ending was to be there. And perhaps Life needed him there.

Rice's doctrinal position for his church came gradually to very simple principles. "Our principles: We believe in the United States. . . . Our Religion is to do good." This statement was put on all letterheads, also the statement that no charge was made for funeral services or the solemnizing of marriages. His acknowledged intention was "to help folks keep themselves out of hospitals, jails and insane asylums and to assist them to live here and now and let the universal law of nature and God care for the future life."

The American creed was adopted as part of the Liberal Church creed, and at one time Rice asked the president of Iliff School of Theology to prepare a set of doctrines for the church which would be in harmony with the findings of modern science. But the request was refused. He finally drew up seven articles of religion—

1. to do good; 2. to learn how to live; 3. to seek the truth; 4. to practice the Golden Rule; 5. to act according to common sense; 6. to try to be thrifty, industrious, saving, and constructively employed; 7. to rationally and intelligently attempt to be healthy, happy, successful, and to assist others to do the same.

Official literature of the church was declared to be: King James Version of the Bible; Wells, *Outline of History; A Receivership for Civilization*, Duren J. H. Ward; *How to Live*, rules for healthy living based on modern science by Life Extension Institution, Indiana; *The Literary Digest*, this being a bible of current events; and *The Denver Post*, "America's greatest, most democratic and fascinating daily newspaper, a friend and protector of the Masses."

Rice insisted upon there being no tax, no dues, no charge, no collections at any service of the church and that the attendance of the members be regulated by their own convenience. No wonder Bishop Rice was destined to look jealously at Alma White's Temple in later years, to know the disappointment of having no church building on the corner of Virginia and South Logan Streets, to be forever consigned to Denver's skid row, and to leave at his death assets amounting to a desk and a chair and a typewriter. Temples and material manifestations are built on taxes and dues, collections and pledges, compulsions and budgets. In these matters he was impractical and visionary.

The runaway bishop was not gentle like his literary counterpart. He was an impatient, impetuous, and sometimes bitter Don Quixote. Rice was fearless in his approach to what he felt to be wrong and had no hesitancy in attacking the Ku Klux Klan as mob law. He offered a course in the methods of sex education for parents of adolescents and younger children. But sex education was frowned upon in 1923. A prenatal clinic and lectures on health and birth control were scheduled, but few women attended and few men cared. Psychoanalysis, the needs of farmers, political issues, did not escape his attention in the lecture field. His fervor extended into other areas of education, law, politics, and the moral aspects of euthanasia. Nothing was sacred. He attacked fallacies wherever they reared their heads. Politics offered a broad target for his jibes. Rice ran for mayor of Denver in 1923 on the Independent ticket but was defeated. Later he repeated his efforts, this time being slated for governor on the Andy Gump ticket. The attorney general ruled the ticket out but a petition with one hundred names then forced the inclusion of Rice's name on the ballot. In the year 1930 he filed as candidate for United States senator on a Liberal ticket. After one election, the board of directors of his own church seemed to sense a rising opposition to his sensationalism and forbade him to run for any political office again. So with his customary reaction, he defied the board and filed as a candidate for all offices, including that of dog-catcher.

To attract Denver's attention he stood on his head—and rocked the city on its heels. Prohibition was one of the balloons he punctured. At one time he applied for ten gallons of wine to be used for communion. Application was refused, whether on principle or quantity is not known. Upon refusal of application he tried to resign as bishop, "What's the use of being a bishop if you can't

276

dabble in sacraments or sacramental wine?" A direct parallel to *Green Pastures* and Noah's firmament! His resignation was refused. With his usual procedure of giving the windmill an extra whirl, he adopted Pabst's Blue Ribbon beer as a sacramental drink with the idea that Whistle and orange drink could be substituted as sacrificial drinks in the event of a shortage of beer—anticipating a dearth of Whistle, he decreed that distilled water could be used, to be turned into miraculous wine by Christ, and then into blood. It was reported that buttermilk had been served in Communion. Conservatives shuddered.

A barber chair was part of the church equipment. His congregation consisted chiefly of men. The surroundings and the creed held little appeal for women. In order to combat this situation he at one time held a lottery at a service at which time a new hat would be given to some woman as a prize. But Bishop Rice was a man with no understanding that a woman does not like a hat drawn in a lottery. Such a hat has no personal meaning and is doubtful as to price tag or label and draws no envious glances. Although completely unaware, there were some things the bishop didn't know. Women and their foibles were a couple of them. According to feminine psychology, a hat should be more expensive than one can afford—entirely devoid of logic and altogether a heady concoction! It should also be selected for a man but not by one! There were no women present at the bishop's service to claim the lottery hat. He had no aversion to raffling within the church and at one time raffled off the down payment on a Flint automobile at a regular service. How the second payment was to be made was not his concern.

In a protest against unintelligible and mechanical prayers, he introduced a practice of praying by punching the keys on an adding machine, often stating that the God of Mathematics would one day translate the meaning.

Rice was conscious that the downtrodden and underprivileged were often inarticulate and with no opportunity to speak or to express themselves. He often held meetings to rectify that lack. A few rules held forth for each meeting. One general rule was that the first speaker should be able to show a certificate of dismissal from an insane asylum. This may have been a mark of distinction. Many of us cannot prove that we are sane.

If a speaker rambled on too long, Rice would step forward and offer him a flower, or tactfully place a screen in front of him. If worse came to worse, he would have the offender thrown out bodily, and then he would give him a glass of buttermilk to assuage his feelings.

One gimmick to increase church attendance was the plan to serve a free lunch at the close of Sunday services; this may or may not have been the forerunner of the present coffee hour.

Whether because or in spite of these eccentricities, his claimed membership for the general movement, which extended far beyond the local boundaries, was a modest 185,000. At one time when church attendance seemed to be dwindling, Rice obtained Mayor Stapleton, Professor Longacre, Senator Garwood, and other notables as speakers. When they failed to draw a crowd, he declared that "the activities at Elitch's Gardens would be the official church activities for the summer."

Among prominent people who became members of his cult, either by their own volition or by "command performance," were Damon Runyan, Gene Fowler, Forbes Parkhill, Babe Ruth, Lee Casey, and Governor Billy Adams. Not to be overlooked, at a later date, was the illustrious name of P. T. Barnum, declared the first saint of the church. William Jennings Bryan did not escape his attention and was promptly canonized "for the impetus he gave to evolutionary hypothesis." One chronicler questioned whether Rice had ever got around to canonizing Eve! The only high priest of the Liberal Church was a harmlessly insane member of the House of David.

The bishop boasted, "We have a bigger percentage of convicted 'vags' and a bigger percent of insanity than any other church in the United States." In another connection he included I.W.W.'s and common-law married people with a claimed insane of 500 in the membership.

It was in 1934 that Rice attracted wide attention when he incorporated his famous "Horsefeathers and Applesauce Society, Scientific." The avowed purpose of this society was stated in this way, on a printed card, "The above-named charter member is hereby authorized to exhibit this membership certificate to any person for the purpose of making it more explicit and clear why said member at this time desires to say, 'No'."

One insurance company office in Denver took out memberships for all their agents. It was suggested, but never materialized, that members of Congress be candidates for membership. The cost of membership was one dollar and it is said "the state of Arkansas alone had 1,000 memberships."

Perhaps the most startling factor in the whole career of the renegade bishop was the amazing manner in which he conferred degrees. Since the church had also been incorporated as a university, he had the legal right to grant any degrees authorized by such institutions. The only exception was Doctor of Medicine. With a lavish hand he created such honors as CSM (Common Sense Man) and CSW (Common Sense Woman) and he hoped to confer one million degrees if he could find the proper candidates. He almost did. *Denver Commercial* refused to run publicity on the ground that it contained religious matter of a sensational nature. It is said that hundreds of degrees were given away in this fashion with no scholastic requirement yet within the law. Rice claimed divine authority, also, because the God of Modern Science had appeared in his office and told him to confer these degrees, and who can gainsay such appearances when the God of Divinity was presumed to have made other earthly manifestations?

The ease with which one could secure such titles was indicated by one interviewer from Iliff who was offered a degree of Doctor of Philosophy with no requisite of study nor expenditure of money. The procedure was simply that Rice would dictate the form and sign it, then the notary public would attest the seal and his signature. The seals of the Liberal Church were made a part of the document and all that was required to make this legal was for the recipient to sign on the line entitled *Received* and then file the certificate with the proper authorities at the courthouse, and for this a charge of seventy-five cents was made.

At one time the bishop estimated he had made some 4,300 ordinations of ministers, and indicated there may have been 200

Ordination Certificate and Degree

THE LIBERAL CHURCH INC.

FOUNDED AT DENVER COLORADO FEB 13, 1915 BY FRANK H. RICE

Our Principles: We Believe in the United States — Our Religion is to do Good

By virtue of my Legal and Divine authority cited and shown hereon

I hereby confer upon

Robert L. Ripley

Founder of Believe It or Not!

the degrees of

Doctor of Divinity and Universal Fact Finding Doctor

By the same authority, I hereby Commission, Empower, License and Ordain Robert L. Ripley, Founder of "Believe It or Not!" Prelatical Bishop in and for The Liberal Church, Incorporated.

By the same authority also, the Diocese of "Believe It or Not!" (International) is duly Created and Established, and the said Robert L. Ripley is fully Empowered to have complete and infallible control over said Diocese. Amen.

July 4, A. D. 1933.

Bishop Frank H. Rice

President, Liberal Church, Inc.

Honorary degree granted by Frank Rice to Robert L. Ripley, founder of "Believe It Or Not." *Photo courtesy Ira J. Taylor Library, Iliff School of Theology.*

or 300 more than this, but that it was not always possible to keep records straight when you ordained 30 to 60 at a time.

He said, "Why go to Iliff for four years when I can *give* you a degree?" Iliff noticed no appreciable decline in enrollment, however!

Among the multitudinous array of degrees one of the outstanding ones was the ordination certificate awarded to Robert Ripley. It read, "By virtue of my legal and divine authority cited and shown hereon, I hereby confer upon Robert L. Ripley, founder of Believe It Or Not, the degree of Doctor of Divinity and Universal Fact Finding Doctor."

At one time he paid a hopeless derelict fifty cents to tack pictures from *Life* magazine all over a wall. On the completion of the task the bishop awarded the vagrant the degree Master of Arts. The man had a hundred copies of the document printed and notaried and mailed to all of his friends, including Roosevelt, who acknowledged it.

An alcoholic was made a Ph.D. and a director of a corporation with very impressive papers. He had come to Rice, drunk, and about to kill his wife. The bishop agreed it was a good idea and offered to accompany him. Instead, they ended up at the psychopathic hospital. But with Rice's assistance and the encouragement of the degree the man made somewhat of a comeback.

Through these citations Rice created "a hierarchy of nuts and freaks." The title of bishop was given to such important figures as Bishop of Atheism, Bishop of Righteous Hell, Bishop of Teeth and Health, Archbishop of the Bull-Pen (the member of the congregation most frequently jailed), and a Bishop of Say It With Flowers. Walt Disney's "Jiminy Cricket" was made an earthly saint and awarded a degree of Doctor of Conscience.

Finding that he could legally charter any church for $3.50, one dollar of which was for a wall certificate, Rice encouraged them in numbers. Some of the organizations went into useful mission work, such as the Church of Sane Civilization, which provided old clothing and fed thirty at a time until upwards of two hundred had been fed at noon and night.

Rice thought nothing of excommunicating three of his cardinals

281

for intolerance toward other religions. He led a march of bums to the City Council to demand their rights, and he opened a soup house on Market Street. Because church officials were exempt from vagrancy laws, he granted degrees of divinity, within his legal power, to a large number of bums. Ministers, he said, could beg without showing visible means of support.

Even animals did not escape his sympathies, and he held services for their baptism. There was room in the Liberal Church's ceremonies to include the lesser creatures. At an Easter service of his church, the sins of the congregation were placed on a scapegoat which was then turned out into the streets. This is not the only time the bishop used the symbol of the scapegoat. In fact, various public officials, such as wardens of jails, were apprehensive when he requested to hold services in their institutions, and on various occasions they stipulated that he bring no animals. One warden, cognizant of Rice's peculiarities, wrote the following letter:

> Letter to Bishop Frank H. Rice, President, Liberal Church,
> April 10, 1930
> . . . . There is, however, a rule which is strictly enforced, prohibiting any animals, other than human beings, brought into this jail. As for the adding machine, which you mention, I think I can save you considerable trouble and work by assuring you that we have such a machine here in the office. Whether or not it would serve your holy purpose, I do not know as it is a Burroughs (I do not mean burro). As I said before, animals are not permitted in jail. . . . I am sure that arrangements can be made for the service which you suggest, with the proviso, however, that no animals be brought into my institution.

Among the curious religious ceremonies which involved the use of animals was the famous one which took place at the grave of Alfred Packer, the alleged man-eater. It was in 1874 that Packer and five companions had taken a trip through the mountains in the Lake City area, despite all warnings of snow. Five bodies were found on a plateau, their flesh partly consumed, and Packer was accused of cannibalism. Because these five men, and Packer himself, had died without being absolved from their sins, Rice took it upon himself to correct the oversight. In 1940 the bishop led six men to the grave of the supposed cannibal, in Littleton cemetery, the six dressed in robes to represent Packer and his victims. Legend has it that the robes were "borrowed" without permission from the choir room of St. John's Cathedral, and the incident forgiven only after the robes had been dry-cleaned and returned. Be that as it may, the procession included a scapegoat, a white one named Angelica, and with due solemnity they proceeded to the grave of Packer where Rice said a few prayers and quoted scripture to prove that the Bible condoned cannibalism.

"In Leviticus, 26th Chapter, 29th verse, the Bible sayeth: 'Ye shall eat the flesh of your sons, and the flesh of your daughters shall ye eat.' And again in Deuteronomy, 28th chapter, 53rd to 57th verses, doth it say: 'And thou shalt eat the fruit of thine own body, the flesh of thy sons and daughters.' Again in Jeremiah and in Ezekial doth the One God proclaim his espousal of cannibalism." *Life* magazine considered the event bizarre enough to send its photographers to the scene.

In later years the incident led to a prank when a group of Denver practical jokers proceeded to print a certificate of membership in the Packer Club of Colorado. The certificate contained pictures of Packer, the Democratic donkey and the Republican elephant, and the fabled famous sentence of the Hinsdale County judge, "They was sivin Dimmycrats in Hinsdale County, but you, yah voracious, man-eatin' son of a bitch, yah et five of thim!" The stipulation for membership in the Packer Club was in the promise affixed to the signature—a promise to eliminate five New Deal Democrats.

Not all ceremonies of the Liberal Church were as elaborate as the one at Packer's grave. The entire ritual of the marriage ceremony consisted of one word, "Married." For this service he would accept no fee. Perhaps Rice felt he could afford to forego any remuneration, considering the brevity of the service.

Compassion had always been the basic creed of the Liberal Church and its founder. With the approach of the depression years Rice's trinity of food, shelter, and clothing became of supreme importance. Years before bank failures had been predicted, the bishop had stressed the necessity of providing the means of guaranteeing all bank deposits. Again the dreamer was ahead of his time. With the first tremor of insecurity Rice played a dramatic role in saving the Central Savings Bank. He took a broad view of the meaning of the word "saved." Already the mob had gathered to withdraw their accounts when the bishop pushed his way through to the window to deposit a hundred dollars, thus stopping the panic and saving the bank from closing. Where he got one hundred dollars is a moot question—probably borrowed from the bank.

The bishop was concerned with the old age pension law, and when Denver raised the tram fares he lectured in protest, though the only man to listen was a janitor to whom he paid fifty cents to do so. Often he seemed to fight alone, but where the welfare of his people was concerned, he refused to keep silent. In the depression year of 1931 his satire again raked Denver complacency with a proposal that a city ordinance be revised to permit hungry persons to eat food from garbage barrels without being charged with vagrancy.

Again he slapped the face of smugness by obtaining an elaborate funeral for a Larimer Street prostitute who had been murdered by her husband. Rice procured money and flowers by sending word around that he himself was the corpse. Truth to Rice was sometimes a means, but never a fetish. Such a notable figure as the bishop could not go to his grave unsung—so florists and undertakers outdid themselves to furnish a lavish funeral as a final tribute to a man who was often a burr under their saddles when alive. Casket, flowers, vault, and mortuary equipment were donated. Denver squirmed when the presumed corpse got up to preach the service!

Certainly the derelicts of the time became his congregation and his burden. Too often he had followed deceased members of his flock to their resting place in potter's field. So much so that he formed a resolution several years later, "It is resolved that any area of dirt where the body of a pauper lies or has rotted is holy earth and every inch of potter's field is as much consecrated ground as is every foot of Westminster Abbey or Arlington Field, or any real or alleged Holy ground. Amen."

Another section of the resolution read, "Resolved, The Liberal Church hereby forgives the sins of and assures a place in heaven for every man, woman and child whose body has or had been placed somewhere in potter's field in Denver, Colorado and if any ecclesiastic dares to question the power of this church to do so let him be and he is, hereby anathemetized and forever cursed until he can produce proof satisfactory to all scientific minds that the Liberal Church has not as much power to effect and improve the status and condition of souls as is possessed by any other ecclesiastical or official or any cultist, medicine man, or Pope, or that the prayers of the humblest member of the Liberal Church are not as effective as those of the most prominent clergymen in any other group or denomination."

To keep the desperate needs of his people foremost in the conscience of an apathetic citizenry Rice put on the garb of the clown again and again. At one time, stowing away on a train, without benefit of ticket and clothed in sack cloth (and probably ashes), he attempted a trip to California to pray for a convicted slayer. He was discovered and put off, but it made a good story, and he loved it and the pictures which went with the account. One paper carried a photograph of the bishop and his associates dressed in sugar sacks plainly bearing the letters "Great Western" across the front. All of them were smoking long black cigars.

Again the fiery bishop continued to flaunt his liberal view in the face of conservative solid citizenry. He offered to baptize the illegitimate quadruplets of an English girl and an American staff sergeant.

He could have been Anatole France's Abbe Coignard instructing the youthful Jacques Tournebroche on the proper path to Heaven: "Repent magnificently; and in order to repent magnificently you must first sin magnificently."

In spite of his gaudy tactics there were some who saw under the grease paint the tears of the clown and detected the glint of sainthood in his eyes. Among these was Henry Hough who wrote in the

285

Denver Post, "Our city has a priceless institution in Bishop Frank Rice. Long may he rave."

A child hungry and cold on the streets would be taken in, bathed, and clothed in warm clothing. Then Rice personally would go to the home to take the child and survey the needs there. For those who were desperately in need he took over the problem of soliciting help for them. If the means of delivery for a donated ton of coal were not available he would borrow a truck, a wagon, or a wheelbarrow and personally distribute it.

Rice had rented a large hall on Market Street and supplied bundles of newspaper to be used as beds. During the depression period he is said to have outwardly derided, but subtly praised, F. D. Roosevelt at a ceremony in the Garden of the Gods near Colorado Springs. The bishop stated that Roosevelt had done more damage to religion than Stalin. He said that there were fewer people in need and going hungry now than there had been and because of this they did not need religion! For this reason Roosevelt was killing the church. A Roosevelt Church of Social Justice was organized under sponsorship of the Liberal Church. All this was in keeping with his determination "to destroy metaphysical religion in favor of humanitarian."

In a lighter vein Rice prodded the slowness of legal procedure and the ham-strung inefficiency of the Supreme Court by offering a horse and buggy to the first of the "nine old men" to retire.

Rice's exhibitionism began to pall on the people and the press. His influence began to wane. Political differences following the election of 1938 made strained relations everywhere. Rice's congregation was no exception. This may have been a reason—on the other hand, it may have been the excuse—for the fifty gallons of beer with which he soothed his straying sheep.

By 1945 the bishop was noticeably showing the effects of a strenuous and ill-starred life. He had championed the cause of every down-and-outer who came to him. From nine a.m. until after midnight he often stayed, keeping a fire going in the room and cooking hamburgers and making chili. In all this time he spared himself not at all. He went home less and less and his wife and daughter, although seldom approving this sackcloth Don

Quixote, were at least passive if not understanding. They must have murmured often the old cliche, "Charity begins at home." But Rice belonged to his flock. There was a strange parallel in his life to that of many of the saints who took the vow of poverty, maybe to St. Francis himself, for he had befriended every man and every animal who needed him, and his blessing was accorded them equally.

There was a gnawing feeling growing in his crusader's mind that he had accomplished little. He became accustomed to ingratitude from those he had helped and learned to expect nothing in return. Even more depressing was his growing awareness that charity accomplishes little in rehabilitation.

At the close of his twentieth year as head of the Liberal Church, a touching self-evaluation took place. It read:

> This year is the twentieth anniversary of the Liberal Church and of my tenure as its highest officer. The good that has been done by it and me could be attributed largely to the help I have received from contributors of small sums. . . . After 20 years I display the same poverty now as I did in earlier days. I do not, like founders of cults live in a mansion. I have no guaranteed salary, nor an assessed congregation. . . . But there was One Man who founded a religion or a church who remained poor in worldly goods. He was called Jesus of Nazareth. The poverty of a founder of a church is some evidence of sincerity and of unpaid service to humanity, to the poor who cannot pay otherwise than in non-negotiable manifestations of gratitude, and if that poverty continues for 20 years, it speaks louder that services were not in exchange for personal gain, but for humanitarian purposes . . . if therefore I plead for funds for the Liberal Church whether in manner of monk or clown, I did so for adults and children still poorer, those who would otherwise be neglected and not cared for, nor advised by other agencies. . . . I freely plead guilty to the charge of being a "crackpot." That is a self serving admission, for people with good horse sense know that only a crackpot would be disposed to serve others more than himself, and remain poor for the sake of a church. Only crackpots undertake to alleviate the poverty of others and to remove the limitations on Liberty. If I appear to be unorthodox, I trust I shall be for-

287

given because operating in an institution for Public sinners, the worthy and unworthy, without endowment is not susceptible to too much formality, dignity, and conventionality.

Signed,

Bishop Frank H. Rice.

But then again, with the support of Bishop Nawyn, a young man who had been chosen to carry on in his place, he took heart. It is said that the young man had been like a son to Rice and that Nawyn often recalled when the bishop had found him selling magazines on a cold downtown street and had befriended him and made him a disciple. The younger man's appreciation and evaluation of his benefactor can be noted in these words, "Today I can say . . . 'There but for the grace of God and the Liberal Church, go I' whenever I see a drunkard or criminal or mentally unbalanced sinner."

Twenty-two years after the founding of the Liberal Church, Bishop Rice died of a heart attack, on Feb. 26, 1945, at the age of 64, with no money in his pockets. But by some strange fortune he had taken out an insurance policy just two months before his death which paid three thousand dollars to his widow—at last he had provided something for her.

Lee Casey, who was said to have understood Rice better than anyone else, wrote a revealing and sincere tribute to the bishop. Casey, associate editor of the *Rocky Mountain News*, said:

> Frank H. Rice was one of the most fortunate men I have ever known. There was no malice in him and no envy, no touch of uncharitableness. He was happy . . . he was blessed with a genuine spiritual longing. He thirsted for religion as many men thirst for fame and wealth. Where some are content with a maximum of an hour's church attendance once a week, Bishop Rice felt it necessary to live his religion every hour of every day. . . . We are aware, just as he was aware, that some regarded him as a good deal of a fraud. He bore no resentment toward those who held such a belief. The truth is, however, that they simply didn't know him. . . . To the undeserving poor, Bishop Rice meant sympathy, a bed, a meal, perhaps a drink—meant what is so often needful, a smile. For Bishop Rice never gave forth charity in the name of a cool and statistical Christ. He gave

288

himself along with the meal or the drink, gave understandingly, gave as a brother, gave indeed, as a fellow sinner. He was possessed by a passion for the poor and lowly. . . . As is always the case, the affection he gave was always fully returned. So Bishop Rice filled a definite need, carried a task in Denver no one else ever quite attempted.

Bishop Rice's real trouble was that he kept right on fighting a battle that was won long ago—a battle which, for that matter, need never have been fought. . . . But Bishop Rice has discovered distinguished company, Mark Twain, and Jack London fell into the same error with consequences tragic to themselves. Bishop Rice, more good natured was saved from the bitter fruitless pessimism of Clemens. Nonetheless, he continued to struggle. The village atheist, once a village oracle, is potent no longer, Clarence Darrow was the last of the species. Bishop Rice wasn't ahead of the times, but behind them. He would have been better off if he had only realized it and caught up with his century. Wit is a perilous attribute and his levity sometimes got him into trouble. But he bore no grudge, even against those who spitefully used him.

On March 1, the Hoffman Mortuary took charge of his funeral. Albert Nawyn, his successor, was in charge of services. It had been the bishop's wish that he be buried in potter's field and in a plain box, but Mrs. Rice and others would not have it so. She had never been in true sympathy with his radical and anti-ecclesiastical methods, yet she had been tolerant of his social work. Perhaps this three thousand dollars was the only money of any consequence he had ever been able to give her. Perhaps she could not bury him in potter's field and accept it without a feeling of guilt. The funeral plans were inexpensive, modest and in good taste, but floral tributes filled one whole end of the mortuary, and it was one of the most impressive funerals Denver ever saw. "Among those present were Larimer Street down-and-outers, justices of the Supreme Court, cripples in wheel chairs, heads of corporations, blind men led by children, professors of universities, police officers, state legislators, children, lawyers, and representatives from every segment of Denver life." In the front row near the bishop's family "seven men who had been in the church from its inception sat ready to carry the man they loved to his grave." The seven were W. R. Blanton, Joe Navarro, Carl Brite, Martin Farrel, George Branish, William Stalling, and Frank Swancara.

A line of cars a half-mile long followed the casket as they awaited its descent to the grave. Reverend Nawyn said, "Friends, this is our last farewell to Bishop Rice, we now commit him back to the earth from whence he came." Quietly, the crowd departed. Barron Beshoar of the *Rocky Mountain News* heard one old man with a three-day-old growth of whiskers and a tell-tale stain about the mouth and a suit that had seen better days say as he left, "Well, there goes Bishop Rice. He was a good man. He believed in the holy trinity of food, clothing and shelter for everyone." A newspaper man was leaving the cemetery and forming the words, "The world is poorer because he is gone, but richer because he lived. And many have realized the shallowness of their shams because of his disconcerting jibes. It is doubtful if any man shall be able to take his place."

The heart of the church was buried with its creator. The ceremony was not elaborate, yet we who have followed his story and know we have gained an insight into the man's character feel he would have preferred a service as simple as his marriage ceremony, one word,

"Buried."

SOURCES

Denver's Cults, Ira J. Taylor Library, Iliff School of Theology, Denver, Colo., Lowell B. Swan, A.B., Th.M., Harold E. Sorter, A.B., B.D., Howard M. Ham, Hubert W. Hodgens and Alvin G. Rowe
The Case of Alfred Packer, The Man-Eater, Paul H. Gantt, University of Denver Press, Denver, Colo., 1952
Denver Post
Rocky Mountain News
Rocky Mountain Herald

Interviews with
The Reverend Harold C. Knudsen
I. B. Bruce, Chief of Police, Colorado Springs, Colo., and a bishop of
  the Liberal Church
Joe Kadish, of Colorado Springs, a cardinal of the Liberal Church
Mrs. Eugene Worth, Grand Little Firecracker of the Order of the
  Saints
and assistance from
The Denver Public Library
The Colorado Springs Public Library
Dorothy and Landell Bartlett

Otto Mears,

Little Man with the Giant Stride

There came upon the Colorado stage, in 1865, a little character who had anything but a bit part to play. Few noticed his entrance but before long he began to upstage larger figures and steal the show with his seven-league boots. Before the final curtain, he was considered one of the chief actors of Colorado's creative period. A nod of his head could elect a governor; a flick of his wrist could resettle an entire "nation," and his "X" on the ballot could name the president of the United States.

This four-foot giant, Otto Mears, was born in Russia, in 1841, of a Russian-Jewish mother and an English father. Orphaned at an early age, Mears lived with relatives in England for a time, then sailed to try his fortune in New York and finally made his way to San Francisco. Uncle after uncle came to his aid enroute, but in San Francisco, at the age of eleven, he began his struggle for a separate existence. First he had to learn sufficient English to enable him to hawk papers on the corner. Later, he picked up the trade of tinsmithing, milked cows for an employer, drove ten miles to deliver merchandise for a storekeeper, and bent his back under loads too big for him.

One more time an uncle figured in his story—Uncle Sam—to whom he swore allegiance. Mears became a citizen and joined the Civil War effort. He served with the First Regiment of California Volunteers, Company H, in 1861, and fought the Confederates in the only major war engagement that took place on Rocky Mountain soil. During his army service he saw action under Kit Carson and helped to break the Navajo resistance. His next experience was in Santa Fe country, where he worked for the firm of Ellsberg and Amberg. A rival firm took notice of the shrewd young man and set him up in business. He also became interested in the cattle enterprise and managed to become the government beef contractor. He kept an eagle eye on his new venture from every angle. His responsibility was with government owned range cattle. Mexican ranchers and menacing rustlers were his problems. At this time he was credited with a personality-revealing statement in explanation of his over-zealous attention to the beef business. Sidney Jocknick in his book, *Early Days on the Western Slope*, quoted Mears as saying, "I don't care a damn how much Uncle Sam gets beat but I hate like hell to get beat myself."

At the age of twenty-four, Mears decided to start out on his own business venture, and in 1865 he edged into the Colorado scene by way of Conejos. In the spare time left over from his general merchandise store, there, Mears took note that there was no sawmill nor grist mill in the county which at that time comprised the present counties of Rio Grande, Mineral, Saguache, Hinsdale, Ouray, San Miguel, Dolores, Montezuma, and Archuleta. He formed a partnership with Major Lafayette Head and erected a grist mill and a sawmill. Since iron was scarce and nails were fifty cents to a dollar per pound, the mill was made entirely of wood except for the "up and down saw." The wooden wheel was tied with a rawhide and the grist mill was built of whole material, using stones of lava found near Conejos. At the time the mills were built, the army at Fort Garland was paying twenty dollars per hundred pounds for flour and eighty dollars per thousand feet for lumber. The nearby Mexican settlers were not raising enough wheat to keep the mill running. Because production was too slow, Mears began to grow wheat himself. He found that hand sickles were inadequate and the native method of running sheep over the wheat to thresh out the grain was too inefficient to satisfy his whip-cracker mind. In 1867 he imported the first mower, reaper, and threshing machines into the San Luis Valley. Jocknick's report of this venture is as follows:

When the machine arrived the Mexicans first refused to have their grain threshed—claimed the machine was stealing it and they went back to the old way of threshing by sheep.

By the time Mears had harvested his crop, the government price had dropped so low that it did not pay to ship wheat to Conejos. He was forced to seek another market. His bright little eyes lit on the new grist mill of Charles Nachtrieb which was being built in the Arkansas Valley near the Chalk Cliffs. From there Mears was in line for a new market for the flour, over the hill to Granite and California Gulch.

There was no road over Poncha Pass, only a trail, and in order to transport his wheat to the mill he began the construction of a wagon road. While he was working, ex-governor Gilpin, part owner of the Baca Land Grant, came along on horseback and was intrigued by Mears's road. He realized the advantage of access from the north. He suggested to Mears that he construct a grade so it could be used eventually for a railroad, which Gilpin said was bound to come. Mears thought it a joke. There wasn't a railroad in a thousand miles. Under the governor's persistent suggestions, Mears gave in. After he sold his wheat, he went to Denver and paid five dollars for his first charter. David Lavender said, "This was the first sprout in the Rockies most fabulous transportation system—a system that in due course would branch out to include some of the zaniest railroads ever built."

There is a story that at one time Mears was driving a load of grain over Poncha Pass and headed for Nachtrieb's mill when the wagon overturned in the creek, getting the wheat wet. Mears's thrifty, tenacious personality would not permit him to waste the wet grain. He gathered it with quiet desperation. To one who had known the full meaning of hunger, every grain was important. It is said that Nachtrieb ground the wet grain with some trepidation as to the result. To his surprise he found the process was better and from that time on the grain was dampened. The old stone grinding wheels of the grist mill are still in Nathrop but have been converted into "flower" planters for the patio on the old Nachtrieb ranch.

Mears homesteaded at Saguache. The only building was a mud-floored store. He was so anxious for Saguache to be voted a town that he gave John Lawrence five hundred dollars to deliver the Mexican vote. Lawrence held out for two hundred dollars more, which Mears felt was excessive; then Lawrence indicted Mears for buying votes, and Mears countered by indicting Lawrence for selling them. The fracas ended in a more-or-less draw. Nevertheless, Mears succeeded in being appointed as first treasurer of the new county. He had drawn his first blood in politics and public office. The circuit court, when called to sit there, required a day of research on the map to locate the remote spot.

There came to be other Mears roads, not always purely for transportation. With the inborn sagacity of a politician, he knew the strategic importance of perfect timing. Anne Ellis said, "I have heard that Mears built this road before an election . . . not that a road was especially needed, but he did need votes."

Anne Ellis also called him a man of wonderful judgment, recalling a time when some of the husbands had overindulged in Mears's store and they were out burying the men who had been killed in a drunken shooting scrape. The wives, all except Nancy Tuttle, who was sick and couldn't go, all marched on the store and smashed the barrels and poured the whisky into the road. Mears looked on, apparently unconcerned. When the husbands received their monthly statements, the whisky was charged on their bills. Anne Ellis said, "Money was so scarce, too. Nancy was sure glad she had that sick spell."

From the same source comes a story of how he gave hams, bacon, and sacks of flour to prospective voters. Much better, Anne Ellis thought, than cigars or whisky.

Mears employed the power of the press and established the *Saguache Chronicle* to advertise the San Luis Valley. When the silver excitement began in the San Juan area, he pooled his energies with Enos Hotchkiss and organized a company to build a wagon road from Saguache to Howardsville in San Juan

County. It was built across Cochetopa Pass to Cebolla Valley and from there to the Lake Fork of the Gunnison and to Lake City.

There were no houses in Lake City when Otto Mears pitched a tent and in company with others published a paper, the *Silver World*. Mr. Wood, the editor, donned his snowshoes and went over the range to Del Norte, carrying the first issue. So began the Lake City boom.

Otto Mears, a trader with the Indians, saw the necessity of speaking their language. Few people bothered with this seemingly unnecessary chore. Hence he became an interpreter and intermediary with the Utes. If he felt disgust or disdain for the unsanitary habits of the Indians, he was shrewd enough not to reveal it in their presence. He could squat by the campfire and share their food with no obvious repugnance. He made a friend of Ouray by such tactics. Ouray did not object to the little man's Russian-Yiddish accent.

It was Mears's rapport with the Ute tribe that brought him into the picture with the Brunot Treaty. The object of the treaty was to have the Indians turn over the area comprising the counties of Hinsdale, San Juan, Ouray, Dolores, Montezuma, La Plata, and San Miguel. The Indians were reluctant to give up this country. Mears suggested a gift to Ouray of one thousand dollars a year for the next ten years. Felix Brunot, chairman of the board of Indian Commissioners was shocked, but Mears explained the semantics by saying it was not a bribe but a salary. He suggested to Ouray that he was "getting along" (Ouray was actually about forty at this time) and that he should take it easier. Mears insisted that the government pay the Utes one million dollars for the transaction in addition to Ouray's proposed salary of one thousand dollars. After all, Ouray might not last ten years and it seemed a good business risk. Ouray accepted and the San Juan was lost to the Utes.

Brunot was elated and in gratitude suggested that the government pay Mears's traveling expenses and the expenses of General Charles Adams, Indian agent, Herman Leuders, his secretary,

296

On the Million Dollar Highway, Mear's old toll road, Mount Abrams in background.

Chief Ouray and Otto Mears. *Photo courtesy Denver Public Library, Western Collection.*

and nine Indians for a three month trip east. The resolution was adopted and Mears joined the $15,000 "gravy train."

The Indians went to the White House to call on President Ulysses S. Grant. Mrs. Grant and daughter Nellie joined the line to be presented. There is a story that Ouray turned to the other Indians and according to the *Colorado Springs Gazette* of April 3, 1901, the following introduction was made: Mears said, "This is the Great Father." Then pointing to Mrs. Grant, Ouray said, "This must be the Great Mother. And if this is the Great Father and this is the Great Mother, then this must be your sister."

The gathering storm over the White River country was shown in an article from the *Saguache Chronicle* of 1875 which was reprinted in the *Colorado Springs Gazette and El Paso County News*:

> Mr. H. T. Bond, Ute agent, Ouray, chief of all the Utes and eight subordinate chiefs left Los Pinos for the Uncompahgre Valley to select a new location for the agency. The present location of the agency is entirely outside of the Indian country but up to the present time it has been impossible to prevail on them, to consent to any change. The Indians now seem to favor a change to some locality near the center of the reservation and it is to be hoped that a site can be settled which will suit all parties. The Uncompahgre is one of the most beautiful and fertile valleys in Colorado and being on the Western slope side of the range the winters are much warmer and the altitude much lower than the San Luis Valley. It is the favorite ground of the Utes, and would, if occupied by the whites become one of the richest and most productive grain and fruit growing countries in the west, is now only a broad beautiful, expanse of meadow land, over which the Utes hold unquestioned control.
>
> The white man who trespasses there is quickly commanded to move on and the painted red wards of Uncle Sam guard every acre with a jealous eye. The Ute Indians control an amount of territory, which divided would give each member of the tribe 3000 acres of land. All of the territory brings no revenue to the government. On the contrary, the natives are supported at a great expense. The same land thrown open to settlement would support many rich and prosperous com-

munities that would return a revenue to the national government. We can well afford to be patient, however, for if any tribe of Indians are deserving liberal treatment on the part of the government, that tribe is the Utes. Ever since Ouray has been chief of the nation it has been at peace with the whites, and in this country while we see hundreds of Indians passing through our country every season, depredations and murders are unknown, and a friendly feeling toward the whites is manifested by the entire tribe.

In 1876 Mears was presidential elector from Colorado and from the newest state in the Union he cast the deciding vote for Rutherford B. Hayes to become President of the United States.

The attempted civilization of the Indians was an unpredictable enterprise. The white man wanted him to become agrarian, honest and thrifty and serious. The red man ran counter to all plans made for him, gambled his allotment at Spanish Monte, cut holes in the seats of his store trousers, made hot-rods out of the mowing machines, and let government doled potatoes rot while he clamored for meat. Once when feed was short in the San Luis Valley, Mears profited handsomely by buying several thousand head of stock from destitute ranchers to feed to the meat-hungry Indians. He made friends and money all the way round.

While he was in Washington he had taken up the matter of mail facilities. Jerome B. Chaffee, the new senator from the new state of Colorado, insisted that every county seat was entitled by law to such service. By coincidence the contract was given to Mears, but he was warned that a heavy fine would be imposed if he did not carry the mail regularly. When winter set in, he began to carry the mail in a toboggan drawn by dogs. With a man alongside on Norwegian shoes (probably skis), no trip was missed until spring when the snow was soft. Eager citizens in Ouray placed orders for tobacco, coffee, sugar, drygoods, and ladies' hats to be brought in by mail. Often the man driving the dogs sat on the toboggan and mashed everything so that tobacco, hats, and sugar were so badly mixed that a complaint went to Washington from the enraged citizenry. The govern-

Millstone from the Nachtrieb mill in the Arkansas Valley.

The old home of the Utes near Montrose. "So long as grasses grow."

ment replied that since the mail of necessity had to be carried on snowshoes and toboggans, it should not be used for hats and general supplies.

When his hired help failed to negotiate the trail, and every one else refused to wade the waist-deep snow, little Mears fastened the mail to his back and spent most of a week and covered the seventy-five miles to beat the deadline.

Marshall Pass came under his enterprising eye and the Gunnison rush enabled him to sell this road to the Denver and Rio Grande for $40,000. This was his first big money.

His private expansion kept pace with the western tide, and his roads began to snake over the San Juans to gain for him the title of the Pathfinder of the San Juans. He held the respect of the people of the western slope. Even Dave Day, the editor of the *Solid Muldoon* of Ouray, who respected no one, had a healthy regard for the whiskery road builder.

After the Meeker Massacre of 1879 the toll roads were choked with troop movements. One general complained of Mears's high fees and threatened to smash the toll gates. Little Mears countered that if he did, it would mean the loss of his commission. The general recognized the power of this half-pint figure and signed the voucher and kept on signing vouchers until it is estimated that Mears finally collected from the war department about $100,000 for the use of his road ruts.

Mears claimed to be instrumental in effecting the rescue of the Meeker women in 1879 with an escort from Ouray. Following the massacre, Mears was placed in charge of eleven Indians who had been ordered to Washington. On the way, Chief Douglas was made prisoner and left at Leavenworth, while Mears continued on the trip.

Back in Colorado, he made an agreement to settle all Utes on one reservation near Grand Junction, but the document was so vague as to geographical location that the Indians refused to sign. As the youngest member of the commission, Mears was best able to complete treaty agreements by covering the area on horseback. His friend, Ouray, died and Mears's task was consequently even more difficult. The Indians insisted on knowing exactly where their new territory was to be, but the commissioners were unable to tell them, explaining simply that they couldn't tell them until the majority of signatures were on the treaty. Mears maganimously offered from his own pocket two dollars per signature. The Indians signed *carte blanche*. Mr. G. W. Manypenny, a member of the Indian Commission, protested this bribery and preferred charges against Mears to Carl Schurz, Secretary of the Interior. Mears was called to Washington to trial, but he stated he paid the money "because the Indians felt that two dollars cash would be worth more to them than $1,800,000 in promises. Government officials told Mears he was quite right and reimbursed him for his farsightedness."

At this juncture, Judge J. B. Bowman of Kentucky resigned as a member of the commission and Judge McMorris of Colorado Springs was appointed in his place. Mears and McMorris had made up their minds that the Utes had to go. The feeling aroused by the Meeker Massacre had sparked a general consensus of that opinion all over the state.

Mears went to look over the choice valley where the Colorado and the Gunnison Rivers come together. At one glance he could see that relocating the Indians here in this beautiful fertile valley would only cause later trouble. Why not interpret the treaty a little more broadly and get them out of Colorado once and for all and let them share with the White River Utes the barren grounds of Utah's Duchesne and White River area? Granted, this was Mormon ground, still it was hoped that the Mormons would take a Christian attitude toward their uninvited guests. After all, Utah is adjacent to Grand Junction, after a fashion, and the treaty implied adjacent territory.

Colonel R. S. MacKenzie was informed by Mears of what had to be done with the Utes. The Indians dallied and refused to move saying that this was not the territory they had been promised. Anxious to get this over with, MacKenzie appealed to the Commission at a time when only two members were available. Strangely enough, the two available members of the commission were McMorris and Mears. They were asked to sign the orders for the removal of the Utes. They complied and MacKenzie issued an ultimatum to the Indians of two hours to pack up and get going. This they did, protesting the shortness of the time for gathering their livestock together. They complained that the hunting season was at hand and they were loath to leave the land of their fathers. The soldiers surrounded them and the hated trek to Utah began. Walker D. Wyman described the tragic march in these words:

> And thus the long drawn out caravan began the thirteen day march along the old Indian trails . . . amid a profusion of autumn color and genuine Indian beauty. Slowly and solemnly they filed along the Uncompahgre down the Gunnison to the Colorado and then westward on that sprawled-out river toward their new land and home. One thousand four hundred and fifty eight Indians including squaws, bucks, braves and children.

> Driving ahead of them over ten thousand sheep and goats, riding, leading or herding eight thousand small ponies. they made their way down the historic river indifferently drinking in the beauties of the late summer sun playing on the mountains. Chief Colorow, famous for his profound stubbornness and resistance to this removal, was the last to leave the valley—a dull prosaic dash of copper at the end of a long Indian sentence . . . if one had stood on Piñon Mesa, what a march of retreating civilization he would have seen.

Among these wanderers went Chipeta, the widow of Ouray. The path bore Indian footprints and the invisible but certain seven-league boot marks of Mears. This time the boots were heavily spiked.

With Mears's efficiency, he had already set up for the Utes, at their new agency, a warehouse, blacksmith shop, doctor's residence, and other buildings. Despite all he had done to help them, when they met him in their new territory, they tried to kill him, blaming him for their relocation.

As soon as the Utes were removed from Colorado, Mears moved into Montrose and helped to incorporate the town and set up its

303

Lizard Head Pass, route of the Rio Grande Southern.

Abandoned station of the Rio Grande Southern.

first newspaper. With the opening up of the new terriory more roads were needed, and he applied his ingenuity to mule packs, wagon roads, and railroads.

Among his developments were the road to Telluride, the road from Ouray by way of Silverton which was to become the Million Dollar Highway, the toll road from Silverton to Animas Forks and Mineral Point, and Durango to Fort Lewis.

He collected toll receipts and covered hundreds of miles each day, dashed about in a silver-studded buckboard, and changed his high stepping mules at every relay station.

He freighted from Saguache to Colorado Springs with ox teams. He ran a mule pack to Silverton. With the acceleration of western life, he started his railroad ventures with the Silverton to Red Mountain, and the Rio Grande Southern. The Silverton Northern was up the Animas to Eureka. (The last little narrow-gauge train operating in the state, runs up the Animas between Silverton and Durango and claims origin with Mears. It has been recently considered by a foundation to preserve this scenic and historic railroad.) Mears took six months to zig-zag the four-mile Ophir Loop up the cliff on the Telluride to Rico run. Legend says that Otto was so terrified at his first locomotive ride over those dizzy tracks that he wanted to get out and finish the journey by carriage. Years later, after Mears had relinquished interest in this road, and when train travel became an economic problem, a Galloping Goose was substituted for the train. This was a hybrid contraption, part Pierce Arrow, and part train. It became the talk of the area, and anyone who ever rode the Goose, or helped to put her back on the track, boasted of the thrills and spills and bruises the rest of his life.

Mears found there were obligations to be met for past favors and privileges to be curried for future plans. What better way could this be done than by granting ornate passes to his friends? First he made the passes of white buckskin. Then there came silver watch fobs. These were followed by silver plates, each with the name of the recipient engraved and the border surrounded by filligree. For some this was not enough and solid gold passes similarly engraved and filigreed were awarded for a lifetime. Undoubtedly the holders of gold passes were given the preference of seats in the plush parlor cars.

It was only fitting that such an outstanding man should be elected to the Colorado legislature in 1884, where he continued for many years as an important influence in Colorado's Republican party. For a long time he served on the State Capitol Commission, and it was due to his suggestion that the gold leaf was employed in ornamenting the dome. Mears served as commissioner by appointment of Governor Job A. Cooper during the construction. It was said to have been one of the few capitol buildings built in the United States without a financial scandal.

In 1901 he was chairman of Capitol Commissioners, and from the San Juan area came a request that his portrait should be placed in the state capitol. This was an embarrassing position for Mears and he felt he must protest the honor, but by unanimous vote of the Colorado legislature the Capitol Commissioners were directed to place the stained glass portrait near the other outstanding pioneers, the only living person so honored.

An amusing story of that period of Denver portrays the relative importance of the little man in the state. The story is that the governor got on a streetcar one day and found he had left his wallet at home. The conscientious motorman forthwith informed him that he couldn't ride without his fare. Said he, "I wouldn't let you ride free, not even if you were Otto Mears."

The panic of 1893 and the collapse of silver were the only things ever to defeat the little man. A receiver of the D. & R. G. took over his seven-league boots.

Mears slipped east to Washington. There he negotiated a contract for the building of a railroad from Washington to Chesapeake Beach. Finding the work behind schedule, he increased the tempo of the languorous colored construction gang by employing two bands to play continuously, one beginning when the other stopped. No record is found of the musical repertoire employed but it is safe to guess the tunes were lively. Mears made his deadline and pronounced it "a neat Jewish trick."

He kept pace with transportation by becoming first president of the Mack Truck Company.

Colorado called him back. The Silverton Northern (four miles) was still operating at a profit. He was tempted to plunge again into railroading. This time his construction gang was Navajo, and he didn't speak their language and felt he was too old to start learning it. So he tried to communicate by gestures and they merely gestured back. He deplored their time-consuming amusement of stoning marmots, so he hired small boys and purchased twenty-five rifles for them to kill the four-legged distractions.

On one venture, his train turned over so many times that "its sole remains ended up as a porch swing in Durango." With persistence he began to regain control of his Silverton railroad to Red Mountain, and by 1915 he added the Silverton, Gladstone and Northerly, but he never managed to reclaim his first love, the Rio Grande Southern.

His greatest dramatic gesture was for the people of the San Juans when the storm washed out the track in October of 1911, and threatened Silverton, whose winter supplies had not been laid in. Snow comes early in the high country and fear mounted for the safety of Silverton. Officials of the D. & R. G. wired for Mears to come and rescue the desperate town. In a few brief hours he had imported equipment from his own railroad and hired two hundred and fifty men to clear the tracks. One problem remained unsolved. His depleted yards could furnish no coal. Mears made a house to house canvass of the town and begged coal from the shivering citizens. Storekeepers sent them all they had hoarded, and even children lugged it to the depot in sacks. They bet their last chance of survival on the ingenuity and determination of the diminutive Pathfinder of the San Juans. An interesting description by David Lavender read:

> White whiskers, frock coat, and all, Otto climbed into the cab of the lead locomotive and roared down the canyon. . . A crew pushing up from Durango met him and joined in the nine weeks race against the snow.

As dramatic as the typical western movie, the hero arrived in

Silverton with winter supplies just ahead of the first snowflake.

In 1917, the lure of mild weather appealed to his aching bones, and his calloused feet were ready for slippers instead of seven-league boots. He moved to Pasadena, California, where he lived until June 24, 1931, and there he died at the age of ninety. His last request was that his ashes and those of his wife should be scattered over the mountains around Silverton. Two daughters survived him and many friends remembered his uncanny accomplishments, his generosity to Jewish charities, his charm, his loyalty to good friends, and his bright and alert mind.

In Washington, today, those in charge of Indian affairs are also remembering a few things as they try to unsnarl the interminable Indian claims.

Many tourists travel the narrow-gauge train from Durango to Silverton each summer. They smile indulgently at the potbellied stoves in each coach and the coal-oil lamps that no longer burn. To some it is a breathtaking adventure of scenery, and high trestles around curves that old timers used to say a jackass could not make without hinges. The black smoke rolls out of the funnel stack of the Jupiter engine and the Animas River outroars the train. Only a few of the passengers know of the Pathfinder of the San Juans.

Over the hill on Lizard Head Pass the railroad ties of the Rio Grande Southern are rotting in the sun and the abandoned station waits in a meadow for the flight of a "goose" that will not fly that way again.

SOURCES

The Big Divide, David Lavender, Doubleday & Co., Inc., Garden City, N. Y., 1948

The Utes A Forgotten People, Wilson Rockwell, Sage Books, Denver, Colorado, 1956

Massacre, Marshall Sprague, Little, Brown and Co., Boston, 1957

Pioneers, Peddlers and Tsadikim, Ida Libert Uchill, Sage Books, Denver, Colorado, 1957

Early Days on Western Slope of Colorado, Sidney Jocknick, Carson
Parker Co., Denver, Colorado, 1913
  dedicated to the Hon. Otto Mears, Pathfinder. (the copy
  in the Colorado Springs public library is autographed by
  Otto Mears to Mrs. E. Gates, Pasadena, California, and
  she writes, "The summer of 1914 I met him and his wife
  at the Maryland Hotel."
Life of An Ordinary Woman, Anne Ellis, Houghton Mifflin Co.,
Boston and New York, 1929
Colorado and Its People, LeRoy Hafen, ed., Lewis Historical
Publishing Co., New York, N.Y., 1948
Stampede to Timberline, Muriel Sibell Wolle, University of Colorado,
Boulder, Colorado, 1949
Colorado, American Guide Series, Hastings House, New York, N.Y.,
1941
Tales of the Colorado Pioneers, Alice Polk Hill, Pierson and Gardner,
Denver, Colo., 1884
Colorado Magazine: "Otto Mears Path Finder of the San Juans,"
LeRoy R. Hafen, Vol. 9, No. 2, Mar. 1932; "The Mission of Colorado
Toll Roads," by Arthur Ridgeway, Vol. 9, No. 5, Sept., 1932; "Grand
Junction's First Year, 1882," by Walker D. Wyman, Vol. 13, No. 4,
July, 1936; "Historic Silverton Railroad," D. B. Sanford and M. C.
Poor, Vol. 23, No. 2, March, 1946; "Preface To Settlement of Grand
Junction," Walker D. Wyman, Vol. 10, No. 1, January, 1933
Colorado Springs Weekly Gazette April 3, 1901
Colorado Springs Gazette and El Paso County News, June 12, 1875
Interview with Mrs. Frank Fielding of Nathrop, Colorado

Ouray, Broken Arrow

It was an augured child of Leo who was born in that year of the "Leonids." From midnight to dawn, one November night in 1833, the primitive residents of the Taos area were awe-struck by the dazzling display of heavenly phenomena. Even their more sophisticated neighbors, such as Kit Carson, were concerned at the sudden and brilliant appearance of two hundred thousand shooting stars that seemed to have their origin in the constellation of Leo. The Taoseños were unaware of an event in their own community which was to have a much more lasting effect on the entire culture and civilization of the west. Some time that same year, Ouray was born near Taos, of Apache and Ute parentage. He was to be the last bright star of the Ute Nation and the Star of Peace for the white man.

His father was named Guera Murah, but sometimes also called Salvador. He was said to have been a Jicarilla Apache who had been adopted by the Utes. Little Ouray and a brother were left with a Mexican family when their parents decided to return to Colorado Territory and their old home in the Uncompahgre Valley. Old Ute Chief Nevava was in need of Guera Murah's help.

Ouray grew up with Spanish as his adopted language. He was a herder of sheep, but he became well acquainted with the culture of the more advanced Mexican families. Although he was not a member of the Catholic church, he attended mass with his foster family and came under the influence of the Christian religion and thereby gained some of that cultural veneer which marked his adulthood.

At about the age of seventeen, Ouray received word of his father's death and the boy went to Colorado to claim his paternal inheritance of a dozen ponies. He decided to remain there with his own people, the Utes.

Sidney Jocknick said of Ouray, in his *Early Days on the Western Slope,* "He finished his education by visiting among friendly tribes, hunting and fishing, and occasionally fighting the hereditary enemies of his people, the Comanches, Kiowas, Cheyennes, Sioux and Arapahoes." He became a vigorous, muscular young brave, five feet seven in height, with an unusually large and well shaped head and regular features. His was the hot blood of youth and the hair-triggered temper of the Utes, combined with all the inborn characteristics of a Leo-born leader.

Ouray's heritage was a blend of two tribes of Indians, Ute and Apache, with an acquired knowledge of two kinds of whites, Anglo and Spanish, and of two faiths, Catholic and Indian, and a competent grasp of four languages.

Jocknick said of him, "He was dignified and pleasing in conversation and took great pleasure in conversing with intelligent and refined white men whose respect he commanded . . . he was a man of broad and intelligent views." One white agent said, "He was a good man and a man who would have measured up to the highest standards of any community."

As a young man Ouray had to learn his own tribal customs. It was at the Bear Dance that a young Ute girl caught his eye and they were married, according to their tribal rituals, in 1853. Four years later his first and only son was born.

What happened to this wife is a matter of conjecture with historians, some of whom say she died in childbirth. Others admit they do not know.

It was the dimpled, diminutive Chipeta who became his second wife, in 1859, the brightest and handsomest squaw in the tribe. Her name, meaning "White Singing Bird," was apt, for she sang and laughed and helped her people. Marshall Sprague in his account in *Massacre* described the sixteen-year old Chipeta as "young and capable, and from dawn to dark, she tanned Ouray's doeskins and elkskins, made his baskets and clay pipes, sewed his clothes and moccasins, prepared dried meat for travel, cooked, hauled wood, carried water, patched his elk-hide tepee, carved wood cups and kept her temper."

311

Chipeta. *Photo courtesy Walker Art Studio, Montrose, Colorado.*

Ouray, Ute Chief. *Photo courtesy Walker Art Studio, Montrose, Colorado.*

Kit Carson knew that old Nevava, the Ute chief, was losing his grip, and Kit hadn't forgotten the bright young man who had returned to his Ute background taking with him a keen awareness of white man's ways and powers. Kit suggested to Ouray that the Utes should make a treaty with the government in order to establish a clear title and boundary to the Gunnison area. Ouray carried the suggestion to Nevava, who was unimpressed and refused to consider such a treaty, since he said the Rockies belonged to the Utes and they need not demean themselves by asking the white man for what was already theirs.

The time came soon when Ouray was forced to take the power out of Nevava's weakened hands. He was the natural one to do this. His authority came first from the old chief's council, who recognized the need for young blood, and secondly from the white man's government because Ouray was the only chief who could make himself understood in English. His power did not come as a birthright but as necessity forced it upon him. Ouray was qualified as the man of the hour to stand at the crossroads of two civilizations, and he was one of the chosen representatives who was sent to Washington in 1862.

Although Ouray was occupied with increasingly burdensome duties as tribal chief, he continued to share the hunting expeditions of his tribesmen. Often they went to the prairie lands in search of buffalo. It was on one such hunt, near the Republican River, that one of Ouray's greatest tragedies struck. On this particular occasion he had taken his small son with him. The lad was kidnapped by a marauding Indian tribe. Ouray was to spend many of his remaining years in an attempt to locate his son and this tragic event was to have bearing on a later Indian treaty. There was no hope of another son. Chipeta could have no children.

The second trip east came in 1868 when Ouray was influential in the forming of the Ute Treaty which was considered at the time to be the most generous bestowal of rights ever granted

313

by the United States Senate to a minority group. This was said to be Ouray's masterpiece.

The wily eastern politicians tried to impress these child-like people with the strength of their armies, the lavish quarters of a Washington hotel, Turkish baths (which must have reminded them pleasantly of the hot springs at home), gifts of candy and cigarettes and bright, but meaningless medals. Ouray was not so easily deceived by gilt and plush. He carefully inventoried a long list of valid grievances which the Indians had suffered over a long period of time and reminded the white men of their half-kept promises, of the wormy rice rations, of black sugar drippings mixed with dirt, of Governor Evans' gift of two (from a promised five) stallions which were to have been the sires of a vast Indian pony herd—and one of which proved to be sterile. Later he was to remind them also of the government's excess of enthusiasm for helping the Ute sheep raising industry, which had led the officials in charge to ship twelve ewes and 1,908 castrated rams.

When a congressman countered with a list of Indian misdeeds, Ouray kept his Ute temper under control—and called for a recess. To the gathered newsmen he made a statement, "The agreement an Indian makes to a United States treaty is like the agreement a buffalo makes with his hunters when pierced with arrows. All he can do is lie down and give in."

The treaty which was supposed to have been so generous with the Utes might have been longer lasting if a few trespassing prospectors had not turned up some valuable ore. The San Juans, on paper, belonged to the Utes, but there were wills and ways—and there was Otto Mears, friend of Ouray.

The first home of Ouray on the Los Pinos Agency, built of hewn logs, burned with all his belongings. He was reimbursed $400 by the government and a new cabin was constructed.

Ouray was not without enemies within his own tribe, many of whom failed to recognize his sincerity of purpose and his deep loyalty to his people. There were numerous attempts to murder him. Even Chipeta's brother, Sapinero, attempted to kill him, and it was only through Chipeta's intervention that Ouray was prevented from avenging himself on his attacker.

With the mining discoveries in the San Juans, the white settlers began to be increasingly resentful of the uncivilized red man camped on their door steps. The trend of opinion seemed to make the red man the intruder. *Out West* of September, 1872, declared:

> The Los Pinos Indian council has failed in its object. The Utes would not resign their reservation, so the fairest portion of Colorado and some of the richest mining country is closed by force of arms. So settled we believe it will be and should be. An Indian has no more right to stand in the way of civilization and progress than a wolf or a bear. The fairest portion of the earth was not made to be occupied by an uncivilized and barbarous race, to the exclusion of civilization, christianity, and refinement and "the logic of events" will prove it so. —So says the *Boulder News* and we cannot contradict it.

An invisible wall seemed to be slowly imprisoning the Utes. Orders went out from Washington to capture or kill all Indians found off their reservations under the premise that, like the wild beasts of the woods, the Indians had no love for civilization. One Indian agent boasted that all his charges had been prevailed upon to remain within their designated boundaries and bragged that there were not enough now of those belonging to his agency outside his reservation "to frighten a cat."

With the Indians gradually being moved off their hunting grounds, the necessity to supplement their increasingly limited food supplies led to an early experiment in governmental doles.

In spite of the bitterness against the Indians as a people and the resentment of a few of his own tribesmen, Ouray was for the most part a respected leader with both reds and whites.

The Colorado Springs Gazette mentioned:

> Among the distinguished visitors to our sanctum during the last week was Ouray, chief of the Tabeguache Utes. We grasped each other by the hand, but our feelings were too deep for utterance. Ouray was on his way to Denver in company with Commissioner Adams, to see about supplies.

Commissioner Adams declared that the report about the Utes having stolen horses in South Park was without any foundation.

The newspaper editor went on to comment, "It was a case, we suppose, of giving a dog a bad name and hanging him."

In July, 1873, Shavano and Little Colorado were in Manitou bearing dispatches from Ouray for Territorial Governor Elbert, and for Washington. (The two chiefs took time out to attend an amateur show at Manitou House.) "These dispatches stated that Ouray has held a council with the bands under his control in reference to Wyoming affairs and that they had accepted his advice to keep perfectly quiet and leave it to the white man to make things right."

It was apparent, by this time, that Ouray's influence extended beyond the territorial boundaries.

During this period the chief heard a rumor that his lost son might be found on an Indian reservation. He made a long journey to check the rumor, but the identifying marks on the young man's body did not tally with those of the missing son.

Ouray never gave up his Indian identity nor failed to take a deep pride in his heritage. He would have preferred that his people not sacrifice their dignity by trying to imitate too closely the white man's ways and dress. He was distressed when the Denver Indians aped the whites in hoop skirts and top hats, made more ridiculous by their mincing mannerisms. It was difficult enough piloting his charges through the mazes of Denver and Washington society without the added burden of affected poses.

Although it was acknowledged that Ouray knew something of civilized manners and customs, one newspaper voiced the opinion that "Some of his brethren still possess the 'untutored mind' which is the peculiar heritage of the 'poor Indian' and need a little watching when in polite society."

Enroute to Washington in 1873, Ouray and other "big bugs" of the Ute persuasion camped at the Munger House in Denver. A news account read:

At the next table surrounded by a party of friends, sat Mr. A. B. Hill, the well known real-estate dealer, who, upon taking his seat, had placed his hat (a fine glossy stove pipe) on the floor behind him. Old Tamserik, a gorgeously clad Ute with a stomach on him like a bay window, and a maw as capacious as the hotel itself, seeing Hill's hat, and supposing, of course, that it was one of the belongings of a first class dining hall, dropped his pea-nut shells, potato peelings and melon rinds plump into it. By the time Hill had finished his dessert, the untutored child of nature had filled his stove pipe brimful of the best the market affords.

The Utes, by the way, very nearly took their departure from Denver by an exceedingly short cut. Four of them were put into a room which was lighted by gas. When they felt a desire for darkness they just blew the gas out and had not Mr. Mears, the interpreter, smelt the escape the gas would most probably have repaid them by blowing them out.

On the way to Washington, that same trip, there were certain reporters who took it upon themselves to describe and quote Ouray without benefit of an actual interview. By so doing they revealed their own prejudices and their abysmal ignorance.

The Colorado Springs Gazette of October 18, 1873, published a rewrite of one such unfair account, headlined "The Utes on the Topics of the Times":

A reporter from the *Kansas City Times* gave a report of an interview with Ouray and other Indians of the Ute delegation that started east last week.

"I call upon you," said the reporter, "in behalf of an anxious and waiting public to ascertain your views and opinions upon the leading topics of the day, the object of your visit to Washington and your views on the money panic, the cheap transportation question, the Memphis Railroad, and other subjects."

Ouray stuffed his scalp locks back into his pockets, smiled benignly upon our reporter's flask of Feineman's best and replied:

"I shall be pleased to give your readers all the information in my power concerning the state of our finances, our cattle prospects, and the view the Ute Nation takes of the cheap transportation question."

Here the old gentleman [age forty] winked at Tepucha and Munchic and Mudo and the rest of the gentlemen as he relieved our reporter of his proffered flask. *[Ouray was almost unique among the Utes of his day—he never touched alcohol or tobacco.]*

"How does the money panic effect the finances of the Ute Nation?"

"Oh, in various ways. We find ourselves very short of currency and during our stay in Denver at Ed Chase's and at Shoaff's bank, found ourselves obliged to suspend payment until after our return from Washington where we expect to draw on sight on Uncle Sam, like we do on all his soldiers, when we get a chance."

"Does it affect the nation to any serious extent?"

"No, not much." ... "We deal largely in horses, cattle, and ha'r and groceries. We draw upon our country correspondents in the valley and give a certified check in payment whenever they protest."

"When do you expect to resume payment?"

"Oh, as to that, we are in no hurry. Our money is invested in government securities such as mining lands, railroad grants, commissary stores, rifles, scalps, knives and ammunition which we can use whenever occasion requires. We are amply secured by the government."

"How does the Ute Nation stand on the Granger question?"

"Square! We all believe in it. We intend to demand free passes for our entire tribe on the Denver and Rio Grande narrow gauge and a controlling interest through the buffalo country. We intend to come out strong on the Grange movement."

"Are you interested in any of the recent suspensions?"

"Yes, we were all much interested in the suspension of cousin Captain Jack of the Modoc bank."

The jibes of the reporters did not penetrate Ouray's calm demeanor. One further disappointment concerning his son was awaiting him in Washington, however. Here he was confronted with a young man believed to be his son. Felix Brunot of the Indian Commission had tried sincerely for years to find the lost boy. When questioned, this young man in Washington could recall nothing of his Ute name or background. He was called

318

Friday by the Arapahoes and the Ute name of Cotoan brought no glimmer of recognition. All who saw Ouray and Cotoan together were struck by the remarkable resemblance and were convinced that they were father and son. Yet, the boy could not believe that he was not an Arapahoe and could not disguise his hatred of the Utes which had been instilled in him from childhood. Ouray could not accept the fact that his son could be so embittered against his own people. Convinced at last of the relationship, Cotoan promised to go home with Ouray "after saying good-bye to his friends in the staked plains country." Unhappily, the boy died on the journey, and "his poor father twice lost his only son."

The Brunot Treaty of 1873 which contained a written promise to help find the lost son of Ouray also guaranteed the Ute chief a salary of a thousand dollars a year. The government insisted upon the salary for services rendered in order that the chief's stewardship might be rewarded and, as Jocknick recorded,

> . . . as an offset to his loss of dignity which he paid for exercising a "straw-boss's authority" over his subjects . . . . Ouray was so entirely devoted to Chipeta that his acceptance of a salary was due alone to the promptings of a conscientious desire to generously provide for her, in order that in case of his untimely death at the hands of his enemies, she would never have to suffer from poverty in her old age.

Although the mineral lands were released, the Utes reserved for themselves their ancestral hot springs which flowed at the head of the Uncompahgre River. The invading hordes of prospectors, however, could not be kept out of the area of the sacred springs. When Ouray protested the violation of the agreement, Agent Wheeler reassured him by promising that in all cases under his observation where the Indian rights were in jeopardy he had been instructed to employ the saving clause, especially in regard to the sacred springs: *The same should remain theirs forever inviolate for as long as rivers might run and grasses grow.*

In the relocation which followed the Treaty of 1873, Ouray was given a homestead on a 160 acre farm about ten miles south of the present city of Montrose. It was the chief's intent to set an example to his people for the change that had to come. His own tribesmen laughed at the chieftain who had become a farmer. Here in their comfortable adobe house, Chipeta and Ouray gathered all the impediments of civilization in the form of the white man's uncomfortable and impractical furnishings. Chipeta took up the white woman's burden of polishing silver and washing china—and turning out the Monday wash. The ritual campfire was hidden in an iron monster that radiated the heat of hell in summer. In one thing the Queen of the Utes refused to conform —the shiny, polished rocking chair made her seasick!

In their home was a piano and a Mexican servant to answer the silver bell and to bring forth the horses and carriage. Ouray was said to have dispensed hospitality in a princely way, to have had all the instincts of an Indian but that he followed the customs of the whites, and that in standing on the verge of civilization and beckoning to his primitive barbarism, he produced a striking figure.

But it was his attempt to pattern after the manners and customs of the whites and his partial assimilation of their culure which was a primary factor in his death.

Although Ouray was only in his forties, his star was beginning to wane and he felt a weakening of his powers, both physical and mental. A deep depression settled over his mind. The white doctor in Canon City diagnosed the chief's physical ailment as chronic nephritis. The feeling of fatigue became more acute, with accompanying back aches and bloated feet. General Adams was constantly sending disturbing news of the Denver and Washington plots to compress the Ute Nation into further restricted boundaries—reports which undoubtedly contributed to Ouray's increasing depression. Nor was he completely unaware of the part Otto Mears, with his uncanny ability for driving a bargain, was playing in the gradual tightening of the net.

Chief Ouray's final years were dedicated and spent in the task of amalgamating two conflicting civilizations. His entire occupation was adjustment with those who refused to adjust and compromise with the uncompromising. He knew he was fighting a losing battle, but he hoped for a miracle. There was no one else with his vision and understanding. He had neither fear of threats nor concern for the schemings of his enemies who could not bribe him to abandon his firm determination to hold the line.

In the White River country Nathan Meeker had been appointed as agent. Ouray did not doubt Meeker's ability as an organizer, nor his sincerity, but the Indian was well aware of the new agent's incapacity for understanding or compromise. Meeker's very insistence upon plowing up the ground was an utter desecration of the Ute beliefs and indicative of the white agent's total lack of comprehension of the Indian mind. The whole Ute situation was a powder keg and every politician or greedy white promoter was looking expectantly for an incident which would furnish the excuse to force the Indian to light his own fuse.

It was inevitable that, pushed to the point of exasperation, the White River Utes, under the leadership of Chief Douglas, would forget all of Ouray's admonitions and throw caution to the wind. They resented the intrusion across their borders of troops, which they had been told were to lead them in chains forever. Fanned to a fury, when Meeker proceeded with his plans to plow up the pony pastures and the race track, the White River Utes retaliated by a complete declaration of war in which every man at the agency was killed and the Meeker women taken captive.

There was true Indian symbolism and a kind of primitive justice in the events which transpired at the agency in those moments when savage and insane fury were unleashed. Some say the Indians tore a stave from a despised flour ration barrel and rammed it down Meeker's throat. Other accounts tell of the Indians tying Meeker's inert body to the sacrilegious plow and racing wildly around the desecrated pony tracks.

As soon as Ouray was informed of the battle raging in the White River area, he experienced a justified desire to retaliate and to join with his own people in the direct protest against the years of intolerance, the cumulative misunderstandings, and the encroachment of government troops. It was said that during that

321

night he suffered more agony of mind than ever before in his life, and it was Chipeta's tears and pleadings for peace which changed the entire course of events and prevented an interminable war, in which other tribes would have been certain to join the Utes. Ouray consented, reluctantly, to call Douglas to retreat, which Douglas obeyed, albeit sullenly.

Ouray assisted in the rescue of the Meeker women and Chipeta took them into her home and cared for them tenderly. Ralph Meeker, son of the agent, termed Ouray a "noble fellow" and, according to W. B. Vickers in *History of the Arkansas Valley, Colorado,* Miss Meeker recalled how "Chief Ouray and his noble wife did everything to make us comfortable. We were given the whole house, and found carpets on the floor, lamps on the tables and a stove with a fire brightly burning. Mrs. Ouray shed tears over us."

A commission was soon called to investigate the trouble for the purpose of bringing the guilty Utes to justice. In the preface to Helen Hunt Jackson's *A Century of Dishonor,* Robert Bent said:

> There are 4,000 Utes in Colorado, thirty-two of them desperately guilty men, have committed murder and rape and three or four hundred of them did, in the convenient phrase of our diplomacy, "go to war against the government," i.e. they attempted by force of arms to restrain the entrance upon their own lands bought—owned and paid for—of soldiers that the government had sent them to be ready to make war upon them, in case the agent thought it best to do so!

The commission heard evidence at the Los Pinos Agency. It was reported in the *Solid Muldoon* of the town of Ouray:

> A death silence fell upon everything. Nothing was said and no one moved for a few minutes. Then Colorow lighted a long pipe and each Indian present drew knife and laid it on his knee . . . just as the pipe had gotten around the semicircle of Indians. Colorow, who had filled and lighted the pipe and passed it to the next man without smoking himself, rose from his seat, glanced at the Utes, and drawing himself up to his full height, jerked his belt around in front of him, drew from its sheath a knife and cast it on the floor in front,

322

where it struck and quivered. Each Indian present dropped his hand down to his waist and laid it upon his knife or revolver. Each white man did the same, and the two parties remained in this position, each waiting an aggressive movement on the part of the other.

. . . The result hung upon a thread and one word would have precipitated a terrible contest which would have ended in the death of every white man in the room. Twenty-five Indians to six whites were terrible odds . . . Finally Ouray spoke: "We cannot deliver up to you these Indians unless they are to be tried in Washington. They must not be tried in Colorado. The Colorado people are all our enemies, and to give our men up to be tried in this state would be as if we gave them up, knowing that they would be hung instantly."

Upon these terms only would Ouray promise to deliver up his guilty chiefs. Jocknick wrote that it seemed surprising to people that Ouray, who had done so much for the recovery of the captives, and had ordered the war stopped by the White River Utes, should now turn and defend the murderers, for of the guilt of a number of them he could entertain no doubt. But, he commented, "it may he said that all he wanted was a fair trial for his people. He looked upon himself as their advocate."

As a grudging compromise to Ouray's firm stand, Otto Mears was put in charge of a Ute delegation to accompany the accused chiefs to Washington; among the group were Ouray, Shavano, Jack, Sowerwick, Douglas, and four others, and Chipeta. Mears was careful to buy only a one-way ticket for one member of the party. For Chief Douglas a stop-over had been arranged in Leavenworth. Later Douglas was reported to have been liberated and to have died insane.

Ouray took time from the governmental proceedings to consult still other white doctors who told him that he had better get done whatever he had to do. His time was growing short.

Secretary of the Interior Carl Schurz was much impressed with both Chipeta and Ouray and in his *Private Memoirs* recalled the conversations they had held during the month-long stay of the Indians in Washington.

Ouray and Chipeta often visited me at my home and they always conducted themselves with perfect propriety. They observed the various belongings of the drawing room with keen but decorous interest and were especially attracted by a large crystal chandelier which was suspended from the ceiling. They wished to know where such a chandelier could be bought and what it would cost; it would be such an ornament to their home.

In official conversation his talk was quite different from that of the ordinary Indian chief. He spoke like a man of a high order of intelligence and of larger views who had risen above the prejudices and aversions of his race, and expressed his thoughts in language clear and precise, entirely unburdened by the figures of speech and superfluities commonly current in Indian talk.

He had evidently pondered much over the condition and future of the Indians of North America and expressed his mature conclusions with the simple eloquence of a statesman.

He comprehended perfectly the utter hopelessness of the struggle of the Indians against the progress of civilization. He saw clearly that nothing was left to them but to accommodate themselves to civilized ways or perish. He admitted that it was very hard to make his people understand this; that so long as they did not fully appreciate it, they should, as much as possible, be kept out of harm's way; that it was the duty of influential chiefs to cooperate with the Government to make the transition as little dangerous and painful as possible; that he, therefore, recognized the necessity of removing the Utes from Colorado, hard as the parting from their old haunts might be, and that he depended on me to bring about that removal under conditions favorable to his people.

Ouray was by far the brightest Indian I have ever met.

Others realized the remarkable qualities of the peace-maker. Sidney Jocknick in his *Early Days on the Western Slope* said of Ouray:

Although one of the savages of North America, he could have taught the Czar and kings of the East much to their interest and to the happiness of their subjects. He was a model in habits, for he never chewed tobacco, abhorred whiskey, took but a sip of wine in company when it was offered, and then only as a matter of courtesy to his friends. He never

324

swore nor used obscene or vulgar language. He was a firm believer in the Christian religion ... and united with the Methodist church.

The treaty made in Washington in 1880 complied with the wishes of Otto Mears and his cohorts in that it eventually accomplished the complete removal of the Utes from the coveted soil of Colorado. One of the state's newspapers gloated that the new agreement had opened up mineral land for prospecting and eleven million acres of land to stockmen. "Eleven-twelfths of the Indian reservation was extinguished without the cost of a life or a dollar to the state by pursuing the peace policy which we advocated."

It was in the late summer of 1880, when Leo was on the wane, that Ouray, with an intuitive knowledge of rapidly approaching death, sought one more peace mission to the Los Pinos Agency. With Chipeta, a white doctor, and Chipeta's half brother, John McCook, he went horseback across the San Juan Mountains for one final look at his homeland. The familiar scenes wrapped around him with the warmth and comfort of a blanket.

He reached Ignacio on August 18 and only his stout heart seemed to keep his swollen body alive. He aroused from a two day rest to take part in the first full Ute commission council with Ignacio's chief. On the 21st and 22nd he conferred with the heads of the Southern Utes, who were reluctant to sign the vague agreement with its undefined boundaries. On the day that Leo relinquished his power in the sky, August 23, Ouray's power also slipped from his fingers. In his final hours, the forty-seven-year-old chief thanked his white doctor and dismissed him, and returned to the faith of his fathers. His white man's religion was laid aside and the medicine man was called in to begin his continuous incantations to drive out the cursed spirits. On August 24, 1880, at eleven a.m., when the white doctor again drew near to offer his assistance, an Indian stepped out of the tepee and motioned him back. Ouray was dead. Within ten minutes after his death, his tribesmen had moved more than a mile away because of their awe of the dead. Within an hour, the dead chief's body was sewed up in new blankets and buffalo robes, tied with cords, and placed carefully across the back of a horse. Accompanied by Chipeta, McCook, Buckskin Charlie, and four other Utes, his body was taken to a cave-like opening two miles south of Ignacio. His saddle was placed beside him. Five of his favorite ponies were sacrificed nearby to provide his transportation to the happy hunting grounds, which would be outside state boundaries and outside the edicts of white men's scraps of paper.

Sapavanaro had been named Ouray's successor.

Some time after news of the chief's death had reached Washington, Carl Schurz was touched by a letter which he received from Chipeta. Because she considered the former Secretary of the Interior her husband's best friend, she wished to send a gift:

> . . . but if he sent one back it would signify he did not value their friendship . . . . The box contained the clothes Ouray had worn in Washington, his tobacco pouch and an old powder horn which he used in younger days.

Schurz commented further:

> It will be admitted that greater delicacy is seldom met with, even in the most refined society . . . the noble savage with chivalrous impulses and fine sentiments, as he occaionally appears in romance, should not be regarded as a mere figment of the imagination.

It had been Ouray's chief concern and his reason for accepting the salary from the government, that Chipeta would always be cared for. But the government forgot, and although Chipeta begged to stay in the Uncompahgre Valley, she was included in those who wound their way through the falling leaves of a mountain autumn in September, 1881. Some may have recalled, as they trudged through the falling leaves, the prophetic words of Ouray:

> We shall fall as the leaves of the trees when winter comes, and the lands we have roamed for countless generations will be given to the miner and the plowshare . . . and we shall be buried out of sight.

A portion of Chipeta's inheritance in the fertile Unchompahgre was purchased, at a bargain price, by Otto Mears.

Much of the record of the intervening years of Chipeta's life has been lost. There is some evidence that she remarried. The widow of General Charles Adams, a former Indian commissioner, located the old woman and wrote of Chipeta that she was

> . . . living on a barren bit of Utah land where even the experienced farmer could not make a living, much less an old woman . . . She was clever at making certain things, but it is late in the day for her to learn to till the ground where Uncle Sam has placed her and said "Make a living or starve." Winter is coming on. Her little log house should be more comfortable.

Mrs. Adams made many fruitless attempts to obtain a pension for Chipeta, keeping in mind that the Meeker women had long ago been pensioned. She begged the women of Colorado to show their compassion, saying that if women could gather together relics to be preserved in museums, surely they could help an old woman.

Outside Colorado the last days of the Queen of the Utes were spent, symbolically, on Bitter Creek.

Dark days had descended on the Utes and for Chipeta it was a total darkness, for she was blind. Friends in Grand Junction had tried to save her eyesight, but to no avail, and so they staked taut ropes around her cabin and down to the brush to guide her steps. Chipeta died in her little home on Bitter Creek, August 16, 1924. News reached Colorado Springs on the forty-fourth anniversary of Ouray's death. Leo had turned again in the sky.

Belated attempts of historical groups were instrumental in bringing the body of Chipeta back to the old homestead near Montrose where she was buried with a permanent marker and where the old home became a shrine. The same concern led to a search for Ouray's body and it is believed that his remains were found and they were transferred to the Ignacio cemetery. Ouray and Chipeta would have liked to be together.

In the dome of the capitol building in Denver, portraits of those who were important in early Colorado history have a place of stained glass permanence. Centering this group and directly facing the Senate chamber on the floor below is a portrait of Ouray, flanked on his right by Father Dyer, symbol of his Methodist faith and on the left by General Palmer, whose westward expansion had helped to seal the fate of the Indian domain. Nearby is the portrait of Kit Carson. Ouray's brown eyes look down to the third floor wall onto the portrait of little Otto Mears, clutching a scrap of paper in his tight-fisted hand. The two face each other for *as long as rivers might run and grasses grow*.

SOURCES

Massacre, Marshall Sprague, Little, Brown & Co., Boston, 1957

The Utes A Forgotten People, Wilson Rockwell, Sage Books, Denver, Colo., 1956

The Big Divide, David Lavender, Doubleday & Co., Garden City, N.Y., 1948

Colorado and Its People, ed. LeRoy R. Hafen, Lewis Historical Publishing Co., New York, N.Y., 1948

Early Days on the Western Slope and Campfire Chats with Otto Mears, the Pathfinder, Sidney Jocknick, Carson-Harper Co., Denver, Colorado, 1913

History of the Arkansas Valley, Colorado, O. L. Baskin & Co., Chicago, Ill., 1881

Colorado Magazine, October, 1928, "Reburial of Chief Ouray," by Mrs. C. W. Wiegel

Colorado Magazine, March, 1939, "Efforts to Recover the Stolen Son of Chief Ouray," Ann Hafen

Colorado Magazine, November, 1924, article by Florence Whittier

Colorado Magazine, May 1930, article by Major James Thompson

Colorado Magazine, September, 1930, article by Mrs. C. W. Wiegel

Out West, August 8, 1872
        September 19, 1872
        December 26, 1872

Colorado Springs Gazette, 1873-1924

and the assistance of

Denver Public Library, Western History Department

Colorado Springs Public Library

Coburn Library, Colorado College, Colorado Springs,

Dr. Ellsworth Mason and

Miss Grace Berger

After Dinner Speech

We hope you have enjoyed the presence of these varied personalities and that their shared experiences have enriched your own. There is something about the breaking of bread that makes a common family. The honor of their presence was ours and our only regret was that we were forced to omit others who would have added to the table talk.

We would have liked to have included H. A. W. Tabor and Baby Doe but we couldn't have left out Augusta—and it posed a social problem. And Baby Doe was a *femme fatale,* the disturbing kind.

A special regret is for the absence of Maggie Brown, one of our favorite eccentrics. She was left out of so many parties!

We considered inviting Isabella Byrd, but she wasn't particularly cordial to Colorado Springs residents long ago—of course the long horseback ride may have had something to do with it.

Then there were the Carltons, the Penroses, the Palmers, and Count Pourtales who were always welcome guests in the historical social register, but it was obvious that they traveled in another orbit.

Lloyd Shaw we remember personally as an imaginative educator, whom we always associate with whirling calico and stamping boots.

Then there was Dr. Florence Rena Sabin, the untiring health crusader.

We especially wanted Langrishe, the matinee idol and father of the theatre in Territorial Colorado, and one who was recognized as a good actor—

Which reminds us of the bad actor, Bob Ford.

Obviously we couldn't include Chivington on the same guest list with Helen Hunt Jackson.

Lily, the Queen of Chinatown, would have lent Oriental color.

We had planned to call on French Blanche, in Victor, bearing a personal invitation, but she died before invitations were issued.

There was William Henry Jackson, pioneer photographer, who focused on infinity.

There was Alfred Packer, who might have found our menu dull —and Fremont, who wouldn't have been choosey.

We remember Tow Walsh and his daughter Evalyn, who would have made us nervous if they had brought the Hope diamond along.

And Charles Fox Gardiner, the peppy pioneer doctor whose stories we heard first hand.

Especially we would have enjoyed Anne Ellis, who was weaned on cornbread and brown sugar.

There may be others we have forgotten, and some we do not know—and some we wouldn't want to invite and some who would not come.

Again we say, the most difficult thing about writing a book or giving a dinner is selection.